Hard
in Herefordshire

Hard Times
in Herefordshire

The effects of the workhouse
and the New Poor Law

by

John Powell

To

Barbara and Barry,

Best Wishes

from,

John

25.10.08

Logaston Press

LOGASTON PRESS
Little Logaston Woonton Almeley
Herefordshire HR3 6QH
logastonpress.co.uk

First published by Logaston Press 2008
Copyright text © John Powell 2008
Copyright illustrations © John Powell 2008,
except as otherwise credited

ISBN 978 1 906663 00 1

Typeset by Logaston Press
and printed in Great Britain by
Cpod, Trowbridge

*Cover illustration: A postcard recording an eviction at Allensmore
on 6 September 1910, by kind permission of Tim Ward*

To
my parents
Cyril and Nancy Powell

Contents

Acknowledgements

The vast majority of the primary research for this book was undertaken at the Herefordshire Record Office and I am indebted to Miss Sue Hubbard, Mrs Elizabeth Semper-O'Keefe and Mr Rhys Griffith and their staff for their assistance, expertise and courtesy throughout my researches. My thanks also go to Miss Elizabeth Teiser, Mrs Helen Hall and the staff of Ross-on-Wye Public Library for their dilligence and persistence in obtaining obscure secondary source materials for me. I thank, too, Mrs Joan Robbins, whose parents, Mr and Mrs Reginald Roff, were the last Master and Matron of Ross Workhouse, for her memories of the working of the poor law system and for allowing me to use some photographs. I am also most grateful to Mrs Virginia Morgan for allowing me access to her work on Nathaniel Morgan's private journals and I acknowledge, too, the kindness of Rowena, Lady Northbrook, the owner of the journals, in permitting me to quote from them. I am similarly indebted to Mr Colin Michael Southall for permission to quote from letters in the Southall Collection. Special thanks go to Andy Johnson and Karen Stout of Logaston Press for their editing suggestions and to Sheila Williams for her eagle-eyed proof reading. My thanks also go to Dr Christopher Williams and, most particularly, to Dr Frank Crompton for his kindness, his expertise and his constant enthusiasm for my research. Finally, my thanks go to Mr Roy Peacock, who first stimulated my interest in poor law history

Preface

In the early 1800s the poor in Britain were supported by a system of relief operated by each parish. Churchwardens and annually elected unpaid Overseers were responsible for collecting the poor rate and distributing it to those in need, in the form of grants or loans, by subsidising rent or paying for basic care in parish poorhouses or workhouses.

Agrarian riots in the 1830s, which happened at the same time as risings in France which brought back memories of the earlier French Revolution, led to the upper and middle classes wishing to review the system. This review saw two principles emerge which shaped what became the New Poor Law: the principle of National Uniformity – that is, uniformity of approach across the country overseen by a national administrative body (the Poor Law Commission), and the principle of Less Eligibility. Under this latter principle only the most basic support would be offered to those seen as feckless, with the idle and lazy (which was how most of the poor were categorized) being discouraged from seeking support by the harshness of new workhouse provision (that under the Old Poor Law had been seen as a bit 'soft') and the limiting of grants and subsidies. They would thus be 'encouraged' to find employment.

The system was enacted in 1834 and began to be put in place from 1836. Over the following ten years, however, people came to realise that not all the poor were feckless or idle, that wage levels were often simply too low, and that age, infirmity, sickness and pure circumstance had their part to play, whilst a scandal at the treatment of those in the workhouse in Andover led to a reform of the system. In 1847 the group of autocratic Poor Law Commissioners was replaced by a Board with wider duties.

This book charts events in Herefordshire from just before the end of the Old Poor Law through the New Poor Law to the creation of the Poor Law Board. The first two chapters provide a broad background to the treatment of the poor, and the change from the Old to the New Poor Law. One aspect of the New Poor Law was to group parishes together in Unions, both to help ensure uniformity of provision and to enable the funding of the new Union workhouses. (A further intention, to spread the cost of administration, was obstructed for decades, and only achieved with the passing of the Union Chargeability Act of 1865.) In Herefordshire this resulted in eight Unions, some of which included parishes in Gloucestershire or Wales. Chapters then cover each of the eight Herefordshire Unions in turn, but with an emphasis on different themes. Thus the two chapters covering Ledbury consider how the law operated under the old system as compared to the new system; that on Ross the social networks out of which the Union's Guardians were appointed and how Guardians and their appointed officers functioned in practice. The chapter on Hereford looks at how a workhouse functioned, and also at how society saw the need for an enhanced role for charity in response to the provisions of the New Poor Law, while the chapters on Kington and Dore consider how the New Poor Law worked in the most rural parts of the county and how different Unions approached the issue of educating their young charges. The chapter on Leominster looks at the Andover scandal and an investigation by the Commission into a case that arose in Leominster shortly afterwards; that on Bromyard covers the use of pauper apprentices; whilst the chapter on Weobley considers the questions of the laws of settlement (by which the parish or Union that had financial responsibility for a pauper was decided) and vagrancy.

1 Parish Relief and Parish Autonomy

In 1760, at the beginning of the long and eventful reign of King George III, the vast majority of his subjects derived their wealth and income from land holdings and agricultural production. By the end of his reign in 1820 the growth of industrialisation meant that the new centres for producing wealth and creating employment were the kingdom's towns and cities. Urban industry had created enormous wealth, but this was very unevenly distributed with great affluence for some citizens and incredible squalor and degradation for others. Uncontrolled building developments erupted in towns and cities, transforming them in a few short years. Men and women who had migrated from the countryside in search of higher incomes often had to endure crowded and insanitary working and living conditions, to the great detriment of their health and quality of life.

Pressure for political and legal reform to help transform this new world came largely from the new breed of entrepreneurs who ran their businesses efficiently and profitably, but reform was slow to arrive. The old landed families perceived the notion of greater centralisation in government as a forewarning of interference in the management of their own estates, where their word had been law. The landowners, Magistrates, farmers, Churchwardens and clergymen controlled employment, poor relief and justice. Ever watchful of violent and revolutionary events in Europe and fearful that such happenings might manifest themselves in England, their nervousness was heightened still further when in 1830 the agricultural labourers of the mainly arable counties of south and east England rioted in protest against low wages and hunger. Village constables, where they existed, were no match for large gatherings of angry and agitated labourers and in the complete absence of a centrally co-ordinated rural police force, property owners felt powerless to protect themselves, their families and their property. The hard-pressed militia could not be everywhere; as soon as one riotous assembly had been dispersed another would spring up a few miles away.

In 1832 there were several different systems in place for relieving poverty amongst the able-bodied poor. In some parts of the country, parishes used the Labour Rate, in others the Roundsman System, and in others the Speenhamland

Scales were the preferred option. They were all forms of wage subsidy for the low paid, financed from the local rates. The system meant that farmers were often accused of paying low wages in order to retrieve some of the money they paid out in rates. They in turn pleaded that they could not afford to pay higher wages unless there was a reduction in the rents they paid to their land-lords and the tithes they paid to the Church. The landlords were, of course, not inclined to reduce their rents, nor the clergymen their tithes. Some of the clergy were further compromised by their private ownership of large estates and the fact that many of them also presided as Magistrates. In the event of disturbance amongst labourers, the local Magistrate presided over a tangled web of relationships of which he himself was likely to be a significant part. As a landowner, some of the farmers who called for lower rents were probably his tenants and he might also be the patron of the clergyman of whom the farmers demanded lower tithes. The farmers were often seen as devious manipulators of the rates, but their position in the village community was sometimes invid-ious and their role in parish affairs was ambiguous. Anne Digby states:

> Norfolk farmers were ambivalent about the problem of surplus labour since, although they wanted a reserve of labourers to meet peak, seasonal labour demands, they disliked the high level of poor rates that resulted from such under-employment. They were fortunate in being able to resolve this conflict of interest by exploiting their position as poor law administrators to pursue a policy with an economical alteration of poor relief and independent income for the labourer. While the changing dimensions of poverty led to variations in the detailed form of relief, the overall policy remained constant.[1]

It is arguable how much farmers were guilty of manipulating the poor rates in order to subsidise their own wage bills, but it is clear that they were often in commanding positions to do so. On the one hand, they had to sustain amicable relations with their own landlord and fellow ratepayers and on the other hand they had to be seen to deal reasonably with their labourers as employees. They were also frequently involved in parish affairs as Overseers and Churchwardens, elected by their fellow ratepayers. They were the dispensers of poor relief and the managers of parish charities.

With all these forces of authority thus arrayed against them in protection of vested interests, it was perhaps inevitable that men who were angry and hungry would turn to rebellion and riot in order to win fairer rewards for their labours.

The Paris Rising of 1830 and fears of a second French Revolution caused considerable excitement in England, with increased fears among the property-owning classes and a 'revival of interest in parliamentary reform'.[2] George IV died on 30 June 1830 and, in accordance with custom, a general election was held. Both Whig and Tory parties were in a factional state, but both realised that parliamentary reform could not be avoided. The Tory Government's position was weakened when Wellington, the Prime Minister, stated that in his opinion 'the state of representation was perfect'.[3] Within a fortnight of the election the government resigned and Earl Grey, the new Whig Prime Minister, 'made the acceptance of a reform bill a condition of forming his ministry'.[4] It was against this backdrop that the agrarian riots took place and continued sporadically into 1832. When the crisis was over, it was clear that the long and vexed problem of poor relief, with its ever-growing cost, would have to be addressed if disorder was to be avoided in the future.

In February 1832, the Whig Government announced that a Royal Commission would be set up to investigate the workings of the Poor Laws of England and Wales. There were numerous existing laws and for generations additions and amendments had been piled one upon another. This had created a complex structure of rules and regulations which, in the absence of a central government department that checked and monitored their activities, unpaid Overseers, often unwillingly in office, interpreted as they saw fit. The situation was further complicated by the fact that much of the existing legislation was of a permissory nature which parish officers and ratepayers might ignore if they so wished. Fulfilling one's moral duty in the office of Overseer for the year could prove to be an expensive, time-consuming and thankless task. Carried out diligently, the role involved assessing applicants' requests for relief and, if necessary, visiting them in their homes, all of which took the Overseer away from his own business affairs. His position was an unenviable one also in that he had to be sympathetic to the needs of the genuinely poor while balancing the expense of meeting those needs against the interests of the ratepayers who financed the relief he dispensed. He would certainly have received criticism from one side or the other, and possibly both. It is not easy to see why men allowed themselves to be manoeuvred into the post of Overseer; the only benefit would appear to have been that the Overseer's influence and standing in his local community was enhanced for a while. Some parishes had a paid official and if the parish could afford the man's wages it must have been very tempting to let someone else deal with difficult paupers and take the criticism. Individual parish interpretations of regulations, coupled with numerous local charities, fostered widespread variations in the relief of poverty, ranging from extreme parsimony to almost indiscriminate alms giving – but parsimony was the more likely.

If those labourers who moved from the countryside to town or city in search of better income and freedom from the restricted world of the agricultural estate found that they had to endure squalor and long hours of work in degrading conditions, the move did open their eyes and broaden their horizons. Previous generations had rarely stirred from the comparative safety and security of their native parishes and, as a consequence, were likely to remain ignorant about how poor relief was managed in other parts of even their own county. It might be argued that the laws of settlement intended it to be so. Migration to towns might bring the agricultural labourer higher wages but if he became unemployed, the Old Poor Law system would not support him in his new parish and he would soon find that he was returned to his parish of origin to seek assistance there.

In 1832 the Royal Commission on Poor Laws in England and Wales sent out a questionnaire to 15,000 parishes of which approximately 10% were returned. The Commission's intention was to produce evidence about how parish officers established an applicant's worthiness for parish relief, the reason for his distress, whether he could have laid aside reserves for possible future difficulties while he had been employed, and whether he was of good character. The details provided by returns from Herefordshire parishes revealed that no standard scale was employed to calculate appropriate relief, nor were the Labour Rate or Roundsman Systems used. Instead, parish officers assessed each case on its merits, relying on their local knowledge of applicants, their needs and, particularly, their characters. While reliance on local knowledge of individuals and their circumstances was likely to be the best approach in meeting the needs of applicants for parish relief in rural areas, it depended for its fairness on a balanced opinion of a man's character amongst those ratepayers who attended vestry meetings and, in particular, the fairness and open-mindedness of Overseers and Churchwardens. Some of those opinions are evident in the detail of the Herefordshire returns which formed part of the Poor Law Report of 1834.[5]

In the city of Hereford there were six parishes – St Peter, St Owen, St Nicholas, St Martin, St John the Baptist and All Saints – and all, with the exception of St Martin, made returns to the Royal Commission. The Overseer of St Peter declared that after enquiries had been made about the applicant, relief was granted or denied on the basis of character. In St Owen parish the Overseers and Churchwardens held the view that those claiming relief while out of work during the winter months could, with care, have provided for themselves with savings from previous earnings. They resented the fact that the unemployed were often granted relief on the order of a Magistrate. This might suggest that the Magistrates thought it was unrealistic for working people of the parish to save against hardship, or perhaps this is just an example of petty point-scoring between two sets of officials. In St Nicholas parish the same relief was given to all applicants of whatever character but 'with greater reluctance and more caution to bad than good characters'. The Overseers of St John the Baptist held a more balanced view; relief was granted depending on the level of distress proved by enquiries and, of course, the character of the applicant. All Saints, almost certainly the poorest parish in the city, had two

Overseers who were usually tradesmen, well known and with good knowledge of the parish's inhabitants. They also had a paid Assistant Overseer who made the necessary enquiries about applicants, and great attention was paid to character. It is likely that in the case of this parish the two Overseers were tradesmen because they were the most affluent people in an area which would have been shunned by businessmen and people of independent means. It was an area full of alleys, crowded courts and lodging houses with, almost certainly, a high level of unemployment and poverty, along with inhabitants who lived an itinerant life bordering on the underworld of petty criminals; for this reason alone, it had need of a paid Assistant Overseer. The parish Overseers' return to the Royal Commission stated: 'Whenever we are obliged to relieve bad characters, as is sometimes the case, we give them as little as we possibly can.' The notion of the deserving and the undeserving poor was very strong; for ratepayers burdened by a heavy poor rate, it was a very logical approach to the problem.

Attitudes in the county's market towns and villages varied widely: Bridstow's Overseers considered an applicant's character; at Credenhill they gave assistance without reference to a Magistrate if the man was known to be of good character; at Eardisland they reported that 'where distress is from bad character we give the least relief which will keep them from starving'. At Almeley no enquiries were made before relief was given and at Ledbury it was provided 'according to circumstances'. The Overseer at Kington reported that 'we relieve bad characters with greater caution and less liberality'. At Ross Overseers stated that relief was refused if they thought the applicant had had chance to provide for himself and the matter was laid before a Magistrate for his consideration, 'but if he has a wife and children, they are not neglected on account of the dissolute habits of the man'. At Brinsop it was admitted that few enquiries were made, often resulting in 'the most importunate succeeding best'. Weobley reported that 'as little assistance is given as possible to bad characters' and at Bromyard, pauper lists were scrutinised very carefully at vestry meetings. The dominant points which recur in the returns completed by Herefordshire parishes are concerning the applicant's character, how deserving he is and the amount of detailed knowledge parish officials have when making a decision about his eligibility for relief.

It was through the vestry meeting that the ratepayers exercised their control over parish affairs, or not, as the case may be. Meetings were held weekly, fortnightly or monthly depending on the wishes of the ratepayers and the volume of business to be discussed and transacted. It is difficult to assess whether the frequency of the meetings illustrated the relative simplicity with which ratepayers could maintain their control, or the pressing problems of the poor in the parish and the need for those difficulties to be addressed. The Overseers and Churchwardens worked with the ratepayers in deciding the poor rates to be levied and also whether applicants for relief should have their claims granted, denied or referred to a Magistrate. Any ratepayers, in rural communities almost exclusively farmers and landowners, could attend and contribute views and opinions on parish business. The autonomy of the parish vestry meetings was jealously guarded, more particularly perhaps in predominantly agricultural counties such as Herefordshire, where village communities were very small and everyone knew everyone. It is almost certain that there would be some rivalry amongst the poor, who would watch to see that neighbours were not receiving more relief than they were themselves. At the same time, there would probably be ratepayers who would watch carefully to judge whether poor relations or aged former employees were being fairly treated in relation to other villagers seeking assistance. In a small rural community it would be very difficult not to be known by all.

In none of the Herefordshire returns made to the Royal Commission was there evidence of poor relief being given on the basis of an established scale of payments. Generally, each case was investigated and assessed on its merits and on the basis of local knowledge of the man, his family and his circumstances. This was an effective means of controlling expenditure and attempting to see that malingerers did not prosper at the expense of the hard-working and industrious as well as the honest deserving poor.

In Herefordshire most Overseers were farmers who, as employers and ratepayers, had a particular interest in seeing that if at all possible, relief was earned or, if not earned, kept to an absolute minimum. If an applicant for relief had his application denied, the decision could be overturned by a Magistrate if he considered it to be unreasonable or unjust. The Magistrates had powers under which a vestry could be ordered to provide relief and at times these powers were used, much to the irritation of Overseers and ratepayers. From the applicant's point of view the Magistrate's powers provided a safety mechanism against hardship in the face of harsh, unjust or possibly spiteful and vindictive decisions made at vestry meetings. He could caution over-zealous or parsimonious ratepayers to think again and remind them of their duty of care to the poor and those in temporary distress. If a man fell foul of his parish officials, it would be very difficult for him to move to another parish for a fresh start, because if he became unemployed he might soon find himself sent back to his original parish or settlement parish to seek help from officials there.

Parishes where ratepayers wished to consolidate their powers in the management of village affairs were given the opportunity to do this by utilising the provisions of the Select Vestry Act of 1819. This Act allowed a vestry to appoint a salaried official, an Assistant Overseer, to run its poor law affairs. Alternatively, it could provide a parish committee to have continuous oversight and control of parish business. The Act also removed the Magistrates' powers to overturn Overseers' decisions. The Select Vestry Act was permissory legislation which can be seen as a direct reaction to public concern about the costs of poor relief, which had risen relentlessly since the beginning of the century, as well as giving ratepayers a legal means of exerting much tighter control over parish spending.

Nine of the 27 Herefordshire parishes that made returns to the Royal Commission stated that they had a Select Vestry. Kington Overseers stated that they had had such a body since 1820 and that 'its affects have been very beneficial to the parish'. At Bromyard they were less enthusiastic, although their Select Vestry had been in operation for ten years. They stated that 'we are not aware of any effects resulting from it, except perhaps procuring rather a more regular attendance at the fortnightly meetings'. Leominster reported a reduction in rates; Shobdon, 'an advantage having a select vestry'; Lyonshall, 'good effects'. Llangarron Overseers confirmed that 'the effect has been a very considerable diminuation of Parish Rates'. At Pembridge, Overseers made a clear and unequivocal statement: 'We have a Select Vestry and Assistant Overseer, and the effect has been that the business has been accurately and satisfactorily done to all parties.'

On balance the responses received by the Royal Commission from Herefordshire parishes showed that those who administered affairs through a Select Vestry were pleased with the improvement in the management of parish business and the substantial reduction in poor rate which ensued. It is important to remember, however, that the views and opinions given to the Royal Commission were those of the ratepayers. The poor may have thought otherwise.

In 19th-century Herefordshire there existed numerous small charities for the benefit of the poor and some of these might have helped to ease any reductions in allowances which resulted from tighter control of parish finances when Select Vestry provisions were employed. Such charities were often specific to particular villages or to particular social groups under the terms of the benefactor's will. Also, more often than not, the management of funds was vested in the hands of those already managing parish affairs: the Overseers of the Poor; the Churchwardens; the rector or vicar; or descendants or relatives of the benefactor. The poor who benefited did so at the discretion of prominent local individuals whose good opinion of them was crucial.

Examples of such charities are numerous. At Brampton Abbotts, near Ross, Edward Stedman left money to fund the distribution of six loaves of bread after morning service every Sunday, the loaves to be distributed at the minister's discretion. John Freeman, of the parish of Whitbourne, left three cottages to be inhabited by poor parishioners, but at the discretion of his son. Alternatively, he could let the cottages at a commercial rate and distribute the accumulated rents to the poor at Christmas.

Inevitably some parishes found more benefactors than others and in this respect Fownhope was particularly fortunate in possessing many charities. They had accumulated over the centuries under the wills of prominent land-owning families such as the Gregorys of How Caple Court and those of prosperous independent farmers. The Reverend Robert Gregory left funds for ten old men and women to be given one shilling each on St Thomas's Day, Gregory's heirs or the Vicar of Fownhope exercising the right of nomination. Francis Brydges left money for the purchase of land to be held by the village in order to provide income for the apprenticing of a boy or girl to a 'respectable trade'. The child had to have been born in the parish, be of the Church of England and be nominated by the son or heirs of Francis Brydges or the minister and Churchwardens.

John Powell, a farmer, left his dwelling, Upper Buckenhill Farm in the parish of Woolhope, and lands in neighbouring villages to his brother Francis Powell under certain conditions. One condition required him to give the minister and Churchwardens of the parish of Fownhope the sum of £60, which was to be invested in government securities to provide funds for the instruction of poor children in reading and writing. Francis Powell was to nominate children to receive this instruction from the parishes of Fownhope, Sollershope and Brockhampton. John Powell also left Lower Buckenhill Farm at Woolhope, plus lands in other parishes, to his nephew Francis Slade. A further £60 was to be invested to provide income for the instruction of poor children of Woolhope – children Francis Slade was to nominate.

The farmers were very influential in their parishes. They were enmeshed in a complicated structure of relationships, all of which resulted from the ties of land: its ownership, its occupation, and its cultivation. Some farmers were landowners and landlords; some were tenants of major landowners, others of independent farmers or the Church. All of them were ratepayers; all were employers. Their social standing meant that in one capacity or another they interacted with all social groups in the community. Their most complicated and uneasy relationship, however, was with the Church and individual members of the clergy.

The Bishop of Hereford, in his capacity as bishop, possessed large estates in Herefordshire, as did the Dean and Chapter and some clergyman as private individuals. Thus, a farmer might be a tenant of the Bishop, the Dean and Chapter or a wealthy clergyman such as the Reverend Henry Lee Warner of Tibberton Court in the parish of Madley; the Reverend Thomas Powell Symonds of Pengethley Court in Sellack parish; or the Reverend Charles Scott Luxmore, Dean of St Asaph and owner and occupier of Cradley Court near Bromyard. The relationship was complicated still further when the farmer's landlord was also the clergyman to whom he paid his bitterly resented tithes. The issue of tithes was always likely to be the cause of conflict, and soured relations between farmer and priest. Despite this potential for discord, however, farmers in rural areas frequently fulfilled the duties of Churchwardens. This role brought them into frequent contact with the parish priest in the management of the local church's fiscal affairs: paying bell ringers, levying poor rates, supporting the itinerant poor, levying church rates and maintaining the church. Tensions were just as likely to arise between farmer and incumbent if the clergyman was a man of very modest means who relied on tithe payments for the support of his family: not all clergymen were wealthy. Rich or poor, the parish priest would not be well-regarded by his parishioners if sour relations existed as a result of wrangles over tithes.

The payment of tithes really amounted to a 10% tax on land and livestock production. Originally payments had been made in kind, but by the 19th century many had been commuted to a fixed annual cash sum which fell heavily on the farmer's income in bad years. By the 1820s dissatisfaction with the tithe system amongst landowners, farmers, clergymen and labourers had created a growing pressure for reform. Agricultural labourers were not immune to the tensions arising from the tithe issue; their calls for higher wages were invariably countered by farmers with complaints about tithes. This may have been a convenient excuse for the farmers, but excuse or not it gave both parties common cause against parsons; labourers also viewed clergymen as harsh Magistrates who did not discharge their pastoral duties to the poor properly.

In 1830, the Swing Riots broke out amongst agricultural labourers in the south and east of England, creating an atmosphere of fear and intimidation amongst the owners and occupiers of land. Haystacks were fired; farm buildings were burnt down; workhouses were attacked; threshing machines were damaged or destroyed; impromptu robberies took place; food and money were demanded with menaces; and some occupiers anticipated personal assault and feared for the safety of their families. Some manufacturing properties and machinery were attacked, but these were few; the main impact of the riots fell on farmers, landlords, parsons, Overseers and justices, because these were the people who could relieve the drudgery and poverty of the lives of agricultural labourers if they were prepared to do so.

The tangle of relationships which had framed and influenced normal life in small agricultural communities in the first half of the 19th century, was in some areas torn apart as local alliances were modified and compromised. The landlords and the Church were generally unsympathetic to the labourers' pleas for higher wages. The farmers' alliances varied, usually depending on whether they were tenant farmers or independent farmers. Large farmers tended to stand in opposition to the rioters alongside the landowners and the clergy, both of whom were members of the Magistracy, while small farmers were inclined to side with the labourers. Indeed, it is likely that some of the very small farmers were little better off than their paid labourers; the very terms 'farmer' and 'agricultural labourer' were, in some instances, almost interchangeable. In their analysis of the causes and effects of the Swing Riots, historians E.J. Hobsbawm and G. Rude suggest[6] that some farmers allied themselves with labourers in an attempt to put pressure on the landlords to reduce rents and the clergy to reduce tithes. If successful, the farmers could then agree to pay higher wages, having effectively manoeuvred landlords and clergymen into footing the bill.

The situation elsewhere in rural England may throw light on Herefordshire. At the Wallops in Hampshire, for example, farmers offered to increase wages from 8s to 10s per week, a similar rate to that paid in Herefordshire, provided that rents, tithes and taxes were lowered in proportion.[7] At Stoke Holy Cross in Norfolk[8] they agreed to raise wages by one fifth if tithes were lowered by a quarter and rents by a sixth. At Horsham, West Sussex, after threatening letters had been received and property set on fire, a riotous meeting of labourers and householders took place in the parish church. The crowd dispersed only when a reduction in tithes had been extracted from the tithe holders and assurances given that labourers would be paid 2s 6d per day.[9]

Farmers who did collude with labourers, or succeeded in manipulating their unruly activities from the shadows, played a dangerous game. Landlords and clergymen who had been intimidated or pressurised into lowering rents and tithes might exact revenge in the future, quietly and surreptitiously, by colluding amongst themselves to create difficulties for a farmer against whom they nurtured a grudge. A tenant farmer might one day need more time to pay his rent; there might be worrying complications and delays over the renewal of his tenancy; his efforts to gain a suitable tenancy for an adult son wishing to strike out on his own in farming might be thwarted.

The Swing Riots started in the southern and eastern counties which were arable areas where labourers were vulnerable to unemployment and the resultant hardship that went with it. Herefordshire's agriculture was more varied and less prone to seasonal variation in demand for labour, and the county was hardly disturbed by the riots at all. Of cases brought against labourers for arson, damage and unruly behaviour, the largest number by county was Wiltshire with 339 cases. Herefordshire's reported incidents during the unrest of 1830 number just four: two for arson and two relating to Swing letters. One case only was brought to court, that of Henry Williams, a journeyman tailor also known as a 'ranting' preacher, who wrote a threatening letter to a farmer at Whitney and was later transported to New South Wales for his trouble. It is quite possible that protest meetings in Herefordshire were impractical because of the county's small and widespread population: the 1831 census gave Herefordshire's population as 110,617, one person to every five acres of land, making the rapid congregation of labourers into large gatherings very unlikely. Also it is probable that the county's remoteness from the main counties of disturbance, its poor roads and the isolation of small rural communities within it, coupled with the generally low level of literacy, meant that the labourers remained ignorant of events elsewhere. In any event Herefordshire had reasonably full employment, so there were fewer causes for discontent or riot than in other counties.

The returns made to the Poor Law Commissioners from parishes in Herefordshire suggest that there was no seething unrest amongst the honest poor. Most lived in cottages owned by farmers or landowners, though some had built their own homes on waste land. The returns also indicate that most of the cottages had gardens, that the rents, which were usually between £2 and £6 per annum, were frequently paid by the parish and that although the cottages were rated, labourers were usually exempted from paying rates. Employment was generally available and in some parishes labourers were able to rent small plots of land of about a quarter of an acre in addition to their gardens for the growing of potatoes. This was the case at Credenhill, Hope-under-Dinmore, Weobley and Pembridge. It is also clear from the return made by Thomas Edwards, Churchwarden of Leominster parish, that some labourers had more land, for he stated: 'Labourers in some instances keep a cow, and if so, they have one to three acres. They also keep a pig or two. Their garden contains from half a quarter to a quarter of an acre; they pay £3 to £4 per acre.' If there were instances of labourers holding two or three acres in other parishes of the county, it is likely that in Herefordshire labourers could feel fairly secure. In addition, wages ranged from 7s to 10s per week, which was not markedly different from other rural counties.

The Board of Agriculture Report produced in 1794 estimated that of approximately 20,000 acres of land in Herefordshire, 3.7% remained unenclosed. Much of this land was in the Golden Valley and along the Welsh border. Close reading of surviving tithe map apportionments suggests that by 1840 the 20,000 acres of 1794 had been reduced to just under 13,000 acres or 2.5% of the county. The poor had been deprived of much, since more than half the parishes, in fact 127, had no waste land or common land at all and a further nine parishes recorded less than one acre. Those parishes where large acreages were yet to be enclosed, mainly parishes along the Welsh border where the land was described as 'common and mountain', included: Craswall with 1,296 acres, Cusop 654 acres, Kington 1,830 acres, Llanveynoe 1,573 acres, Cwmyoy 887 acres, Longtown 356 acres, Clifford 368 acres, Michaelchurch Escley 507 acres, Aymestrey 315 acres and Yarpole 399 acres. Looked at from another point of view, where the poor had received awards of a few acres of land in lieu of common field strips, they were perhaps quite content with a low-level subsistence style of life which made few demands on them and still provided a few common rights. If all but 3.7% of the county had been enclosed by 1794, the process must have been developing over many generations by agreement.

The Board of Agriculture Report of 1805 states that only one third of Herefordshire's land was held as leasehold, copyhold or under other ancient agreements, and two thirds were held as freehold. This tends to support the view that piecemeal enclosure by agreement had been going on for generations with the result that a larger proportion of the poor in Herefordshire would have owned a few enclosed acres of land at the time of the 1830 riots than in other counties where enclosures were less advanced or were only just beginning to proceed by Act of Parliament rather than by agreement. Open fields in Herefordshire, still worked under the ancient strip system, were relatively small, often with fewer than ten tenants, so agreement could be achieved fairly easily. This meant that the need to resort to an Act of Parliament was rare; indeed, just 31 Acts were used to enclose the 13,000 acres mentioned above, while Oxfordshire, for example, used 158 Acts to enclose 37% of the county's acreage.

The vast majority of enclosures in Herefordshire had therefore taken place a generation and more before the agrarian riots of 1830. Commoners had not just been turned into wage labourers with a few enclosed acres of their own; sufficient time had passed to allow the population to adjust to a new way of life and adopt different methods of working. Yet it was against this backdrop of the agrarian riots of 1830 that the Poor Law Commission carried out its investigations into the workings of the Poor Laws of England and Wales and produced its report. Herefordshire was to become part of a new national system.

2   Union Relief and Union Control

At the beginning of the 19th century many agricultural labourers and their families lived in the enclosed world of large estates. For many generations the landowners and tenant farmers had successfully controlled their labourers' social conditions at a level just sufficient to avoid serious protest or disturbance of the peace. As industrialisation and the accompanying urbanisation moved rapidly forward, however, some labourers looked towards the cities for a higher income and a better way of life. The long-held allegiances between master and labourer began to crumble, but the social controls remained unaffected. The labourer who migrated to the city for work and who later became unemployed could soon find himself returned to his parish of origin by the laws of settlement and perhaps somewhat out of favour with his former master. The host parish which he inhabited whilst he was working in the city was under no obligation to relieve him and his family if he was laid off work during a trade slump or even if he was ill and could not work. He was the responsibility of his home parish and any relief he received had to be paid for by the ratepayers of that parish. He might be allowed to remain in the parish in which he had been working during temporary unemployment, but only if the Overseers of his home parish agreed to repay the cost of the relief he received. After the disturbances of 1830, however, the landowners realised that if they refused to relieve poverty, the result would almost certainly be further riot, loss of property and perhaps loss of life too. Amongst themselves they accepted that the relief of the poor was the lesser of two evils; to the world in general they would acknowledge that it was a public duty which accorded with their station in life. The need for reform was recognised by all sectors of society. The poor called for the just relief of poverty; the ratepayers called for relief from ever-growing poor rates.

The investigations of the Royal Commission of 1832 showed that parish autonomy in the management of poor relief had created widely differing practices and that the need for reform and greater uniformity was urgent. The report which followed the Commission's work formed the basis of the Poor Law Amendment Act of 1834, which heralded a major change of direction in the administration of public aid. Parish autonomy was replaced by central government control. Ever since Elizabethan times the property owners of each parish had been required to hold an annual meeting, usually at Easter, to set a rate for the relief of the old and the sick, widows and orphans, and children who had simply been deserted by their parents. Parish relief was dispensed by an Overseer of the Poor who was elected annually. The post was not popular because it involved a great deal of work if carried out diligently, and was unpaid. It was seen as a parish duty and ratepayers were expected to take a turn.

After the passing of the Poor Law Amendment Act of 1834, at local level, the management of poor relief was taken away from parish officers and placed in the hands of Boards of Guardians who administered the affairs of a group or union of parishes. The Guardians, in turn, were supervised by three Poor Law Commissioners at Somerset House, a system of dual control which, it was hoped, would provide uniformity. The changes were, however, not always as sweeping as might be first thought, because under the New Poor Law the Boards of Guardians often employed the same parish officers as had administered the Old Law.

All major changes of political direction bring advantages for some people and disadvantages for others and in this respect the New Poor Law was no different. The ratepayers lost some control over parish affairs, but some could gain greater influence than before by being elected to Boards of Guardians. Under the new legislation the landowning qualification was no longer a bar to those seeking office, which meant that men who earned their income through trade were as eligible to be elected Guardians as the gentry. As a result of this change a much wider spectrum of society was represented on Boards of Guardians. Grocers, shoemakers, maltsters, timber merchants and wine merchants could participate, sitting with farmers, landed gentlemen, doctors and clergymen in a way that would have been impossible under the old administration. Overseers and Churchwardens lost immediate control of parish relief but were absolved of many time-consuming and often vexatious unpaid duties, and could quite properly refer difficult paupers and their complaints directly to the Boards of Guardians.

In rural areas Boards of Guardians usually held their meetings in the market town which formed the nodal point of the Union, but might be up to ten miles from where the pauper lived. This had the effect of removing difficult situations between Overseers and paupers from the immediate vicinity of the parish, and made control more remote and more anonymous. It was more difficult for a pauper to complain to the Union Relieving Officer who visited the parish weekly or fortnightly than it was for him to accost the village Overseer. Many paupers would have been daunted by the prospect of presenting themselves before the Board of Guardians to complain, particularly if it meant a long walk in bad weather. It is likely that this was one of the intentions of the new arrangements. Paupers who lived in parishes where officers had been weak or malleable or over-generous were likely to feel deprived under the new tightly-run regime. Those paupers who were genuinely needy, however, may have felt that they were more fairly treated post 1834, particularly if they had been subjected to the whims of uncaring Overseers and parsimonious ratepayers. The New Poor Law, however, embraced parsimony as an organising principle and it might therefore be argued quite reasonably that relief was more for the ratepayers than for the paupers.

The New Poor Law was established on Benthamite principles, known as Utilitarianism. Jeremy Bentham (1748-1832) was the founder of a school of political philosophy which questioned many of the established notions and practices of the law, religion and economics. Bentham's view was that the poor were of value for their labour and should be made to work for their keep as well as to make a profit. In order to prevent malingerers from benefiting from poor relief, the New Poor Law enacted that able-bodied adults should only be allowed relief if they resided in the Union Workhouse. This was known as the 'Workhouse Test', because it was assumed by the poor law authorities that only the utterly destitute would contemplate entering the workhouse, as the relief given within its walls was to be less than that which an independent labourer could provide for himself and his family through his own travail. This was defined as the 'Principle of Less Eligibility'; that is, paupers in the workhouse were to be less eligible for the world's resources than the poorest labourers outside the workhouse, as a deterrent to the idle.

Entry to the workhouse for the respectable and normally hard-working poor who found themselves in unfortunate circumstances was therefore a devastating and demoralising experience. Shelter and minimal food, the absolute necessities of life, were often grudgingly provided, whilst the pauper suffered a loss of dignity and self-respect, and a total loss of personal autonomy. Once within the workhouse walls paupers were examined by the Medical Officer, bathed and put into workhouse clothes. Husbands and wives were separated, rigid routines were imposed, and the process of institutionalisation was under way. It was virtually imprisonment without trial and, most essentially, without crime. Even the alleged criminal was entitled to have a fair hearing in open court; the pauper, on the other hand, could be consigned to the workhouse on the word of the Union Relieving Officer. Boards of Guardians did sometimes countermand the orders of the Relieving Officer but in general his orders were followed. It is true that the pauper could leave the workhouse on giving three hours' notice of his intention to do so, but if he had no other means of providing for himself and his family, he had very little option but to remain.

It is difficult not to see the workhouse as being imposed on society as a means of social control; that is, control by the wealthy classes of those whom they considered disreputable simply because of their lack of worldly resources. Respectability appears to have been measured on a scale which paralleled the measure of wealth, and critics of the New Poor Law argued that in the new and prison-like workhouses 'poverty was to be treated as a crime'.[1]

Under the Old Poor Law many parishes, though by no means all, kept a parish poor house or workhouse, and in the early years of the New Poor Law, it was common for old workhouses to be used, but these did not provide enough space for the Boards of Guardians to ensure that the rules regarding the segregation of the different classes of pauper could be enforced. There were clear guidelines which required that respectable women should be housed in different wards from prostitutes; that young women with illegitimate children should be accommodated away from other single girls; that those with venereal disease were kept in separate wards which were generally known as the 'foul wards'; that orphans and abandoned children were kept away from adults; and that the old and the sick were protected from the rowdy behaviour of other paupers. The Boards were therefore encouraged to erect new buildings designed to meet the requirements of the new law. Most of the new workhouses resembled prisons, with imposing edifices and an aura of power. As Assistant Poor Law Commissioner Sir Francis Head said in 1836:

> The very sight of a well-built efficient establishment would give confidence to the Poor Law Guardians; the sight and weekly assemblage of all the servants of their union would make them feel proud of their office; the appointment of a chaplain would give dignity to the whole arrangement, while the pauper would feel it was utterly impossible to contend against it.[2]

It is a paradox that the new law which promoted the swift reduction of pauperism and dependence on parish help as its major aims in fact created more paupers by insisting that relief, in most cases, be provided only in workhouses. Under the Old Poor Law families often received relief from their parish as a subsidy to supplement low wages. This usually took the form of a quantity of flour or bread, a small sum of money or possibly shoes and clothing. Many also had their cottage rents paid for them which meant that they could retain some semblance of self respect and continue to live as a family. The New Poor Law swept this type of assistance away and forced many families into the workhouse, thus making them paupers. It is also ironic that many respectable widows and their children continued to be relieved in their own homes after 1834, probably as an expedient to prevent overcrowding, and thus avoided the stigma of being a pauper. Those who were relieved in the workhouse, however, endured the humiliation of knowing that every quarter the Relieving Officer responsible for their parish was required to pin a list of their names to the door of their church. This was clearly intended to name and shame paupers in the eyes of other parishioners in order to deter them from ever entering the workhouse again. It is arguable, however, that the deterrent effect of entry to the workhouse diminished with each succeeding admission.

Within the confines of the workhouse system an upper-class morality was imposed upon the labouring classes. Despite the fact that Roman Catholics were emancipated in 1829, the moral and religious teaching of the workhouse was that of the Church of England and therefore promulgated an Anglican morality. Indeed, the Royal Commission which had collected the information on which the 1834 Act was based was chaired by Bishop Blomfield of London and included Bishop Sumner of Chester. The fact that such senior churchmen were activists in the New Poor Law shows that the collaboration between church and state in the moral improvement of the lower classes was established at the very highest levels. In this context it is reasonable to argue that the Workhouse Chaplain was an agent of social control; his Anglicanism made him trustworthy and he could be the 'eyes and ears' of the Boards of Guardians and perhaps of the Poor Law Commissioners too. Of all the workhouse appointments the Chaplain held the highest social status and often received a salary as large as that of the workhouse Master, although he was required to perform far fewer duties for his money.

Clergymen varied in their attitude to the New Poor Law, but many agreed that the old system encouraged idleness, immorality and increased bastardy and should be amended. In his study of the Victorian Church, Owen Chadwick states:

> Anglicans liked the provisions for religious instruction in workhouses. Divine service must be celebrated, the Bible and catechism taught, and a chaplain might be appointed. The Dissenters were pleased that their pastors might visit the workhouse to teach their own people. An assistant commissioner claimed that few persons outside universities had better opportunities for religious instruction than inhabitants of the new workhouses. 'Some of the paupers, I was assured, had complained that they had too much divine service.' It was also observed that under the old system nine-tenths of the paupers never entered a church, and therefore the new system was bringing them to worship.[3]

At the beginning of the New Poor Law the appointment of a Workhouse Chaplain was at the discretion of the Board of Guardians, but within a few years of the 1834 Act's being passed, an appointment became a legal requirement. Close reading of the minute books of the Boards of Guardians for the Unions of Ross and Hereford reveals very few references to the work of their Chaplains, perhaps four or five for each Union during the period covered by the Poor Law Commission of 1834 to 1847. This suggests that although the Chaplains were appointed early in the establishment of the New Poor Law, their role in Herefordshire was far less dominant than in other areas of the country. The explanation for this might be that they were considered less important, as in a number of the Herefordshire Unions the Chairman was a clergyman of high position in the Church and, in some cases, also a major landowner. It is difficult to say whether it was his status as a landowner or as a churchman that was the more important in his role as a Guardian, but it is clear that some of these clerics were diligent in their attention to poor law affairs. The Reverend Archer Clive, for example, was the owner of large acreages along the Welsh border and also Chairman of Dore Union for many years; Canon John Underwood was Chairman of Ledbury Union; and the Reverend Watson Joseph Thornton was Chairman of Hereford City Union for over a decade. In addition to these gentlemen, there were usually five or six elected or ex officio clerical Guardians on all of the county's Union Boards. Some of these churchmen were of very high standing, perhaps in some ways diminishing the status and confidence of the Workhouse Chaplain in the presence of such powerful individuals. The Dean of Hereford Cathedral, the Reverend Doctor John Merewether, a man of strong and forceful personality, often attended the meetings of the City Union, and the Reverend Charles Scott Luxmore, Dean of St Asaph, attended the meetings of Bromyard Union as a local landowner.

In his study of the care of children in Worcestershire workhouses, Frank Crompton has shown that the Unions of that county appointed Chaplains from the very beginning of the New Poor Law and that they appear to have asserted themselves quite forcefully in respect of the selection of workhouse teachers, the supervision of those teachers and, of course, their religious teaching. Children who had been in the workhouse since infancy because they had been abandoned or orphaned would know no other influence than that imposed on them by the workhouse system. Frank Crompton states:

> In some unions the chaplain was so powerful that he overruled the judge-
> ment of the Assistant Poor Law Commissioner. He did this by influ-
> encing the attitudes of the Board of Guardians, the group that controlled
> the Poor Law locally and in a case such as this, the Poor Law Inspector
> could only invoke a complex procedure to get a decision changed.
> Whilst this sometimes led to the Poor Law Central Administration
> ordering the local Guardians to comply with orders and regulations, this
> procedure was very protracted and was only invoked in cases of serious
> disagreement. Thus in most cases the Guardians' decisions, often much
> influenced by the opinion of the chaplain, were not questioned by the
> inspector.[4]

Far from introducing a new and rigorous system of public aid, recent analyses of the poor law reform reveal a considerable degree of local interpretation and implementation. In Bedfordshire, for example, in the Unions of Biggleswade, Luton and Woburn male heads of households were sometimes taken into the workhouse while their wives and families were given relief in kind. This was a very practical step in that it meant that more families could be brought under the control of the poor law without the workhouses being filled to overflowing.[5] In parts of Yorkshire the New Poor Law was never fully implemented and at Thorne Union in the West Riding, the Guardians wrote to the authorities expressing the view that they desired to administer the new system 'not in the restrictive ideological manner demanded, rather in an innovative way aimed at curbing the local problem of vagrancy'.[6] In Norfolk the Principle of Less Eligibility was clearly ignored, for Anne Digby writes:

> There is no doubt that the material standard of living of the inmate of a
> rural Norfolk workhouse was superior to that of the labouring poor in
> the surrounding countryside.[7]

In her lengthy study of poverty Gertrude Himmelfarb argues that it was the stigma of pauperism which provoked so much opposition to the new law in the 1830s and the 1840s. This opposition from below came not from the paupers, because they were quite powerless, but from the poor who felt degraded by the idea of the workhouse. Opposition also came from the parochial powers who resented losing control of local affairs.

In Hereford City the opposition to the New Poor Law was orchestrated by a gentleman by the name of George Wythen Baxter who wrote a book, published in 1841, in which he highlighted the evils of the new law by including newspaper articles drawn from all over the country which told lurid stories of cruelty and starvation in the new workhouses, which he described as 'bastiles'. The book has subsequently been described as 'a compilation of alleged incidents of cruelty and abuse'[8] and as 'tales'.[9] In addition Baxter petitioned Parliament for the repeal of the New Poor Law on the grounds that it was causing great hardship and cruelty within the City of Hereford. He also made allegations against the Hereford Board of Guardians and specifically against the clerk to Hereford City Union, Mr Nicholas Lanwarne. Baxter described him as 'the Commissioners' man-servant',[10] made personal comments about his voice and physical appearance and then mocked his integrity, calling him: 'Electioneering Go-Between ... ladies man, and everybody's six-and-eight penny lacky ...'.[11] He also pointed out in a rather deriding manner that the Union Clerk was also Coroner, Tender Agent and the Contractor for Pauper Coffins. Considering that he was a lawyer it is perhaps surprising that Nicholas Lanwarne seems to have taken no action and no word is recorded about the subject in the Union minutes. In addition to the comments about Nicholas Lanwarne and perhaps including Lanwarne as a guilty party, Baxter claimed that the more corrupt inmates of Hereford Workhouse were given preferential treatment:

> As for the ladies of the pave, it is well known that they, perchance, through their former commercial relations with the officials, are much better treated in the Hereford Union Workhouse, than the old and respectable folk who are taken in and done for.[12]

The Guardians of Hereford Union must have decided not to give the comments any additional importance by commenting on them or contesting them, nor did they seek the advice of their Assistant Commissioner. They probably took the view that the less the Poor Law Commission knew about such allegations, the better it would be for Mr Lanwarne and for the Board of Guardians. The first Assistant Poor Law Commissioner for Herefordshire under the New Poor Law was Sir Edmund Walker Head, who remained in post until September 1840, when he returned to London to become one of the Commissioners at Somerset House, in the company of his academic and political friend, Sir George Cornewall Lewis.

As the New Poor Law became established, the principles of National Uniformity and Less Eligibility underwent subtle changes. There were many interpretations to accommodate local situations, whilst attitudes towards Less Eligibility were softened as Guardians and public alike accepted that some groups of paupers, such as the aged, the sick and children, were not culpable with regard to their impoverished circumstances. Indeed, abandoned and orphaned children in workhouses gave a troubling conundrum to the administrators of the New Poor Law. They could see the logic of educating pauper children in workhouses if it enabled them to seek employment and become independent adults rather than being conditioned to a life bound by pauperism, but at the same time, to be provided with such education gave them advantages over

Sir Edmund Walker Head, when Governor-General of New Brunswick, c.1848

the children of independent labourers outside the workhouse and thus broke the Principle of Less Eligibility. Those who upheld the Principle above all else would therefore seek means to avoid providing workhouse children with an education. The Guardians of Ross Union successfully avoided appointing a properly qualified teacher until 1855 and did so then only under pressure from Somerset House.[13] It would appear that by 1850 the Central Authority at Somerset House had accepted that the Principle of Less Eligibility in the

Sir George Cornewall Lewis by H. Weighall
(© National Museums & Galleries of Wales)

case of pauper children's education was not tenable and were actively working against it. The Poor Law Board (1847-1871) was, however, in a very awkward situation from a political standpoint because elementary education for the population outside the workhouse did not become law until 1870. They were, though, quite prepared to smooth over regulations in order to achieve their aims when it suited them and this is illustrated in a case cited by Sidney and Beatrice Webb when writing their enormous work on the New Poor Law in 1910.

In 1856 the Poor Law Board was urging on the Holborn Guardians the wisdom of educating pauper children in separate schools in order to free them from any undesirable influences and habits encountered in the workhouse and to give them sufficient education to enable them to earn their own livelihood. The Webbs claim[14] that the Central Authority at this time took every opportunity to urge this course on all Unions. When some Unions raised objections on the basis of giving pauper children unfair advantage over the children of the independent poor, the Central Authority replied that 'the provision of good education for the children was not likely to encourage voluntary pauperism in the parents, and therefore there was no need to apply the principle of less eligibility in this case'.[15]

It is clear from the minute books of Ross Union that the same education policy – which will be given more detailed consideration in a later chapter – was being advocated in rural areas as well as in cities. At a Guardians' meeting held on 8 January 1849, the clerk to the Guardians read out a letter from Jelinger C. Symons, Inspector of Workhouse Schools, inviting Ross Guardians to consider the provision of a district school with the neighbouring Unions of Newent in Gloucestershire and Ledbury in Herefordshire. It also suggested that the Guardians of all three Unions should meet to discuss the possibility of providing such a school. There is no mention of the proposed meeting and it is quite reasonable to assume that, apart from their reluctance to spend money on providing good education for workhouse children, the Guardians did not think that the provision of one school to cover such a large rural area was practical and, in that respect, they would have had a strong argument on their side. The minutes also show that at a meeting held at Ross on 21 January 1850, the Chairman drew the Board's attention to the details of an entry in the visitors' book made by Jelinger C. Symons in September 1849, when he had expressed his views about the poor standard of educational provision in Ross Workhouse. The Guardians were certainly not intimidated by the Central Authority and maintained their stance on education for pauper children until 1855.

The two major principles of the New Poor Law, Less Eligibility and National Uniformity, which were often so rigidly applied in the early years of the new law, were soon softened for both practical and political reasons. The new law had been the subject of enormous controversy both in Parliament and amongst the general public because of the severity with which some Unions applied these principles, and the resultant harsh treatment of the respectable poor. This was brought to a head in 1845 when the plight of the paupers in Andover Workhouse was discovered, to the shame of all those men involved in the running of that Union. The 'Workhouse Test' had been applied so severely that the paupers were reduced to gnawing the bones they were given to crush for fertilizer. The very fact that there was considerable criticism of those Unions who were thought too zealous in their application of the new law brought the concept of National Uniformity into question and showed that it was seriously compromised. Yet it had been compromised from the very beginning because the Poor Law Commissioners had not managed to establish strong and effective mechanisms in order to ensure uniformity. Similarly, when the Boards of Guardians asserted themselves and applied regulations as they saw fit, providing extra resources for particular classes of pauper, the Principle of Less Eligibility was also compromised.

The problem was that the central government was experimenting with a new form of control over local affairs and, in many respects, they were feeling their way. There was much opposition to the notion of centralisation and the Poor Law Commissioners could not really control the Boards of Guardians in their day to day management of Union affairs even with the supervision of their Assistant Commissioners to help them. Frank Crompton makes this point clear in the conclusion to his study of the care of children in Worcestershire Workhouses. He states:

> The Principles of Less Eligibility and of National Uniformity – the major Benthamite tenets of the New Poor Law – thus caused problems from the outset, particularly regarding children. However, some Worcestershire Guardians continued to adhere to these outmoded ideas, so that Less Eligibility differed from place to place, particularly in relation to child paupers. Some Guardians, such as those at Martley, over a long period of time resisted innovation in the treatment of child paupers for this reason.[16]

In many instances, the attitudes which Boards of Guardians displayed with regard to innovation and change probably reflected the attitudes and opinions of one or two Guardians or perhaps a small group of them. These were men of particular wealth and influence whose standing in the community allowed them to manage or steer the decision making at Guardians' meetings. The New Poor Law was an experiment with a new approach to the management of public aid and was clearly seen as just that by some of the politicians who sought to implement its principles. Writing from London on 6 August 1848,

Sir George Cornewall Lewis was able to say to his friend Sir Edmund Walker Head, by then Governor of New Brunswick, that:

> The Poor Law of Ireland is exercising a most powerful influence on the social state of the country. In England the Poor Law is no longer heard of. The experiment of direct responsibility to parliament has been decidedly successful. This is Graham's opinion as well as mine.[17]

England was being changed by the process of industrialisation; the growth of towns and cities created greater and greater concentrations of people and the old ties of paternalism were breaking down. The centralisation of political power had begun.

3 The Old Poor Law in Ledbury

The Overseers and Churchwardens of Ledbury were fortunate in retaining the services of a succession of diligent Vestry Clerks who recorded their decisions and kept the minutes of their meetings in good order. This was not always the case in other parishes, making any attempt to compare the workings of the Old Poor Law and the New Poor Law almost impossible. In Ledbury, however, the precise work of the Vestry Clerks (1804-1834) and of the clerks to the Board of Guardians (1834-1865) provides sufficient detail over a 30-year period for a comparison of the two systems to be attempted.

Parochial independence, flexibility of management and an inadequate system of auditing always made the Old Poor Law vulnerable to exploitation both by the idle who claimed unwarranted assistance and by unscrupulous merchants who tried to make easy money by charging high prices for inferior goods. Ledbury experienced its share of these problems, but for the most part the Overseers and Churchwardens managed to sustain a generosity of spirit towards the poor often absent in other parishes. They generally gave them the benefit of the doubt until precise details of an individual's circumstances gave them cause to reconsider their award decisions. The records also indicate that they were rarely overruled by Magistrates when relief claims were refused. This suggests that for the most part they acted reasonably in their dealings with the poor, even though the only real incentive they had for administering poor relief was that of being in a good position to influence spending in order to hold down the poor rate. They were already heavily burdened by other taxes: church rate, militia rate, county rate, statute duty, and fines for the deficiency in the army reserve force; and hop growers also had to pay hop duty. Some of them, however, were clearly motivated by the notion of public duty, because over a period of two or three decades the same names occur in the records again and again. They included some of the major landowners in the district and many of the most prominent merchants, surveyors, insurance agents and bankers in Ledbury. The minutes of their meetings, read in conjunction with the town's response to the Poor Law Commission's enquiry in 1832, paint an interesting picture of the problems they faced as they struggled to manage the ever-rising cost of poor relief in the first three decades of the 19th century.

The return[1] was compiled by a land surveyor and auctioneer named Charles Share who was described as 'Vestry Clerk and Acting Overseer'. It shows that between 1801 and 1831 the cost of poor relief in Ledbury per head of the general population rose broadly in line with that of Ross, Bromyard and Kington, all market towns with populations of a similar size. For Ledbury the costs per head were: 7s in 1803; 16s 11d in 1813; 13s in 1821 and 11s 9d in 1831. The issues surrounding the dramatic rise in costs, both locally and nationally, have long been debated by historians, but owing to the inconsistent nature of the surviving records, the real reasons for the increase in expenditure remain obscure and contentious. The particular issue here, however, is not so much why costs rose, but how the Overseers and Churchwardens of Ledbury responded to the situation and attempted to control costs in a manner that was fair to all concerned. The system of finance was simple and effective so long as everyone behaved responsibly. Each year a new Overseer, a ratepayer, was elected, and throughout the year the Churchwardens and ratepayers who attended vestry meetings granted him three or four sixpenny rates at a time. This meant that he could go to the occupiers of property to collect a poor rate of 6d in the pound based on the poor rate assessment for their property on a number of occasions without further reference to the vestry. It also meant that the ratepayers did not have to pay the whole rate at one time. The Overseer could then pay for supplies for the workhouse, out relief and all other expenses connected with maintenance of the poor. At Easter, the Overseer's accounts were examined, deficiencies made good and cash balances handed on to the new Overseer, whose term of office ran until the following Easter. It was a time-consuming and arduous task, particularly since it was unpaid and considered a public duty.

The most significant difference between the administration of the Old Poor Law and the New Poor Law in Ledbury was in the use of the workhouse for the able-bodied poor. Before 1834, the emphasis was on keeping them out of the workhouse as far as possible by assisting them to live independently in their own homes. For that reason, the core of the inmates usually comprised the aged and the sick who were acknowledged to be beyond work, abandoned or orphaned children, and at times, single girls with infants. In July 1803 the inmates, from infant to adult, numbered 13 males and 25 females;[2] in September there were 13 males and 19 females;[3] in June 1804, 5 males and 14 females;[4] in October, 8 males and 17 females;[5] and in April 1805, 7 males and 10 females.[6] The general population of the workhouse rose and fell as able-bodied men and women came and went in response to the seasonal availability of field work. These were, however, likely to be single people, because the Overseers generally managed to sustain their policy of relieving families in their own homes. If they were genuinely homeless they might be found lodgings or, if absolutely necessary, taken into the workhouse, but they were not allowed to do nothing. If regular work was not available, they might be sent out to labour at the direction of the Overseer and their earnings were supposed to be paid to him as a contribution towards their maintenance.

After 1834, however, the system of relief was far less flexible. Able-bodied men and women, apart from respectable widows with young children, were supposed to be either unemployed and in the workhouse or entirely independent in the community. In some respects, this was a backward step, because it made paupers of respectable men and women who genuinely just needed a little help from time to time, but the rules said there were no half measures. At the beginning of the 19th century the parish of Ledbury owned almshouses in several parts of the town and a number of pieces of land on which parish officers planned to build more. It also owned most, if not all, of the properties built on the finger of land situated between Church Lane and Back Lane. It was here, very close to the church and the centre of the town, that Ledbury Workhouse was to be found. In 1803 its domestic management was in the hands of a Mrs Mason, the Matron, and under the general control and management of the Overseer of the poor and a board of eight assistants, four of whom were replaced each year. They were all ratepayers and men who regularly attended vestry meetings and took turns in inspecting the workhouse. They appeared to accept, probably through their knowledge of local families, that most of the people seeking relief were indeed the deserving poor, the sick and the moribund. Parish records suggest that Ledbury Workhouse was indeed a last refuge for the utterly exhausted and destitute; deaths often occurred within a few days or weeks of admission.

The case of Frances Newberry[7] suggests just such a life of toil and drudgery ending in poverty. She was admitted to the workhouse on 20 August 1803, seemingly possessing only the clothes she was wearing, and died four days later, just 40 years of age. In the normal course of events she would have been given a pauper's burial at the expense of the parish and her clothes and meagre possessions, if she had any, would have been sold to offset some of the costs. On this occasion, however, since Frances Newberry had not received any previous help from the parish, the Board of Assistants agreed that her clothes should be sent to a Mr and Mrs Baker, possibly former employers, who had said that they would arrange the burial without any expense to the parish.

Admission to the workhouse at this date did not appear to engender fear. Indeed, some of the able-bodied poor who managed to gain admission were inclined to become a little too comfortable there and had to be urged to leave. Some who were thought to be malingerers just taking advantage of the situation were simply 'dismissed' if they refused to leave of their own accord. At the beginning of July 1803, a man named George Cotterell, his wife and three children, were admitted to the workhouse, 'being destitute of lodgings'.[8] At a meeting held the following day the wisdom of admitting the family was questioned, because it was thought that it might encourage other families to seek admission. The Cotterells were deemed to be in good health and quite capable of work and it was felt that it would therefore have been wiser to make some other provision for them. As a result the Overseers were recommended 'to be particularly cautious in their orders for admission into the House'.[9] The concern seems to have been quite justified because it appears from the records that the Cotterells were abusing the situation. After about a month in the workhouse George Cotterell had been found work but later it was noted that 'having been at work for the last fortnight without bringing his wages to the Overseer',[10] it was ordered that the family should be expelled from the workhouse.

The system of sending able-bodied men and women out of the workhouse to work on a daily basis was very lax and open to abuse by both employer and employee. The labourers were often sent out before any price for their work had been fixed and the farmers and tradesmen who employed them were often very slow to pay the Overseer. This resulted in large sums of money remaining outstanding, when prompt payment would have eased the general burden on ratepayers. Some no doubt took their time in the hope that the inadequate accounting system might allow them to escape payment and thus retrieve some of their own poor rate expenses. The case of Mary Dix, however, indicates that other employments arranged from the workhouse were more straightforward and proved to be satisfactory to all parties – the parish, the employer and the employee. In July 1803 Mary, probably in her early teens, hired herself out to a Mr Benjamin Johnson and his wife for one year. She was to be allowed 'a proper sufficiency of meat, drink, washing, lodging and clothing on being first provided with proper clothing by the parish'.[11] It was also agreed that at the end of the year Mary's clothing should be as good as that allowed by the parish at the commencement of the agreement. In July 1804 a minute recorded that having completed her year's employment Mary had been received back into the workhouse 'with a proper change of apparel agreeably to the terms of her engagement'[12] and that Mrs Johnson had also left 'a written character of her good behaviour during the time of her service'.[13] In the right situation Mary had proved that she could do well, despite previous criticisms of her behaviour whilst working in the pin factory attached to the workhouse.

Amidst the clamour of the ratepayers to put the poor to work, the Overseers were constantly in search of suitable employment for them, but it was not always easy to find, particularly when field work was unavailable. The establishment of Mr Watts' pin factory, attached to the workhouse, must have seemed the ideal employment solution for the winter months, and with strong management it might have worked to everyone's advantage. His business was, however, beset by problems caused very largely by his unusual workforce. As well as employing adults and children from the workhouse, he employed some of the independent poor, but his failure to keep firm control of these groups led to considerable unrest. The independent poor accused the paupers of abusing them with improper language; Mr Watts accused them of leading the children astray and passing on their own bad habits. 1803 appears to have been a particularly trying year of complaint and counter-complaint, but most of those recorded were concerned with the behaviour of the children in the factory. There is no record of the children's ages, the hours they worked or what was required of them, so it is not possible to judge whether their tasks were suitable for them, or whether they were mistreated. At the beginning of May, Mr Watts presented the Overseers and Churchwardens with his account of the children's earnings for the previous two weeks. They amounted to £1 7s 11d, of which the children were allowed to share 4s 'as an encouragement to their future exertions'.[14] Their share varied slightly from distribution to distribution, but the general pattern indicates that they were allowed to keep approximately 2d in every shilling. This was forward thinking, but the incentive did not engender the hoped-for work ethic in all the children and some were punished quite frequently. The distribution of earnings did continue, however, for those children who were deemed to be deserving of them.

In July, it was reported to the Board that six of the children had not carried out their proper tasks, and Mrs Mason, the Matron, was ordered to give them only bread and water for their meals for a day. The other children ate as normal and shared 3s of the 18s they had earned in the past two weeks.[15] A week later Board Assistant Daniel Saunders visited the factory and was informed that Mary Dix, Elizabeth Napper, James Parker and Edward Parker had again not done their work. They were admonished by Mr Saunders and again the Matron was ordered to give them only bread and water for their dinner. At a Board meeting held the same day it was resolved that 'in future the Assistants who made daily visits to the workhouse should also visit the pin factory to see how the children are working'.[16] This was a recurrent theme throughout the summer, with other names being added to the list of miscreants: Hannah Cotterell, Thomas Morgan, William Pitt, John Pillinger and others. Later, Elizabeth Napper was discharged for stealing flax and was thereafter directed to do spinning under the supervision of the Matron. Not all the complaints came from Mr Watts and the Board of Assistants. Late in November Edward Parker complained that Mr Watts had struck him and he had received 'a violent blow on the face, without giving any cause of offence'.[17] The matter was investigated and thought to be without foundation, but it had given the Board serious cause for concern. Four days later, the Overseer, John Slade, signed a minute which stated that upon reviewing the 'trifling sums of money earned by the children, which is not nearly equal to their maintenance',[18] and the many complaints about them, the Board recommended to the next vestry meeting 'the propriety of placing them out to the farmers which we think would be more beneficial to the interests of the parish and serviceable to the children themselves'.[19] Sent out to farmers, some of the children would no doubt have been treated fairly, but others were quite likely to have been condemned to a life of drudgery and a very sad existence.

Records suggest, therefore, that at the beginning of the 19th century Ledbury Workhouse was firmly but fairly regulated and that life within its walls might be very reasonable for any pauper who respected its rules and behaved himself. He was provided with shelter, clothes and regular meals. Indeed, his general welfare was probably more assured than that of many of the independent poor. The workhouse was inspected almost daily by a member of the Board of Assistants who recorded his findings and reported any serious issues at the next board meeting. He checked the building for cleanliness, witnessed the weighing of portions of meat and cheese, and examined the quality of the bread. He listened to the complaints of the Matron and the inmates and dealt with problems as quickly as possible. Troublesome inmates were questioned and cautioned that if their behaviour did not improve they might be expelled from the workhouse to fend for themselves. Some paupers undoubtedly found the firm routine of the workhouse alien to their previous mode of life and, consequently, found it difficult to conform.

The vast majority of paupers, however, received out relief whilst living in their own homes for the Overseers and Churchwardens of Ledbury did everything they could to keep people out of the workhouse by helping them to remain independent. Their relief came in the form of a weekly sum of money and an allowance of bread, occasional grants of shoes, clothes and bedding, simple medical care, an entitlement to buy subsidised coal in the winter months, and the full payment of cottage rents or occasional help with rent arrears. All in all, Ledbury's poor seem to have been treated very fairly, but, perhaps inevitably, some of them abused the situation. As the first decade of the century passed into the second, and poor relief costs escalated, the minutes of the meetings of the Board of Assistants indicate a marked tightening of procedures, a closer scrutiny of individual cases and a distinct hardening of attitude. Parish expenditure was running out of control; those paying the poor rates were being overburdened, the parish had substantial debts at the bank, and something had to be done to make savings. There was a sense that the men administering poor relief in Ledbury were beginning to feel overwhelmed by the magnitude of the problem.

The placing of pauper children as parish apprentices appears to have been a relatively simple expedient to reduce parish expenditure, but the distress it caused to children and their families must have been considerable. The vast majority of them were not orphaned or abandoned children living in the workhouse, but from families where parents were unable to earn sufficient money to keep them and were in receipt of a weekly cash subsidy in aid of low wages. Parents who refused to let their children be apprenticed had their allowances reduced or stopped completely depending on the number of their children. A minute dated July 1816 showed that the same rule was applied with equal firmness to widows: 'Ordered that the Widow Hooper of Wellington Heath be relieved with three shillings (per week) but in case she applies for further relief that her eldest child be put out apprentice'.[20] Widows and couples with large families had little choice but to watch their children's future be settled by the degrading process of a public ballot, not unlike an auction. They were caught in a trap. They lost their oldest children just when they were likely to be able to start contributing to the family's income, but if they refused to let them go, their problems were increased as they tried to provide for the same number of children with a smaller income. William Graves had his weekly allowance reduced to 1s 6d 'in consequence of his keeping his son, about 16 years old, at home'.[21] The true nature of this man's circumstances was not recorded, but the Board's decision was clear and unambiguous. In March 1804 17 boys and girls were selected to be apprenticed by ballot and 'a like number of Paymasters to the rates of the largest rentals were selected'[22] to take them. The ratepayers could absolve themselves of their obligation by paying a £10 fine; the parents could only await and accept the outcome of the ballot.

In the first three decades of the 19th century the Overseers and Churchwardens of Ledbury apprenticed hundreds of children in this way, but they were far less harsh than some of their counterparts in other parishes in two important ways. They did not apprentice any children under ten years of age, nor did they send batches of children to work in cotton factories many miles from Ledbury. It is impossible to say just how many children were apprenticed, because it is clear from the Overseers' minutes that large groups of 40 or 50 were apprenticed locally but were never properly indentured, probably to save money. The survival of an apprentice register[23] covering the years 1805-1825, however, provides a glimpse of activities in those years. It listed 133 children: 66 boys and 67 girls. Each apprenticeship was approved by the Overseers and Churchwardens and also sanctioned by two Magistrates. The children's ages ranged from 10 to 16, but the average for both sexes was just 11. A little more than half were apprenticed to farmers and the rest to an assortment of professional men, tradesmen and merchants, but few are likely to have received any systematic training in acquiring real skills because apprenticeship fees were paid in only seven cases. Twelve ratepayers elected to pay a fine rather than take an apprentice and one mother, whose 11-year-old daughter had been directed to join the household of a ratepayer who described himself as a farmer and butcher, simply refused to let her go.

Once the children had been apprenticed and provided with new clothes at the parish's expense, the parish officers probably assumed that they would incur no more costs for them for years ahead, but this was not always the case. Some children ran away from their masters and after their circumstances had been investigated, were usually returned to them. Others were turned out and if their masters did not give just cause for their actions they were duly summoned to attend the Magistrates' court to explain themselves. A few children were simply dismissed and, since they did not have proper apprenticeship indentures, could be placed with another master, subject to the approval of two Magistrates. One such case was that of James Pritchard,[24] a lively lad who had been apprenticed to a Mr Taylor at The Feathers Hotel in the centre of Ledbury. He was dismissed for riding one of the horses stabled there beyond Hereford. In a few cases, children were apprenticed to tradesmen either by private agreement or on completion of formal indentures. At the beginning of December 1817, John Bowkett, a shoemaker of Ledbury, offered to take Thomas Andrews, an orphan pauper living in the workhouse, to provide for him and teach him his trade on being paid a £4 premium. It was also agreed that the poor rate on Bowkett's house which had recently been increased from £3 to £3 10s, should be reduced to the original sum.[25] Later that month, Thomas Miles was formally indentured for seven years to Charles Beech, a glass-toy maker of Birmingham;[26] and in February 1818, Edward Hooper was allowed 15s to buy an indenture for his son, William, who was to be apprenticed to a carpet manufacturer at Kidderminster.[27]

The maintenance of children was a heavy burden on the poor rate, not least those born to single mothers. They were, of course, supposed to be supported by their natural fathers, but ensuring that this happened was often more easily said than done. A register[28] of the putative fathers of base-born children for the years 1803-1830 listed 170 cases. A succession of Vestry Clerks kept precise records for each man, detailing both payments and arrears. The sums involved generally ranged from 1s 3d to 2s per week, but the zeal with which the men were pursued to keep their accounts up to date had waxed and waned depending on the attitude and the efficiency of the men managing poor law affairs. In December 1818, a review of parochial accounts revealed that the sums received from putative fathers had been trifling and that for years the parish officers had failed to take appropriate steps to compel them to meet their responsibilities. It was resolved, therefore, that Mr Slade, the current Overseer, must take all proper means to enforce payment without further delay.[29] There was, however, considerable delay, probably while the Overseer made enquiries about the men's ability to pay. There was little point in paying 3s for a warrant to bring a man to court if he was unemployed or already receiving poor relief to help in the support of his lawful wife and children.

In April 1819[30] the Overseers were instructed that in future payments for bastards must not exceed 2s per week, as the Magistrates had directed that larger sums should come from affiliation orders. Early in June[31] that year, the Board of Assistants ordered the Overseers to see that putative fathers in arrears were brought before the Magistrates' Court at the next sitting, but two weeks later[32] they were again told to get on with the issuing of warrants. It is unclear when the first warrants were issued, but the first to be minuted were not served until the beginning of March 1820,[33] when warrants were issued against 25 men and it was ordered that the 3s it cost to procure the warrant should be added to their arrears. More were issued in August 1821,[34] this time against women who had deserted their children as well as putative fathers. There was a distinct hardening of attitude and, perhaps for that reason, some men came forward voluntarily to arrange regular weekly payments and also to pay what they could to clear or reduce their arrears. Despite the Board's attempts to enforce payment, the Overseers' accounts showed that in 1822 the parish expended £222 10s on the support of base children alone, an average of £18 10s 10d per month.[35] There was still a long way to go before receipts and expenditure were likely to balance. As the diligent members of the Board of Assistants and the Churchwardens wrestled with the problem of settlement cases, deserted families, outbreaks of fever, vagrants, malingerers, pauper employment, reducing parish debts and the difficult issues surrounding the management of the workhouse, their efforts were sometimes seriously undermined by the incompetent or unscrupulous methods of their own Overseers.

Thomas Bosley and Stephen Baylis were two such men. Thomas Bosley was a miller and baker of Ledbury who had a contract to supply bread to the town's workhouse, but appeared to think that anything would do for paupers. At the beginning of December 1816, Samuel Rickards, the Visiting Assistant, tasted the latest delivery of bread and found it to be 'very ordinary and heavy'.[36] In March 1817, Thomas Webb, another Assistant, sampled the bread and declared it to be 'scarcely wholesome'.[37] Mr Bosley appeared before the next vestry meeting and pledged that in future only good quality bread would be supplied, but his words meant very little because less than a month later Samuel Rickards sampled the bread again and made some damning remarks: 'Monday visited the House – bread very inferior in quality, and weighing heavy, having by its appearance and taste a large quantity of bran flour intermixed therewith'.[38] He also inspected another batch of bread, presumably just delivered, and found it to be short of the weight charged and again very inferior in quality and 'such as ought not to be brought into the House'.[39] Complaints continued throughout the summer and autumn of 1817, and in December it was minuted that a pauper or paupers in the workhouse had complained to a Magistrate about the quality of the bread provided for them. Overseers and Churchwardens in general bridled if Magistrates interfered in poor law matters and the Ledbury Board of Assistants are unlikely to have reacted differently. As a result of the complaint to the Magistrate the bread was tasted by all members of the Board and found to be 'of sufficient quality,'[40] but an order was made that any future complaints should be made to the Matron and that she should give potatoes to those who complained at their next meal instead of bread. A week later the Board decided that in future, bread for the workhouse inmates would be baked in the workhouse. They perhaps thought this the most expedient solution to the problem, but parish politics were almost certainly a factor too, because on 3 December that year, Thomas Bosley was elected Overseer of the Poor.

This was not as odd as it might seem because, as a ratepayer, Bosley had a moral duty to take his turn in the job and also had a right to put his name forward for election. It was unusual for elections to take place in December, but at that particular time the structures of the Old Poor Law were crumbling and parish finances were in chaos. Overseer Stephen Baylis had been suspended from duty and was later removed from office.

The Board of Assistants constantly sought ways of saving money in order to reduce the demands on the already overburdened ratepayers and in February 1815 had decided to advertise for a Workhouse Master: 'a man of respectable character who is capable of employing the poor in some useful manufactuary'.[41] Proposals were to be sent postage paid, if by letter, to the Churchwardens and Overseers and likely applicants were reminded that no person should apply whose character would not stand the strictest scrutiny. A month later Stephen Baylis's proposal was discussed, agreed and made binding for one year, at a Board meeting held on Lady Day, 25 March 1815, when Baylis stated:

> I will make myself responsible for all monies granted by Rates for the maintenance of the Poor ... and I will undertake the general management of the Poor both in the workhouse as well as those who receive out pay, for the sum of one hundred pounds per annum.[42]

The Board may have breathed a temporary sigh of relief that someone else was going to take charge of the day to day administration, but this was a bold and ambitious undertaking for both parties and if anything went wrong, it was still the Board's responsibility to set matters in order. In January 1816 they were forced to intervene and no doubt had to acknowledge to themselves, if not to Stephen Baylis, that the arrangement entailed too much work for one man. Decisions had to be taken and it was ordered that 'a proper woman be appointed to superintend the workhouse,'[43] which suggested that its supervision was unsatisfactory. There had long been problems with able-bodied paupers coming and going as they pleased and suspicions about the theft of food and other provisions and, without a resident Matron monitoring activities, the situation had probably become even more untenable. In addition it was ordered that 'three respectable people of the parish be appointed visitors to look over the affairs of the workhouse'.[44] It was also agreed that Stephen Baylis would, with the active help of Overseer Caleb Hankins, continue to collect the rates until next Lady Day for £50, in order to reduce parish expenses.[45]

By December 1816 the crisis in Stephen Baylis' financial affairs had deepened and since his fiscal problems were so intertwined with his incompetent handling of poor rate revenues, parish finances were in a dire state too. In fairness to Stephen Baylis, it is not entirely clear whether he was actually dishonest or just over-confident in his ability to fulfil the proposal he had formulated and presented to the Board in March 1815. It was clear, however, that by the end of October 1817 he was in debt to the parish for poor rate revenues amounting to £374 6s 9d and was suspended from office.[46] A week later, on 5 November 1817, the Vestry Clerk recorded the following minute:

> It appearing to this meeting that Stephen Baylis, the Assistant Overseer or Guardian of the poor of this parish is considerably indebted to this parish for monies received by him for the use of the parish which he has improperly applied and he having admitted that he is insolvent and unable to pay any part of it, resolved that he is therefore become an improper person to intermeddle further with the affairs and concerns of this parish.[47]

It was further resolved that, with help from the Board of Assistants, the elected Overseers and Churchwardens would continue to manage parish business without the aid of a paid Assistant Overseer; a decision which led James Holbrook, attorney and Clerk to the Magistrates, to withdraw from the Board. His letter almost certainly voiced the thoughts and opinions of many other ratepayers:

> I must request that my name be expunged from the list of members now constituting such Board; because I consider it utterly impossible for the

individuals forming the same to acquit themselves and give satisfaction to the parishioners without the assistance of such an officer: unless they devote a considerably greater portion of their time to the management of the poor than they can afford or reasonably be expected to do, as it appears there are near three hundred paupers (exclusive of casualties) whose cases and complaints are at least weekly and many daily requiring attention.[48]

The volume of work had recently caused problems for there had been occasions when so few of the members of the Board of Assistants had attended meetings to assess the needs of the poor that proceedings had to be adjourned and the paupers turned away with nothing, no doubt adding greatly to the misery and distress of the genuinely needy. The system was in decline because it depended too heavily on the voluntary work of men who had pressing business needs of their own.

In March 1818 a public meeting was held to consider the possibility of indicting Stephen Baylis for fraud. The Board concluded, however, that whilst his conduct 'merits the severest censure and renders him unworthy of any office of trust,'[49] it was not practical to prosecute Stephen Baylis for fraudulent practices because it would be very expensive and 'not advisable ... considering the great burden of parochial taxes so severely felt at this time by the paymasters of this parish'.[50] This was not the end of the matter, however, because in May that year creditors were pressing for the immediate payment of £217 7s 3d[51] for goods supplied during Baylis' term of office, and it was resolved that the only way the current Overseers could discharge the debts was by obtaining a loan from Ledbury bankers Thomas Webb and Son. Later, the accounts of the Surveyor of Roads[52] suggested that Baylis was entitled to receive £53 he had expended for labour and his wife was owed £20 for stone purchased to employ the poor in the winter months; and attempts were made to have these sums transferred to the parish to offset some of his debts. The fact remained, however, that he still owed the parish well over £500, money which would ultimately have to be made good through future poor rate revenues. Records suggested that the greatest crisis in Ledbury's poor law administration was during the years 1815 to 1818 and, whilst it would be all too easy to make Stephen Baylis the scapegoat for all the problems, it was probably not entirely coincidental that they were the years of his period of office. There were very clearly great weaknesses in the mechanisms for collecting and spending poor rate revenues which rendered the system open to abuse and perhaps none more so than in the management of the workhouse.

Lady Day 1815 marked the beginning of Stephen Baylis' agreement with the Board of Assistants to manage the poor and assume the role of Master of the workhouse, but it was not clear whether he and his wife lived on the premises or in their own home. If they did live at the workhouse, it would appear that they presided over a very lax regime which was open to abuse by able-bodied paupers and unscrupulous merchants alike. In January 1816 the Board had to intervene and assume responsibility for the management of the workhouse once more. At the beginning of May, a Mrs Nott was appointed as Matron and with her help the Board attempted to regain control of the workhouse. She agreed to furnish her own room and to provide tea and sugar for her personal use at her own expense, but was to be allowed meat, bread, vegetables and beer as part of her salary of £30 per annum.[53] Mrs Nott was to devote all her time to the poor, keep precise records and ensure that the workhouse rules were properly observed.

The Matron was given firm guidance about her general duties and in particular she had to see that no food was wasted or stolen. She was to keep a provisions book and present it to the Board for inspection at every meeting and it was also to be open to any parishioner who wished to see it. She was to take particular care to see that coals were not wasted with the lighting of unnecessary fires. She was to 'inspect the persons who are appointed to instruct the children to read',[54] and Mrs Nott herself was to instruct the girls who had spent the morning working in the pin factory 'in sewing, reading or some useful domestic employment'[55] during the afternoons. Finally, she was to see that she called 'the whole family that are in the House who are not prevented by sickness to be assembled previous to their going to bed every night to whom she shall read prayers'.[56] In June that year an inventory was taken of everything in the workhouse, including paupers' own garments, and the Board of Assistants was increased from eight to twelve, suggesting a further tightening of procedures and a need to keep a very close check on everything. Visiting Assistants Samuel Rickards and Daniel Saunders made a routine inspection of the workhouse at the end of June[57] and found it to be very clean and well ordered.

Mrs Nott died that summer, and in September a Mrs Ann Ward was appointed on very similar terms, but, perhaps because of the Board's deepening suspicions about the financial stability of their Overseer, Stephen Baylis, she was informed from the outset what might happen if she gave any cause for complaint. In the event of her misconduct she might receive a warning and a further month's employment on trial, alternatively a special meeting of ratepayers might be called to consider her conduct and, if a majority of them thought it prudent, she might be removed from office.[58] She signed the minute book to confirm her acceptance of these conditions, but left after just over a year and was replaced by a Mrs Stephens.[59]

In the autumn of 1816 and throughout 1817 the Board of Assistants embarked on a careful review of the circumstances of the able-bodied men and women in the workhouse and whether their admission had been appropriate. In past years admission to the workhouse for such adults had been approved only when there appeared to be no other solution, but since Stephen Baylis had been Master of the Workhouse, some had adopted a very comfortable existence there and seemed to be using the establishment as a free boarding house. They apparently came and went as they pleased and often used their earnings for their own indulgence instead of handing them to the Overseer to contribute to their keep. In a small town like Ledbury this would soon be well known and no doubt caused resentment amongst the ratepayers and considerable criticism of the Board of Assistants. The Board began, therefore, to clear the workhouse of malingerers, bringing to an end an existence which quite possibly assured them greater security and comfort than that sustained by the poorest independent parishioners who were struggling to pay the poor rate.

Stephen Baylis had agreed to arrange suitable employment for the poor as part of his contract with the Board of Assistants and it was therefore his responsibility to collect their earnings or to ensure that a responsible person did so on his behalf. He clearly failed in this duty on some occasions because Richard Berry and William Morris were in the habit of collecting their wages themselves and arriving at the workhouse in a very drunken state, causing great disruption to the smooth running of the establishment.[60] They were warned about their behaviour and told that they would be turned out of the workhouse if it happened again. The warnings went unheeded and the Overseer was ordered to take them before the Magistrates to answer for their behaviour. Richard Berry was, however, still in the workhouse eight months later, possibly because he was there with his children. The Magistrates and the Board were probably well aware that if they turned him out his children would suffer greatly or, more likely, he would simply disappear and leave his children to be provided for by the parish until they were old enough to be apprenticed. Deserted wives and children were a frequent and particular problem for parish officers because the cost of supporting the family whilst tracing the husband and bringing him to court could be considerable. If the man was found guilty and sent to prison then the expense of maintaining his family continued for the term of his imprisonment.

Some paupers were helped on their way with cash allowances and the provision of a few essential household items. On leaving the workhouse William Underwood and his family were given 15s for immediate needs, a quantity of herdin, a strong material used to make pillows or mattresses, sometimes called ticks, for a bed and an allowance of 7s 6d per week.[61] George Smith and his family were provided with a bedstead and bedding;[62] and Elizabeth Green was given 20s to purchase household items, a weekly allowance of

2s and the loan of a spinning wheel.[63] At the same time, other paupers had their personal circumstances investigated, perhaps more thoroughly than ever before, and were quickly presented with clear ultimatums. It was ordered that Elizabeth Poole, having left the workhouse of her own free will to search for a place of employment, was not to be readmitted without the permission of the Overseer.[64] The provisions supplied to Samuel Load and his son John were to cease – for the father until he gave an account of his earnings for the past four months and for the son because he was apprenticed to Mrs Bond of Stone House and must return to his mistress.[65] Despite the Board's best efforts to reduce pauper lists and to remove malingerers from the workhouse, expenditure remained burdensome, and in September 1817, thirteen 6d rates had to be granted in order to keep the relief system running.[66] At that time the number of inmates in the workhouse averaged 45 to 50, a large number for the Matron to monitor on a daily basis amidst her other duties, and it was clear that abuse was still a serious problem. It was ordered, therefore, that all current and future inmates must give up their own clothes and 'wear the livery of the house',[67] presumably to make it easier to spot interlopers, particularly at meal times. The Board, probably under pressure from ratepayers, appeared to be intent on reform and the drive for economy continued unabated. A week later, after close scrutiny of the pauper lists, it was noted that 'there are many of the inmates of the house who have been declared improper subjects for the workhouse, but still refuse to leave'.[68] It was resolved, therefore, that at the next parish meeting the inmates would be divided into three classes, the old and infirm, the children, and the able poor and that 'the utmost attention shall be paid to persons of the latter from having any further allowances than the customary rations, and also to prevent their being supplied with tea or any other indulgences'.[69] It had apparently been customary in Ledbury for those men and women working from the workhouse who regularly handed their wages to the Overseer to receive a small amount for themselves but, in November that year it was ordered that in future they should receive no part of their wages until their earnings were equivalent to the cost of their main-tenance and that of their families, 'and all other persons in the house able to work be sent to labour in the garden'.[70]

In the spring of 1818, there were evidently still serious problems at the workhouse because at a meeting held at the end of March, strict new rules were introduced to prevent the paupers removing food from the dining room. It was ordered that if paupers did not finish their meal it must be saved for them to eat at the next meal before they were allowed anything else. To ensure that no food was pocketed, Richard Tree, James Griffiths and his wife were deployed around the dining room at the Matron's discretion as food inspec-tors. Only the sick and the infirm were to be allowed to eat in their rooms and the most vulnerable inmates in the dining room were to sit next to the Matron to ensure that they had sufficient to eat. It was also ordered that anyone who was a nuisance or refused to follow the rules should miss the next meal as a punishment.[71] Food taken from the dining room might have been kept to eat later but might also have been supplied to friends outside, because at that time Ledbury was experiencing particular problems with vagrancy. Although no direct connection has been discovered, the problem was hinted at in another order recorded at the same meeting. It was ordered 'that the Parish Officers do apply to the Magistrates at their next meeting, to appoint proper persons to superintend the lodging houses; much danger, expense and inconvenience having arisen from the numerous tribes of vagrants that resort to this town'.[72] It appears that the Board of Assistants was beset with the problems of poverty from all directions.

Throughout the records of the Board of Assistants there are regular references to the inmates of the workhouse as 'the family'. The Board had long sustained a fairly benign attitude towards the poor and had only hardened their approach and tightened controls out of necessity as a determined group of inmates abused the system. Even then, few were simply dismissed without any effort to provide for them in another way. John Pritchard, for example, described as 'a very disorderly man and guilty of ill behaviour,'[73] was interviewed and admonished by the Board, and since John Bibbs, a local butcher and member of the Board, had agreed to employ Pritchard, and the parish had provided him with a house, he was ordered to remove himself, his wife and his children from the workhouse immediately. Paupers for whom the parish had no legal responsibility, such as sisters Louisa and Sophia Haws, had often been treated quite gently, but here, too, attitudes were changing. They had already been removed to Bradfield in Norfolk, their rightful settlement parish, but had returned, and Ledbury was faced with the problem of removing them for a second time.[74] By April 1818, the Board's efforts to remove malingerers from the workhouse could be seen to good effect because it was reported that inmates then numbered 28 males and 28 females, most of whom were 'proper objects for the house',[75] and to prevent any nuisances or malingerers from establishing themselves again, inmates had to wear new and very noticeable workhouse clothes. The new garments were blue gowns and grey jackets, both with yellow cuffs and collars, and with the letters L.P., also in yellow cloth, emblazoned on the right arm. At no time were they to wear any other outer garment.[76]

In May, John Evans was summarily dismissed from the workhouse for receiving his wages directly, without leave from the Overseer. Several women described as 'working to their own advantage'[77] were also under close scrutiny and the Matron was informed that she must see that the workhouse rules were obeyed and that 'in the case of trouble or nuisance or resistance'[78] she must call the parish Constable.

It was at this time that the depth of Stephen Baylis' insolvency was being exposed and the effect on parish finances continued to rumble on throughout the summer. By the autumn, the Board had concluded their deliberations, and at a meeting held at the beginning of November 1818 the following announcement was made:

> A careful examination of the present heavy expenditure of the workhouse amounting for the last half year to the sum of £358 or thereabouts, the number of inmates therein averaging 47 it is the opinion of this meeting that the expenditure of the parish ought to be reduced and that no means will contribute thereto so essentially as by changing the system of managing the workhouse. It is therefore resolved that housekeeping of every kind at the expense of the parish shall cease on the 16th day of this month and that such inmates who really need assistance shall have a weekly allowance in money for their support subject to the approbation of the Magistrates if dissatisfied with the offer of the Parish Officers.[79]

The workhouse was closed 15 days later; Mrs Stephens, the Matron, was paid £6 5s for the quarter ending at Christmas, and henceforth all paupers considered eligible for help were to be provided with out relief. The clearance of the workhouse, however, was not a simple matter; there were 12 cases of able-bodied couples and individuals who proved reluctant to leave. These were induced to go by helping them to find lodgings and by loaning them beds, bedding and other household items to help them to set up their own homes. The aged and infirm were each given an allowance of 3s 6d per week; children under ten years of age living with their parents were given 2s per week and the same allowance was provided for orphans farmed out to families in town. Children over ten years old were to be apprenticed as soon as possible, and adults able to do some work were to be assisted at the discretion of the parish officers.[80] Eight months later, in June 1819, the Board of Assistants recorded that they were convinced that closing the workhouse had been 'beneficial to the interests of the parish',[81] and that it should remain closed.

At the same meeting it was agreed that the workhouse buildings would be reallocated for particular parish needs. The former dining room would be reserved for general parish business and for the Magistrates' meetings, the two rooms used as schoolrooms would be held in trust for that purpose, and a small room would be set aside for Ann Baggott, a parish servant, who would look after the rooms and the furniture. One building was to be dismantled and rebuilt as two dwellings in the Horsefair at the Homend for the use of 'persons labouring under contagious disorders'.[82] The Board could not escape the fact that the homeless sick poor had to be provided for somewhere and that responsibility for that provision would almost inevitably fall upon them.

It is evident that the Board of Assistants had achieved much in clearing the huge debts left behind by Stephen Baylis, but there was still much to be done. Despite the vigorous pursuit of putative fathers of illegitimate children, men who deserted their lawful families, children who failed to support their elderly parents, parish tenants with rent arrears and the almost permanently defaulting ratepayers, the parish continued to be burdened by substantial debts. In January 1820 it was resolved that:

> This inclement season of the year whereby the wants of the poor are become very pressing and also in consideration of the £200 debt at the bank, that there be seven sixpenny rates granted to the churchwardens and overseers to enable them to meet the necessities of the poor and to liquidate the debt aforesaid and that one sixpenny rate be also granted them for the payment of a Shire Hall and County Rate.[83]

By the autumn of that year, it was clear that the financial situation had not really improved, so a sub-committee was set up to examine accounts and produce a precise statement of parish debts. The final figure for sums already advanced was £429, of which £200 was still owed to the bank and the remainder to Overseers and other Board members.[84] The drive to reduce expenditure continued: paupers could no longer expect their cottage rents to be paid as a matter of routine and settlement cases were scrutinised to ensure that the parish did not unwittingly become responsible for paupers who had no right to claim settlement in Ledbury. In November 1821 the Vestry Clerk noted: 'It appearing that Sarah Egerton some time ago clandestinely lay in, in this parish, resolved that in the event of her applying to the overseer for relief that she be taken before a Magistrate to be dealt with according to law.'[85] Sarah Egerton was not going to be allowed to claim settlement in Ledbury simply because her child had been born in the parish.

Regular reviews of pauper lists in the years 1818 to 1821 often resulted in large numbers of paupers having their weekly cash payments of 2s to 7s reduced by 6d or 1s per week, depending on individual circumstances, and some groups received particular attention. In March 1821 it was resolved that all paupers receiving weekly pay who 'have sons idling their time away and not getting anything towards a livelihood'[86] should be put to work for the benefit of the parish or have their allowances reduced. At the same time, it was ordered that all labourers who were currently unemployed and chargeable to the parish should work from 6am until 6pm or have their pay discontinued. The Board did not, however, indicate how such employment was to be found for them. In August that year the parish constables were asked to put up a list of all the paupers receiving weekly pay in the tap room of every public house in the parish and at the same time, 'to inform the landlords that if they allow any paupers named in the said list to tipple in their houses their conduct will be reported to the Magistrates',[87] which can only be seen as a hint that it was something to be considered when they applied to the Magistrates for the renewal of their licences. Action was sometimes taken against landlords for keeping disorderly houses and the vestry minutes indicated that paupers and paupers' wives who drank in public houses on Sundays, involved them-sevles in drunken street brawls, or were abusive to parish officers, had their weekly pay stopped or suspended for a while in an attempt to modify their behaviour.

Throughout the 1820s and the early 1830s the same issues returned again and again, but the Board of Assistants, some of long standing, had learned much about managing parish finances since the disastrous period from 1815 to 1818. In order to keep a closer check on the poor and to distinguish between the genuinely needy and the idle, Ledbury had been divided into four districts, each with its own Overseer, who seems to have held office for just six months at a time. This arrangement proved to be very effective. In October 1822, Thomas Baylis, a retiring Overseer for the half year ending at Michaelmas, had achieved very considerable deductions in the weekly cash allowances paid to paupers and had stated that in his opinion, 'by proper investigation of the situation of the paupers, a further reduction may be made by succeeding officers'.[88] After due consideration the Board resolved that 'it is therefore recommended to the overseers for the ensuing half year that they do proceed with such investigations and make all proper and necessary reductions'.[89]

The division of the parish into four separate areas made it much easier for Overseers to investigate individual cases and gather information, and as a result they were more alert to possible abuse and the Board much more deci-sive in taking appropriate action. Settlement issues were investigated more quickly, removal orders obtained from the Magistrates, and if there was any likelihood of another parish challenging their decision, they did not hesitate to instruct James Holbrook, the parish solicitor, to defend the case. Women with illegitimate children were pressed to name the fathers and affiliate the children, and the putative fathers were vigorously pursued to agree payment terms, even those living in towns and cities far from Ledbury who might have thought that they had escaped pursuit and payment. It was now much more difficult for malingerers to prosper and remain undetected. The able-bodied unemployed were placed under the authority of the parish surveyor and were required to carry out whatever tasks he gave them, more often than not the breaking of stone for the roads, or risk having their weekly allowances stopped. Others who had secured work for themselves in other towns were helped with travelling expenses, and young single men were sometimes provided with passage to make a new life in the colonies.

The employment of children remained a particular problem because of the numbers involved. In the early 1820s the routine of sending them out to farms as parish apprentices was suspended, almost certainly because many farmers were struggling to stay in business and maintain their own families. The system was reintroduced a year or two later but the children were not bound to their masters, so they could be sent back to their families if circumstances changed. Apprenticeship fees for lads wishing to enter skilled trades were also paid less frequently, but the Board would sometimes make a contribution as in the case of one Edward Hodges. John Jauncey, one of the Overseers, collected £5 in subscriptions towards apprenticing the boy as a tailor and the Board agreed to pay a further £7 to complete the fee of £12, half to be paid when the boy had been bound and the other half after two years.[90] Other boys were less fortunate; those over ten years of age had to break stone.

The paying of pauper rents had long been a vexed problem, because of the possibility of collusion between landlord and tenant. A man who could not pay his rent stood the risk of having his household possessions distrained by his landlord, leaving him and his family with nothing. If he applied to the Overseer for help, with luck his rent would be paid, his goods restored and life could go on as before; if there was collusion, the landlord's rent was paid in full, the tenant escaped all payment and the ratepayers were saddled with the bill. If the Overseer refused, however, he might then have to find lodgings for the man and his family, which was likely to prove more expensive than paying the rent for him. The number of paupers seeking parish payment of rents grew substantially throughout the 1820s and although the Board continued a discretionary policy of looking at each case individually, there appears to have been a distinct hardening of attitude, no doubt because of the fear of widespread collusion between landlord and tenant. In January 1831, Thomas Smith of Wellington Heath, whose rent was £5 per annum, claimed that his furniture had been distrained for arrears of rent amounting to £8 10s; after considering the case the Board granted him £2 15s towards settling his debts.[91] A few weeks later it was resolved that in all future cases where the annual rent was above £4, rather than pay arrears, the Board would 'let goods be seized',[92] and in 1835, on the eve of the New Poor Law, landlords were informed that it would no longer pay rents for paupers on parish relief.[93] There can be little doubt that the payment of rents was a significant factor in the escalation of parish expenses and provided opportunities for a major abuse which had to be stopped.

Although the closing of the workhouse had considerably reduced parish expenditure, it had caused some difficulties in managing the care of the sick and the elderly who could no longer look after themselves. The Board still provided basic needs such as beds, bedding, clothes, shoes, coal and simple medical care, but did not have a building specifically for the treatment of sick paupers, despite the plans to provide one in the horsefair when the workhouse was closed. The problem was managed by paying respectable female parishioners to look after the infirm, the sick, and children who had been abandoned, orphaned or whose parents were in prison. There was clearly a need for such a building because there were regular outbreaks of fever and in November 1831, Congreve Selwyn, the dispensary surgeon, reported that between March and November the dispensary had seen 1,086 patients, including 171 fever cases, of which 20 were still receiving treatment. His report continued:

> This fever is of the typhus character and in some instances is of a very severe form. But it had, generally speaking been found among the poor, in close, confined, unhealthy situations in the neighbourhood of pig styes, ditches etc. and where there appeared to have been a want of cleanliness.[94]

The Overseers and Churchwardens duly embarked on vigorous cleansing of the town. In March 1832[95] a letter from the Privy Council urged them to provide a receiving house where sick paupers could receive treatment and in July they were ordered to do so by the Board of Health.[96]

The Old Poor Law was essentially a very humane system of providing for the poor, but it relied on everyone concerned, ratepayers, Overseers, Churchwardens and paupers behaving reasonably and honestly. In Ledbury the parish officers had endeavoured for generations to administer the system fairly and humanely, but by the 1820s it had often been undermined by fraud and other minor forms of abuse. By the 1830s the records convey the sense that, owing to the very parochial nature of its administration, the system was in almost constant danger of being completely overwhelmed, and that it was indeed time for radical change. In July 1836, as the responsibility for relieving the poor was passed to the Ledbury Board of Guardians, Edwin Allgood, dispensing chemist and Overseer, wrote with obvious relief the following minute:

> Finis of Parish Meetings held by Paymasters in consequence of the said parish with its neighbouring ones being formed into a union for

the better administration of relief to the poor – Therefore Gentlemen, I have the pleasure of consoling myself that I shall not be called upon to meet you again on such troublesome business I bid you farewell. Adieu.'[97]

4   The New Poor Law in Ledbury

The first meeting of the Ledbury Board of Guardians took place at the beginning of June 1836[1] in the comfortable surroundings of the Feathers Inn. Sir
Edmund Walker Head was in attendance and no doubt he was pleased to know
that elected Guardians from all the 22 parishes which comprised Ledbury
Union were present, with the exception of Eggleton and Little Marcle. In
addition, he would have been relieved to see that 11 ex-officio Guardians of
high social standing were present, Guardians who would provide the Board
with leadership and direction. It had been the common complaint of Assistant
Commissioners that in rural Unions, Boards lacked the necessary zeal to attend
properly to poor law business because, for whatever reason, some had failed
to attract the support and leadership of the wealthiest and most influential men
in the district. This was clearly not the case in Ledbury. At the opening of
proceedings Col. James Money temporarily took the chair[2] and Union business proceeded very briskly. Major Thomas Heywood was duly unanimously
elected Chairman, the Reverend John Underwood Vice Chairman. Mr Thomas
Webb, a Ledbury banker, was elected Union Treasurer, and Mr William Reece
was appointed as Union Clerk at a salary of £65 per annum. Three Relieving
officers, John Hammond, William Thomas and Christopher Jones, each responsible for his own designated area, were appointed at a salary of £52 per annum,
and the two medical districts were to be served by surgeons John Tanner and
Charles Cooke, each receiving £75 per annum. All the proposals taken forward
at this meeting came from affluent landowners and wealthy clergymen: the ex-
officio Guardians, the Magistrates, had already taken control. It was generally
the case that the ex-officio guardians, the magistrates, steered Union business
at meetings.

That first meeting took the decision to build a new workhouse and by
the end of June they had chosen a plan submitted by Mr George Wilkinson,[3]
who had also designed the new workhouses in Weobley and Bromyard. At
the front was an entrance block and behind it, radiating from a central hub,
were accommodation blocks which created four segregated exercise yards for
the different classes of pauper: male and female, young and old. The Poor

Law Commissioners quickly approved Mr Wilkinson's plans for a building to accommodate 150 inmates[4] and also authorised the necessary expenditure. Land in the Horsefair at the Homend was purchased from John Martin for £125[5] and a building tender of £3,000 was accepted from John Matthews.[6] A very neat schedule of work was drawn up by the architect, giving tradesmen precise details of what was required of them and the quality of materials to be used,[7] and Mr Edward Wood was appointed Clerk of Works to ensure that the work proceeded smoothly.[8] The whole enterprise was to be financed with a loan[9] advanced by Mr Richard Heywood, approved by the Poor Law Commissioners and underwritten by future poor rate levies.

Eighteen years had passed since the old workhouse in Church Lane had been closed, and the poor of the town had grown accustomed to collecting their relief in the form of 4lb loaves of bread and small allowances in cash. For the time being, that system was to be expanded to cover the Union's three relief districts with collection points at various church vestries and farms. It is highly likely that the collection arrangements were made deliberately inconvenient in order to deter malingerers with only two, three or four collection points in districts which were comprised of between five and eleven parishes. The Guardians then embarked on a detailed review of the pauper lists and shortly afterwards all those who had been receiving relief before the formation of the new Poor Law Union were brought before the Board to be examined about the true nature of their circumstances.[10]

At the Guardians' second meeting[11] the Clerk had been instructed to inform the Overseers and Churchwardens of all the parishes in the Union that payment of cottage rents was to cease from 2 February 1837. In Ledbury especially the issue was confused because the parish owned or managed properties which were provided rent-free for some of the poor because they had either been bought or built with parish revenues, or left for the use of the poor by generous benefactors. A small committee of Guardians was therefore appointed to establish the current position and then seek advice from the Poor Law Commissioners. The Commissioners' opinion was that parish officers and Guardians were not obliged to pay cottage rents, and that they should not feel bound by any agreements outside their own period of office.[12] Shortly afterwards, Sir Edmund Walker Head wrote to Ledbury Union and pointed out that to maintain some of the poor in rent-free parish properties would complicate the notion of the deserving and the undeserving poor and would also be inconsistent and unfair.[13] The new policy of not paying rents for the poor, however, was guaranteed to undermine the independence of otherwise perfectly respectable people: arrears would build up, landlords would distrain household goods, and the tenants would have no alternative but to seek admittance to the workhouse. The reality of the situation was that an ideology intended to reduce pauper numbers would have exactly the opposite effect.

By the beginning of January 1837 the new workhouse was nearing completion and later that month Mr James Hughes and his wife, Ann, were appointed
as Master and Matron.[14] The first group of paupers to be admitted had been
listed and the Overseers of their respective parishes had been notified to bring
their paupers to the workhouse, 'properly clean', on prescribed mornings in
the last week of February.[15] If any of the paupers anticipated the indulgent and

*The new workhouse in Ledbury, long since converted
into separate dwellings, as photographed in 2008*

often lax atmosphere of the old workhouse, they would soon realise that the New Poor Law was unerringly rigorous and that the Guardians appeared to be imbued with a missionary-like zeal to ensure that the system was managed with irrefutable efficiency and economy. In those early days of Ledbury Union the Guardians appear to have had all aspects of poor law administration under constant review. They kept a close eye on the performance of Union officers, reminded Overseers of their responsibilities, pursued putative fathers for maintenance, and summoned various individuals to explain why they did not assist impoverished relatives.

In September 1836 the Medical Officers were reminded that they must attend patients immediately, or very soon after receiving orders from the Relieving Officers,[16] and were also cautioned to keep their records up to date. It was not long, however, before they were called before the Board to explain why patients had not been treated promptly. In December that year Charles Cooke was required to attend the Guardians on Board day to explain why his records suggested that he had visited patients more regularly than he really had,[17] and in April 1837 John Tanner was required to explain why he had not attended a sick pauper in the workhouse, although he had been asked to do so four times in two days.[18] His explanation was that he had been performing an operation on another seriously sick patient. Whilst this may have been the truth, the records of the Medical Officers appear to have been rather poorly kept and the Guardians instructed that in future they must provide the Board with weekly returns of their patient care.[19]

A general warning was sent out to the Overseers of all parishes to remind them that the union auditor, Mr Thomas William Davies, would require full details of money collected against affiliation orders and clear explanations of lapses in payment. The Guardians also pointed out that they were 'persuaded' that in the past these matters had been neglected and now precise records must be kept so that individual accounts were accurate and unequivocal.[20] In November 1836 the Overseer of Colwall was summoned before the Magistrates for not ensuring the prompt payment of parish poor rate contributions to the Union Treasurer[21] and in January 1837 the same indignity befell the Overseers of Mathon, Aylton, Bosbury, Castle Frome and Coddington.[22] In August 1836 the Overseer of Bosbury was instructed to summon Mr Trehern and Mr Homes, the grandfathers of widow Trehern's children, to appear before the Magistrates for an assessment of their capability to make contributions to their grandchildren's maintenance.[23] Curiously, despite the Guardians' general efficiency, the results of enquiries and court appearances were often not recorded in the minutes of their meetings; perhaps the decisions were not what the Guardians wished to hear.

There were some early casualties amongst Union officers, either because they were no longer needed or because they resigned of their own free will.

None appear to have been dismissed for misconduct but, as will become all too evident later, some were directed or persuaded to resign. At the beginning of May 1837, less than six months after their appointment, James and Ann Hughes resigned their posts as Master and Matron.[24] The Board appeared to think highly of them and shortly afterwards Mr Hughes was elected Union Clerk on the resignation of William Reece.[25] The Board had no criticism of Mr Reece, indeed, they praised his work, but he stated that for a salary of £65 per annum there was too much work for one man to do without assistance, particularly since he was not allowed to conduct any business other than that of Ledbury Union.[26]

Mr and Mrs Hughes were soon replaced as Master and Matron by William and Sarah Dyer,[27] and with their appointment the Guardians decided to rearrange the relief districts in order to reduce costs. Under the reorganisation, Relieving Officer John Hammond's district, which included Ledbury and four small parishes, was split up and although the Guardians made no criticisms of his work, Mr Hammond was simply informed that his services were no longer required. The four small parishes were added to the districts of Relieving Officers William Thomas and Christopher Jones and the new Workhouse Master, William Dyer, was given responsibility for Ledbury, for which he would receive an additional £15 per annum.[28] Shortly afterwards the medical districts were reorganised and the number of Medical Officers was increased to four, indicating an acceptance by the Guardians that the workload was too great for two men. Despite their complaints about them, the Guardians heaped praise upon Charles Cooke and John Tanner 'for the manner in which they have discharged their duties under circumstances of peculiar difficulty as Medical Officers for the year.'[29] The contracts of Union Medical Officers were readvertised every year, giving them little more security than other Union officers.

Once the new workhouse was open, some parishes in Ledbury Union were left with redundant workhouses and the Guardians turned their attention to the possibility of raising capital from them. The Poor Law Amendment Act made provision for the sale of such properties and in most cases matters probably proceeded without difficulty. Once the properties were sold, the funds realised might be used to meet parish contributions to the servicing of the loans raised to build the new workhouse or to settle accumulated debts. Parish properties were often sold by auction; for example, in September 1837 the sale of buildings in Stretton Grandison, Aylton, Ashperton, Bosbury and Much Marcle was advertised to take place at the George Inn in Ledbury.[30] Legal complications sometimes arose, however, when the true ownership of 'parish' properties was obscured by the passing of time; long-term use or management of a property by parish officers could not be taken to indicate parish ownership. The proposed sale of properties in Ledbury became a seriously contentious issue for just that reason.

Just before Christmas 1838 a parish meeting was called to consider a proposal to allow Ledbury Union to sell all the parish properties in Church Lane plus a freehold plot of land and four cottages at the Homend, but so many parishioners attended the meeting that the committee room in the old workhouse was too crowded and the meeting had to be adjourned to the room used by the Boys' National School. Eventually a vote was taken and resulted in a clear majority of 49 in favour of selling all the properties under consideration.[31] Before matters could proceed any further, however, Mr John Biddulph, a local landowner and London banker, intervened to express his concern about the legality of what had taken place at the meeting, and made the following comments in the vestry minute book: 'I doubt the authority of the parish to dispose of the property situate between the Church and Backlanes for the purpose of paying the parish debts and relieving the ratepayers.'[32] He was clearly of the opinion that it was not theirs to sell, for he added: 'The said property having been purchased and built expressly for other purposes: not with parish money but by and with the money of a few private individuals'.[33] Warming to his subject, he pointed out that on the spurious authority of a former parish officer, part of the building complex was now used as a warehouse to generate income to relieve the rates, quite against the original instructions of the people who had purchased it specifically for use as a butter market. The National School, which was financed entirely through private subscription, was also housed there, and its closure would deny a valued education to 300 children who would find themselves displaced and left out in the streets. In addition, the town committee room, formerly the workhouse dining room, served Ledbury's inhabitants very well as a venue for many important pursuits: the transactions of the Friendly Society and the Savings Bank; parish meetings; the Magistrates' Court; and, because the church vestry was very small, vestry meetings too. If the buildings were indeed closed and alternative ones had to be purchased or built to accommodate these services, it would mean enormous expense for the parish ratepayers. If the Poor Law Commissioners had been given the full facts of the case, they would never have sanctioned the sale.

John Biddulph's precise analysis of the situation must have left some ratepayers squirming in their seats as they realised how close they had come to implicating themselves in a transaction which might well have been perceived as little short of fraud. The controversy continued, but as a result of Biddulph's intervention, the full facts of the case were sent to the Poor Law Commissioners who tactfully suggested that perhaps just part of the property might be sold. Their response was discussed at a parish meeting held in April 1839 which ended with a resounding majority in favour of keeping possession of all the property, but allowing some of it to be let so that the income could be employed, at the direction of the Poor Law Commissioners, 'for the permanent advantage of this parish'.[34] The Ledbury Guardians do not appear to have become involved in the sale debate, but they later became embroiled in a dispute about who should manage the lettings, the parish officers or the Guardians. Valuable income was, of course, being lost while they haggled over the issue, so the Overseers and Churchwardens requested John Biddulph to write to the Poor Law Commissioners once more, in order to seek permission for the parish officers to administer the properties without further delay.

The minutes of their meetings suggest that for the most part the Guardians continued to administer Union affairs in an efficient and businesslike manner. Problems and complaints were assessed quickly and well-reasoned decisions were implemented without delay. In November 1837, for example, when there were complaints that the heating system in the workhouse was consuming enormous quantities of coal without producing a corresponding amount of heat and hot water, they did not hesitate to instruct the Union solicitor to write to the heating engineers, Eckstein and Son, to require them to attend to the problem immediately.[35] Putative fathers were routinely pursued through the Magistrates' Courts for maintenance, warrants were quickly obtained for the apprehension of husbands who deserted their wives and families, and disorderly workhouse inmates were admonished and cautioned. If there was no improvement in their behaviour they too could soon find themselves in court. Some Guardians, of course, regularly presided as Magistrates and their court experience was often revealed in their attitude to poor law administration, particularly with regard to removal orders. In the past Overseers had often procrastinated over applying for removal orders, but Boards of Guardians were ruthless in their defence of Union finances.

The Guardians' zealous efficiency and their intense scrutiny of all Union business may have worked against them in one important respect. They appear to have found it difficult to retain staff. Schoolmistresses and nurses came and went with great frequency and in the first ten years of the Union's existence numerous couples were appointed as Master and Matron, some lasting only a few months. It is possible that the Guardians imposed such exacting standards on their workhouse officers that few could withstand the watchful visitations of the Workhouse Chaplain or the probing vigilance of the Board's Visiting Committee for very long. To be quite fair, they also demanded high standards of themselves; a hint of this is evident in the wording of a detailed finance report compiled by Mr James Collins, a Ledbury attorney, in November 1842. The Guardians had become aware that between the years 1838 and 1842 the Union's expenditure on poor relief had risen by 25%, and they had set up a committee to examine the reasons for the dramatic increase. In particular, they wanted to know whether it could be attributed to a general rise in pauperism and to causes beyond their control or whether it had resulted from 'a relaxed vigilance on the part of the Guardians in the administration of the law'.[36] The accounts of the two largest parishes in the Union, Ledbury and Bosbury, were compared for the years 1838 and 1842 and after a detailed analysis of pauper maintenance costs had been completed, it was concluded that the number of paupers had doubled in both parishes but the proportion of workhouse inmates and paupers receiving out-relief had remained the same, which was seen as an indication of constant and uniform management. The rise in pauper numbers was explained by a marked increase in food prices during 1840, 1841 and 1842, particularly in the price of flour, bacon and potatoes, the staple foods of the poor, an increase which had also 'compelled the Guardians to abandon the scale of relief which they originally prescribed for themselves, in cases of aged, infirm and bedridden paupers'.[37] The increase in pauper numbers was also attributed, in part, to the decline of the glove trade. Many elderly women had garnered modest incomes from gloving, a source of income that was now lost to them.

In addition, the committee looked at the accounts for Ledbury and Bosbury for the years 1837, 1838 and 1842 and compared the expenditure incurred for those years in the first week of October; that being the time of year when agricultural labourers began to lose employment and go in search for parochial relief. The comparison revealed an increase in pauper numbers which the committee found so disturbing that it described it 'as an evil so serious as to demand all the care and attention of the Board and, through the Guardians, of all the owners and occupiers of lands and houses in the union'.[38] In the conclusion of the report the point was emphasised once again and employers were urged to continue 'to present to their labourers the alternative of work, at wages proportionate to the times, instead of consigning them to the workhouse, during the winter months'.[39] Employers could not escape the fact that they either had to continue to employ their labourers and pay them wages to keep them out of the workhouse, or pay increased poor rates to maintain them inside it. The report also drew to the attention of the Guardians the cost of Union officers' salaries, the servicing of loans, building alterations, the construction of new classrooms and fever wards, the care of lunatics, and the support of bastards.

Indeed, the Guardians had discovered, as their predecessors under the Old Poor Law had discovered, that providing support for illegitimate children was a highly contentious issue and an extremely vexing practical problem. Under the New Poor Law, women with illegitimate children were not supposed to receive any assistance unless they were admitted to the workhouse, because it was thought that helping them in the community would only lead to further immorality and more illegitimate children. In rural areas, however, Unions usually paid single mothers so little that it was hardly likely to encourage bastardy. Forcing single mothers and their children into the workhouse was expensive and it is evident from the Guardians' minutes that 'accommodations' in the law were apparent from its inception. Illegitimate children were, of course, the responsibility of their natural fathers and, whilst some accepted their liabilities and paid maintenance directly to the mothers, others were persuaded to pay through the Union and others had to be compelled to pay by the Magistrates' Courts, if they could be found. At times, the Guardians appear to have acted as mediators in an attempt to avoid legal costs, as in the case of Thomas Norris. In October 1837, Margaret Stevens asked the Overseer of Ledbury for relief for her two children, the natural children of Thomas Norris of the Talbot Inn in New Street. The Overseer granted the mother 2s temporary relief and approached Norris to persuade him to contribute to the support of the children, but he refused. The Overseer referred the matter to the Guardians and, after giving the case some thought, they disallowed the 2s relief and sought legal advice themselves.[40] Discussions continued and in January 1838 it was minuted that Norris had agreed to pay 1s 3d per week for one child if the mother supported the second child herself, and the Board of Guardians agreed to the arrangement.[41]

In cases where men made regular payments the Guardians could argue that paying out-relief was far more economic than maintaining mother and child in the workhouse. This point was emphasised in the report compiled by James Collins and others which stated that a child could be supported for 1s 6d per week in the community, while in the workhouse the cost was 3s per week.[42] In June 1838 the Board announced that all payments for bastards of seven years and above would cease immediately, but mothers would be given the opportunity to let their children be received into the workhouse[43] – clear evidence that throughout the 1830s and the 1840s Ledbury Union had supported women with illegitimate children on out-relief, though clearly against the law, and allowed them to live as families in the community on economic grounds, and hopefully on humanitarian grounds too.

The children in Ledbury Workhouse benefited greatly from the Guardians' positive attitude towards education, possibly the most enlightened attitude of all the Unions in Herefordshire. The Ledbury Board had an education committee when many Unions refused to educate pauper children at the ratepayers' expense and justified their position with reference to the Principle of Less Eligibility. They either procrastinated about appointing a Schoolmistress at all or employed a person, sometimes a pauper, who was hardly more literate than the children in her care. In April 1839, the committee reported very favourably on the kindness with which the discipline of the school was enforced and they saw no reason to believe that Miss Bowkett was not fully competent and willing 'to carry into execution any plans which the Board may direct in order to render the present system more efficient'.[44] In many workhouses the Schoolmistress appears to have been left very much to her own devices, but clearly not at Ledbury.

It was evident that the education committee had been undertaking a review of the facilities provided for the children and possibly a comparison with those provided at Bromyard Workhouse. At that time there were 31 boys and 32 girls in Ledbury Workhouse, most between 6 and 9 years of age, but despite the fact that the workhouse buildings were new, the children's recreational opportunities were severely restricted by its design. In the playground, which was small and covered with sharp stones, the girls were supervised by the Matron and the boys by the Porter, but there was little incentive for them to play because no walls were suitable for ball games and marbles were taken away because of their wear on clothes. Daily physical exercise was difficult, so apart from occasional walks in the countryside, there was little to occupy the children, unlike their counterparts at Bromyard, where a selection of games was provided and space was available for physical exercise. There was clearly concern for the children at Ledbury, but the Guardians took pleasure in the fact that Miss Bowkett treated the children well.

They did, however, disapprove of the nature of Sabbath readings, though it was unclear whether their disapproval was levelled at the Schoolmistress or the Chaplain. They considered that the reading of the church service each Sunday morning by an 11-year-old pauper boy, using the other children to make the responses, as 'highly improper'[45] because they took the rather advanced view that children should not be made to repeat anything they did not understand. Miss Bowkett obviously continued to meet with the Guardians' approval, because she was still at her post six years later. In May 1843, however, the Board decided: 'That instead of the present dayly [sic] schoolmistress, a person be appointed who shall reside in the workhouse, and take active charge of the children'.[46] This meant in effect that the Schoolmistress would be on duty for 24 hours a day, and all for the cost of her keep and the princely sum of £16 per annum. Miss Bowkett left. A stream of residential Schoolmistresses followed, but few lasted a year and several only survived for two or three months, a problem not unnoticed by the officials at the Poor Law Commission.

The appointments of all Union officers had to be sanctioned by the Commission, so officials there would have been well aware that there had also been many changes of Master and Matron at the workhouse, and for some reason the Ledbury Guardians were still unable to retain the services of key members of staff. This problem was certainly not unknown in other Herefordshire Unions, but it appears to have been a serious problem at Ledbury and it is evident that the details of many resignations or dismissals went unrecorded. There were numerous occasions when the only indication of one officer's departure was a minute noting the appointment of his or her successor. The reasons for the relentless coming and going of officers were probably many and varied, but the rather high-handed and dictatorial manner in which the

Guardians altered and augmented officers' duties and routines may have been significant in causing unrest. In August 1844, for example, Miss Andrews, the Schoolmistress, was informed that in future she would be required to teach Sunday School to the children in the workhouse for one hour in the morning and a further half hour in the afternoon.[47] Miss Andrews resigned a few weeks later. Schoolmistresses at Ledbury Workhouse grappled with an almost impossible task – to teach 60 or 70 children from infants to adolescents during the day and supervise them generally during the evenings. Life must have been both monotonous and exhausting because they were, to all intents and purposes, on duty all day every day. Any serious disruption in the schoolroom would have drawn the Master away from his workhouse routines and his duties as Relieving Officer for the parish of Ledbury, almost certainly engendering staff tensions and discontent, particularly with the Visiting Committee and the Chaplain peering over their shoulders. The Schoolmistress probably did not appreciate the fact that the Chaplain kept a careful note of his schoolroom observations, but his journal was to prove very useful to the Board when, in October 1846, Assistant Commissioner Edward Gulsin visited the workhouse and his report did not find favour with the Guardians.

In 1845 the Poor Law Commission had been rocked by revelations of the scandalous neglect of inmates at Andover Workhouse in Hampshire and, whilst charge and counter charge continued to reverberate, in October 1846, the potential for more undesirable publicity emerged at Leominster Workhouse (see chapter 9). A literate pauper inmate wrote to the Poor Law Commission complaining of corrupt management and ill-treatment of paupers and Assistant Commissioner John Graves was sent urgently to Leominster on what amounted to a damage limitation exercise. It is reasonable to suggest, therefore, that although officials at Somerset House may have been monitoring the alarming number of officer appointments and departures at Ledbury Workhouse as a barometer of the Guardians' management of the Union, the precise timing of Edward Gulsin's inspection of the workhouse, also in October 1846, was perhaps more significant than was generally appreciated, being prompted by the fear of further revelations and scandal. It was more than likely that Edward Gulsin's brief for Ledbury was not markedly different from that of John Graves at Leominster.

The particulars of Edward Gulsin's report on the general running of Ledbury Workhouse were not included in the minutes of the Guardians' meetings, even though they must have discussed the report in some detail. The omission could simply have been an oversight on the part of an overworked clerk, but a more likely explanation is that he was given precise instructions on the subject. If Gulsin's comments had been generally favourable they would without doubt have been recorded for posterity, and their absence may well be significant in the light of a resolution minuted early in November 1846, soon after the inspection had taken place. It was moved by the Chairman of the Board, the Reverend John Hopton, and seconded by the Reverend John Hanmer Underwood, that having listened with great pain to the statements of the Master and Matron, William and Sarah Law, and the Schoolmistress, Miss H. Yates, and having weighed those statements very carefully, the Board had unanimously agreed that it was impossible for the future business of the workhouse to be conducted satisfactorily 'under the guidance and supervision of those officers'[48] and they were recommended to tender their resignations. It was quite possible, of course, that the three officers had been guilty of neglect of duty, incompetence or immorality, but since no specific charges of misconduct were levelled against them, it is more than feasible that they were simply being made scapegoats to allow the Guardians to save face for their own lack of supervision. The Guardians' minutes were, of course, always written from the Guardians' point of view.

Edward Gulsin's report on the standard of education provided at Ledbury workhouse appears to have been highly critical: he considered it to be 'defective in quality and system'.[49] Although compared with the other unions in the county the Ledbury Guardians were very positive towards the education of workhouse children, they simply expected too much of their schoolmistresses, hence the constant criticism. Although the full report was not recorded in the Guardians' minutes, the essence of it may be gleaned from their response. In Gulsin's view, there were too many children for one Schoolmistress to manage; the hours of tuition were too few; all the children should attend lessons morning and evening; none of the children understood the common rules of number; the girls should be taught arithmetic as well as the boys; and the schoolroom was poorly located. He recommended that two new classrooms should be built, that a Schoolmaster should be appointed to teach arithmetic to all the children and that two new vagrant wards should be built because the present arrangements, whereby vagrants gained access to their wards through the children's yard, were unacceptable.

A small committee of Guardians considered Gulsin's criticisms and, in a firm but measured report, rebutted each one. The Guardians did not accept that there were too many children for one Schoolmistress to manage and pointed out that in National Schools working under the monitorial system it was common for 100-150 children to be managed and controlled by one person. They explained that in Ledbury Workhouse the children under 5 were looked after by a 'responsible woman'; boys and girls above that age were cared for the Schoolmistress; and the older boys of 12 to 16 spent part of the day gardening and doing sundry workhouse jobs under the supervision of the Porter. Those arrangements appeared to work and allowed the Schoolmistress to have an average of about 50 children to teach, so the guardians did not think her 'overtasked'. They considered three hours of lessons, morning and afternoon, to be quite sufficient and saw no necessity for the appointment of a Schoolmaster, because they were satisfied with the children's progress; and they quoted at length from the Chaplain's register of classroom observations to emphasise the point. They were impressed by the fact that they received frequent requests from masters and mistresses in the district for permission to employ workhouse children and took such requests to signify public approval of the children's level of education. They did not think it appropriate for 'stout boys' of 14 to 16 to be confined to the schoolroom for long periods while the lads of independent labourers often began their careers as ploughboys at 11 or 12. They would, however, appreciate advice from the Commissioners on the apprenticing and training of boys for employment. They countered Edward Gulsin's criticism of the location of the schoolroom by pointing out that it was located where the Assistant Commissioner, Sir Edmund Walker Head, advised it should be when the workhouse was opened, but they did agree to consider the construction of additional buildings. In conclusion the Guardians stated their regret that Mr Gulsin thought the educational arrangements at Ledbury Workhouse insufficient but emphasised that they were happy in the knowledge that:

> The ratepayers and Guardians (including the Magistracy, the Clergy of the District) who are conversant with the habits, and requirements of the neighbourhood, and the entire system of rural economy existing in this county, are satisfied with the present system.[50]

The Guardians' confidence in the system was, however, not endorsed or substantiated by the record of events, because officers continued to arrive and depart as rapidly as in previous years, a situation almost certainly exacerbated by the interference of the Reverend W.J. Morrish, who had been Chaplain since 1838. He appears to have been a rather unusual character and, for a man of the cloth, particularly adept at causing difficulties. He was, however, not beyond reproach himself. At the end of January 1844, for example, the Chairman of the Board, the Reverend John Hopton, had been dismayed to learn that Morrish had been practising Mesmerism on some of the inmates of the workhouse, proceedings which he considered to be highly improper and greatly to be regretted. The Board instructed the clerk to write to the Chaplain to inform him that he had exceeded his duties and to request that he would, in future, 'abstain from such reprehensible practices'.[51] The matter was not mentioned again, so it might be presumed that, having been rebuked, he did indeed concentrate on his proper duties, if a little too zealously as far as other officers were concerned.

Just before Christmas 1846, Mrs Jane Powell was appointed as Schoolmistress,[52] but at the end of January 1847 the Chaplain reported to the

Board that the children were not making satisfactory progress under the new Schoolmistress.[53] He also complained that she had refused to pay attention to certain regulations which he had thought proper to suggest. The Guardians responded immediately by asking the Reverend Underwood and the Reverend Dowell to look into the matter, and shortly afterwards the Guardians were gratified to hear that, in their opinion, the children were making 'due progress in religious instruction, reading, writing and arithmetic',[54] and stated: 'That this Board do not see the necessity of imposing additional duties on the Schoolmistress not ordered by the Poor Law Commissioners or the Board of Guardians'.[55] Mrs Powell had obviously been working hard, but perhaps she found the task too great and too exhausting to sustain, particularly if relations with the Chaplain had become soured. She resigned in February 1847[56] and was followed a month later by Miss Amelia Hickman.[57]

In April 1847 the Guardians called a special meeting to consider 'the needfulness of appointing a Schoolmaster to instruct and have care of the boys and teach the girls arithmetic'.[58] Soon afterwards a decision was taken to build two new classrooms with bedrooms for a Schoolmaster and a Schoolmistress and also two new wards for vagrants.[59] It would appear that the Guardians had at long last accepted that no Schoolmistress, however good she was at her job, could or would endure the regime at Ledbury Workhouse for very long and that the appointment of a Schoolmaster could no longer be avoided. It could, however, be delayed, because in September 1848 the Guardians were still prevaricating over plans to alter the boys' dormitory to make a bedroom for a Schoolmaster. The first Schoolmaster to be appointed, at a salary of £30 per annum, was one Joseph Swinton, and his name first appeared in the list of quarterly salary payments in October 1848.[60] He resigned in January 1849[61] to be followed by Richard Elton in April,[62] who in turn was replaced, by October that year, by George Stanton.[63]

The Guardians' judgement in appointing and retaining staff appears to have remained woefully inadequate, because the lamentable procession of Masters and Matrons continued unabated. At the departure of William and Sarah Law, Henry and Eliza Elkerton began their duties on New Year's Day 1847,[64] but Mrs Elkerton died in July 1848[65] and there then followed an unusual arrangement whereby Henry Elkerton's services as Master were retained at £50 per annum and a Mrs Stone was appointed Matron at £20 per annum.[66] Both of them resigned at the end of November 1848.[67] Thomas and Drusilla Longstrath were appointed in their place but did not survive for very long because, although no reasons were minuted, in May 1849 the Board decided to dispense with their services at the end of the quarter.[68] In July, William and Mary Benwell became Master and Matron but, along with the Schoolmistress, Amelia Hickman, they were forced to resign just three months later in deep disgrace.[69]

At the end of October 1849 the Board had had 'cause to suspect that there had been much irregularity in the conduct of the master, matron and schoolmistress of the workhouse'.[70] In their attempt to ascertain the truth, they decided to question the Porter, the nurse, and the Schoolmaster. William Eley, the Porter, stated that he had often seen all three in an intoxicated condition, so much so that they needed to support each other in order to walk. On one occasion they had consumed an almost full half-gallon jar of beer in the Relieving Officers' room before breakfast, and drinking sessions often took place there in the afternoons when the Schoolmistress should have been teaching. He also stated that Miss Hickman and Mrs Benwell frequently went out for a couple of hours in the evening and 'came back rather lively'.[71] As a result, Miss Hickman was sometimes absent from the school in the mornings, having 'left it to the girls'.[72] Elizabeth Rose, the nurse, confirmed that Miss Hickman was often seen 'the worse for liquor'[73] and said that she had frequently observed her entering and leaving the Benwells' private rooms, sometimes straightening her apron as she left. George Stanton, the Schoolmaster, made similar comments and said that he could tell when Miss Hickman was absent from her classroom by the noise the girls were making. He also informed the Board that, until he cautioned her against the habit, she was inclined to send one of a number of the older boys out into the town in the evenings to bring in beer. On other evenings, as the Porter had stated, she went into the town herself in the company of Mrs Benwell, and on one occasion, as he returned to the workhouse after visiting friends, he found the two women at the gate with Oakley and Matthews, two local carpenters, all talking excitedly. Oakley was so drunk that the women asked the Schoolmaster to take him home as he was not safe to go alone. He also stated that he had seen 'the master in the sitting room playing with the schoolmistress in an improper manner'.[74]

Mr and Mrs Benwell and Miss Hickman were all suspended from duty whilst the Guardians sought the advice of the Poor Law Board. There could have been little doubt in anyone's mind about the outcome of events, but in the meantime, the management of the workhouse was placed in the hands of the Union Clerk. At the beginning of November 1849, the Master, the Matron and the Schoolmistress were allowed to resign, and a little before Christmas, Mr and Mrs William Dowle were appointed as Master and Matron with a joint salary of £60 per annum plus their keep, and Miss Caroline Bennett was appointed as Schoolmistress with a salary of £16 per annum plus keep.[75] It appeared that the Guardians had grown lax in the day to day supervision of their workhouse officers. If the level of drunken behaviour had indeed been as described, even allowing for an element of vindictive exaggeration, it should have been obvious to the Visiting Committee and to the Chaplain, and their apparent silence on the subject must have raised some questions about the value of their observations and reports. Miss Hickman had, after all, freely admitted to the Guardians that there 'was much irregularity in her conduct'.[76] The Guardians could not deny that they did not have proper control of the workhouse or that their lack of day to day supervision was a factor in the constant coming and going of staff.

The Chaplain's role should have been pivotal in alerting the Board to potential problems, but in the case of Ledbury Workhouse, he appears to have been part of the problem. He interfered with the duties of the workhouse officers, neglected his own duties and at times overstepped his authority. In 1844, as has been noted, he had been admonished by the Board for practising Mesmerism on some of the inmates and on another occasion he had been asked to explain why he had failed to read the Litany at several Sunday services.[77] He had also been awkward about the time set for worship on Sundays and Tuesdays. A number of Masters had complained that the Chaplain's insistence on taking services at 8.30am caused the workhouse officers a great deal of inconvenience, and also made the point that many of the aged and infirm inmates could not be ready to attend at that hour. In February 1847 he was requested to conduct the Sunday service at 9am,[78] but if he did comply, it was not for long because by May of that year both services were once again held at their former time. At the end of May 1849 the Guardians reviewed the Chaplain's duties and, perhaps with a saving of £30 per annum in mind, seriously considered dispensing with the services of a chaplain completely.[79] This was feasible because there were five or six clergymen of wealth and high social standing who were diligent in their attendance as Guardians and the devotional duties of the workhouse might have been shared amongst them. After due discussion, however, it was decided that, supervised by a 'proper person', able-bodied inmates would attend morning and evening Sunday services at the parish church and benches would be provided specifically for their use. The Chaplain would continue with his other duties to the sick and infirm and be responsible for catechising all. The paupers were so badly behaved in walking to and from the church, however, that the arrangement had to cease, and the Chaplain was directed to perform one full Sunday service at 8am from Lady Day to Michaelmas and at 9am from Michaelmas to Lady Day.[80]

In January 1850, the Chaplain reported the Schoolmaster, George Stanton, to the Board for what he felt was undue severity towards the boys, and on investigation the Board agreed that one of the boys had been corrected in a very 'improper manner'[81] and contrary to regulations. The precise details of the offence or the punishment were not recorded but on being brought before the Board, 'Mr Stanton expressed his sorrow'[82] for what he had done and was reprimanded by the Chairman, the Reverend John Hopton. The matter could not have been too serious, because it was not referred to the Poor Law Board, which it most certainly would have been if the Guardians had thought that they needed to protect themselves. In March, George Stanton was summoned before the Board again, this time to explain why, according to the Chaplain, the children had made so little progress. Stanton defended himself and made the point that in arithmetic the children could answer better than the Chaplain. He also added that the children disliked the Chaplain because he had failed to keep promises of rewards to them on several occasions.[83] The Board agreed that Stanton's charge should be investigated, adding that the breaking of promises 'cannot but have a bad moral effect on the minds of children',[84] but nothing more on the subject was recorded. In June 1850, George Stanton resigned from his post as Schoolmaster;[85] the Reverend W.J. Morrish, however, remained in office to oversee Stanton's successor.

At that time the management of the workhouse appears to have been particularly lax because in September 1851, the clerk minuted that on the 6th of the month, six small girls had left the workhouse and three days later they had still not returned. The Master, William Dowle, was questioned by the Board as to how such an incident could have happened and also about what action he had taken to find the children, but his answers were considered to be 'insufficient'.[86] A week later the Board questioned him again, rebuked him for not having taken immediate steps to find the children, and entered a minute to the effect that in their opinion 'greater care and attention is required from Mr. Dowle in the general management of the workhouse and that without it he must not expect to retain his appointment'.[87] The fate of the little girls was not mentioned again so it might be presumed that they were found and safely returned to the workhouse. William and Victoria Dowle resigned in September 1852.[88]

In the early 1850s the stream of workhouse officers of all levels, from baker to Master, who stayed for only a short time, continued as in past years and it is clear that Mr Hughes, the long serving Union Clerk, had grown both adept at and accustomed to presenting the Guardians with appropriately sanitised minutes of which they would approve. The evidence for his selectivity sometimes becomes apparent when issues which had obviously been simmering for days, weeks or months suddenly came to a head and thorough investigations revealed a trail of incidents not previously mentioned. This should perhaps have raised questions in the minds of the Guardians about the content of his verbal reports at Board meetings, but they appear to have had supreme confidence in his ability and his integrity. In March 1856 his probity was finally questioned when the workhouse Master, Daniel Eaton, accused him of falsifying the workhouse stock book, but although the Guardians thought it necessary and perhaps prudent for their own safety to refer the matter to the Poor Law Board, they were more than happy to give Mr Hughes the benefit of the doubt.

The weekly examination of the Union officers' records was one of the clerk's main duties and his findings, good or bad, were reported to the

Guardians at each meeting and routinely minuted as evidence of their having been completed. In May 1856 the Master again questioned his probity when he wrote a report in his stock book that accused Mr Hughes of having removed a page dated 15 April 1856 to cover up a deficiency in the workhouse stock of flour. The Board ordered that a copy of the Master's report be sent to the Poor Law Board and requested that one of their inspectors be sent to Ledbury to investigate the matter as soon as possible, 'as the Board are unwilling that so serious a charge should remain uncontradicted against the Clerk who has so long assiduously served them'.[89]

In August the Guardians received a letter from the Poor Law Board[90] reporting the findings of their inspector, Mr John Graves, when he visited the workhouse and questioned the officers. From his investigations it appeared that the Master had first mentioned his concerns about the flour stocks to the Chaplain but, as nothing had been done, he decided to write the memorandum in his stock book, presumably to protect himself against the possibility of future accusations of theft. The clerk had, it was alleged, read the Master's memorandum but had said that it was pointless to present the matter to the Board unless he could also provide a satisfactory explanation and, probably for the same reason, he had also altered the Master's baking account without the Board's knowledge. The Poor Law Board concluded that the clerk must have cut the page from the book as the Master had said, and suggested that the Guardians should consider whether it was still appropriate to allow Mr Hughes to retain his post, despite his long service to the Union. The Guardians discussed the situation and agreed that they would indeed retain the clerk's services, and they conveyed their decision to Somerset House. A week or so later they received a courteous reply to their letter. The Poor Law Board[91] made the point that from the evidence they could not have come to any other conclusion than previously expressed, but said that they would respect the Guardians' high opinion of Mr Hughes and, out of deference to their unanimous decision, would not object to their retaining his services.

The Guardians' apparently unshakeable confidence in Mr Hughes may have been well placed in terms of his administrative ability, because he was certainly very efficient in handling Union business. A few of them may however secretly have wondered how often he had kept information from them in the past, and how many appointments and departures might have been avoided in the previous two decades if they had been in possession of the full facts of individual cases. As clerk to the Guardians he was ideally placed to filter information and to choose how and when he would present it to them, secure in the knowledge that his word was unlikely to be questioned. The minutes he wrote were in a consistently neat hand, very precise in detail and indicative of a highly organised man who might prove to be a formidable adversary in any debate or dispute, a man of whom other Union officers might be a little in awe.

At the beginning of October 1856, just a few months after the altercation over the Master's stock book, Daniel Eaton was again at the centre of controversy. The Guardians wrote to the Poor Law Board seeking advice about his removal because they were frequently called upon to arbitrate in the continual disagreements which arose between Mr Eaton and the subordinate officers of the workhouse, to the point where 'such a state of things exist as to make his continuance here most unsatisfactory'.[92] They also stated that although he had requested testimonials in pursuit of office in other Unions, when they asked him to resign Mr Eaton refused to do so. They were, however, 'perfectly satisfied from his irritability and violent conduct, as often displayed in the presence of the Board, his remaining in office is entirely incompatible with the due regulation of the workhouse'.[93] The matter was not mentioned or referred to again, but the following week Daniel and Harriet Eaton resigned their posts.[94]

Ledbury Union's first Board of Guardians attracted the interest of some of the wealthiest and most influential men in the district, a number of whom continued in office for many years. The Reverend John Hopton, for example, was a Guardian in 1836 and was still taking a turn as the Chairman of the Board three decades later in 1866. Yet the constant stream of workhouse appointments and departures must raise questions about the Guardians' apparent inability to select suitable men and women for important posts and retain their services for more than a few months or, at best, a few years. They appear to have assumed that once appointed, officers would know how to carry out their duties and, perhaps somewhat naively, that they would do so efficiently, honestly and consistently without the need for day to day supervision. It is hardly surprising that staff problems arose, because the workhouse was almost as much of a prison for the officers as it was for the paupers. They were almost permanently on duty and could not leave the premises, except at prescribed times, without the permission of the Master. This restriction must have made it very difficult for young men and women to enjoy a social life and perhaps explained why bouts of drunken behaviour sometimes occurred. Even the Master and the Matron could not enjoy an occasional evening out without the express permission of the Board, because they were generally not permitted to be absent from the workhouse at the same time, a restriction rarely mentioned in the records of other Herefordshire Unions. The only officers who served the Union for many years were Mr Hughes, the clerk, and the Reverend Morrish, the Chaplain, who lived in their own homes. Mr Edwin Allgood, the workhouse dispenser, also did long service, and although he lived at the workhouse for a while, for the most part he had his own premises in New Street.

The trail of frequent appointments and departures continued throughout the 1850s and the 1860s, partly because of the Guardians' unrealistic expectations of their officers and partly because of the high-handed manner in which they altered agreed terms of appointment, without consultation, in their zeal to do everything possible to hold down the poor rates. For example, when food was plentiful and relatively cheap, they expected Union officers to accept reductions in their salaries. In April 1849, the Board resolved: 'that in consequence of the low prices of agricultural produce and corn now being at the price it was forty years ago, therefore with a view to the reduction of the poor rates, it is deemed expedient that the salaries of the union officers be reduced'.[95] The idea was raised several times but dropped on the advice of the Poor Law Board, but it gives an indication of the Guardians' attitude towards Union officers – an attitude very much the same as that held by the Board of Assistants under the Old Poor Law – and perhaps explains why they incurred so many problems.

5   Confidence and Independence at Ross

Once the Poor Law Amendment Act of 1834 had become law the government appointed three Poor Law Commissioners who were to be responsible for the implementation of its provisions throughout England and Wales. The three appointed were: George Nicholls, a former sailor who had risen in the world to become the governor of the Birmingham branch of the Bank of England; J.G. Shaw Lefevre, formerly bailiff to Lord Althorp, the Chancellor of the Exchequer; and Thomas Frankland Lewis, a country gentleman with an estate in Radnorshire. Nicholls had been active in poor law administration for some years and had earned himself the title of 'the depauperiser of Southwell',[1] while Lewis had served as a member of the Sturges Bourne Committee whose enquiries and recommendations had resulted in the Select Vestry Act of 1819.[2] Shaw Lefevre, however, had no experience of the Poor Law. His appointment resulted from what can only be described as 'aristocratic jobbery'.

Edwin Chadwick, who had written much of the Poor Law Report of 1834, had expected to be appointed as a Commissioner but was passed over, being offered the position of Permanent Secretary to the Poor Law Commission, a post he accepted on the assurance of Lord Althorp that he would be considered in effect as a fourth Commissioner.[3] It is evident, however, that the assurance was not meant and soon tensions were growing between Commissioners and Secretary. Thomas Frankland Lewis in particular considered Chadwick to be over-stepping his powers and position.

The Commission was based at Somerset House in London and much of the routine work became Chadwick's responsibility. He was a brilliant administrator and in the early years the Poor Law Commission benefited greatly from his expertise. His strength lay in his ability to set up procedures by which the policies of the Commission could be made workable throughout the country on a day to day basis. He was zealous in his wish to see the Utilitarian principles of the new law enforced quickly, but whenever a policy of 'the greatest good for the greatest number' is adopted, flexibility in the treatment of individuals is lost; then such a policy might assume a greater importance than the welfare of any individual's case. Yet when individual cases of injustice and cruelty arise, however, they may assume great significance in the public perception. When such cases were highlighted and the Commission attracted criticism, it was easy for the Poor Law Commissioners to blame Edwin Chadwick.

The Commissioners were empowered to appoint Assistant Commissioners whose function it was to liaise between Somerset House and the local Boards of Guardians in the formation of Unions of parishes and the implementation of the new regulations. The first Assistant Commissioner for Herefordshire was Sir Edmund Walker Head, who liaised with the eight Herefordshire Unions: one formed around the City of Hereford, six more around the market towns of Ross, Ledbury, Bromyard, Leominster, Kington and Weobley, and one other, Dore Union, around the village of Abbey Dore. County boundaries were ignored in the formation of Unions when it was practical to do so; parishes were included in Unions formed around the market town most often used by their inhabitants in the transaction of their business affairs. Thus, the Herefordshire parish of Whitchurch was added to Monmouth Union; Ruardean parish in Gloucestershire was made part of Ross Union; the Herefordshire parish of Aston Ingham was included with parishes in the Gloucestershire Union of Newent; and a number of Radnorshire parishes formed part of Kington Union in Herefordshire.

Sir Edmund Walker Head[4] was a close friend of George Cornewall Lewis, the elder son of Thomas Frankland Lewis, and no doubt this family connection was instrumental in Sir Edmund's appointment. What would be seen as nepotism or favouritism now was seen as patronage in the 1830s. When Sir Edmund took up his duties in 1836, aged 30, he received a salary of £700 per year plus expenses. Lewis's family estate lay at Harpton Court in Radnorshire, a few miles from Kington, and this would have made it easy for him to arrange personal introductions between Sir Edmund and many of the prominent local figures involved in the administration of the New Poor Law; Lewis had numerous familial, clerical and political connections with many of the major landowning families in Herefordshire. This patronage soon extended, by design or by chance, to other figures in many of the Herefordshire Unions. Samuel Peploe of Garnstone Castle, near Weobley, was Chairman of Weobley Union and his wife and Lewis's wife were sisters;[5] Sir George Cornewall of Moccas Court was his brother-in-law[6] and patron of Lewis's younger son, the Reverend Gilbert Frankland Lewis, who was elected Guardian for Monnington-on-Wye in Weobley Union.[7] The Clives of Whitfield Court were close friends of the Lewis family, and Edward Bolton Clive, MP for Hereford, was the first Chairman of Dore Union[8] and in due course was succeeded by his heir, the Reverend Archer Clive.[9] Colonel Edward Clive, another son, attended as an ex-officio Guardian.[10] Edward Bolton Clive's son George was Assistant Poor Law Commissioner for Monmouth.[11] In 1838 Sir Edmund increased his social connections in Herefordshire when he married Anna Maria Yorke, who was the daughter of the Reverend Phillip Yorke of Lincoln Hill House near Ross, the second son of James Yorke, Doctor of Divinity and Bishop of Ely, and grandson of the first Earl of Hardwicke.[12] Her mother, Anna Maria Cocks, was the daughter of Charles Cocks, first Earl Somers and later Viscount Eastnor[13] of Eastnor Castle.

A statistical return[14] produced by the Poor Law Commission reveals that by 25 March 1838 all the parishes in Herefordshire had been put into unions and the business of the Boards of Guardians was proceeding.

Ross Union was comprised of Ross parish, which had four elected Guardians, and 28 rural parishes, all of which had one elected Guardian, with the exception of two very large parishes, Llangarron and Walford, which had two Guardians each.[15] All these men were present at the first Guardians' meeting, except the Guardian for the Gloucestershire parish of Ruardean, which did not have a Guardian attending meetings until 1837. The reasons for this are unclear; there might have been an element of local resistance and resentment attached to the parish's having been added to a Herefordshire Union, but it might simply have been that none of the eligible ratepayers was prepared to be elected to perform an unenviable task. Guardians' meetings usually commenced between 10am and 11am and as Ruardean was a remote parish of woodland and farms approximately eight miles from Ross, in winter a Guardian would have had to sacrifice a whole day's daylight hours from his own business affairs in order to attend the meeting. As 59 meetings were held in the first year, from April 1836 to March 1837, this may have been enough to put anyone off wanting to represent the parish. Attendance at meetings, perhaps not surprisingly, varied widely with one parish Guardian managing just five meetings (8.47%) while, at the other extreme, another attended 53 meetings (89.83%).

In addition to elected Guardians, each Union had unelected or ex-officio Guardians who were Magistrates. The New Poor Law gave Magistrates in rural areas an automatic right to serve as Guardians,[16] so long as they had been duly sworn in and were presiding in court on a regular basis. Ross Union had a varying number of these Guardians, usually between 15 and 20. Their attendance varied too, from one meeting in the year up to 56 meetings.

In 1836, Ross Union had 51 elected and ex-officio Guardians and of these 49 have been traced through the 1841 census, tithe map apportionments and contemporary trade journals in order to create a profile of them in terms of their occupations and their ownership of land, their professions and their relative status in society. Twenty-seven were farmers, of whom 13 were independent farmers owning their own land and 14 were tenant farmers, four of whom were tenants of fellow Guardians. The other 22 comprised: six clergymen; three lawyers; two doctors; five gentleman landowners; four gentlemen described in the 1841 census as being 'of independent means'; one banker with numerous business concerns; and one Member of Parliament, Daniel Higford Burr of

Gayton Hall, near Ross. A small group of ten Guardians were continuously in office from 1836 to 1844, regularly attending at least 75% of meetings in any one year. Of these, eight were continuously in office to 1847 and a few further still into the 1850s. The reason for such long periods of service might simply have been that the number of eligible ratepayers who could be elected was very small or, alternatively, that having found someone who was prepared to be an active Guardian year after year, parishioners with a right to vote were more than happy to just let him get on with it. It was, after all, a time-consuming and unpaid job.

The Guardians' remit was simply to administer poor relief in accordance with the 1834 Act and, in many respects, they were left to their own devices. They were, of course, volunteers, performing an important public duty which meant that the Poor Law Commissioners could not interfere too much because they needed their co-operation and good will to make the system work. In their correspondence with the Boards of Guardians they advised, suggested, persuaded and sometimes directed, but were unfailingly polite. The Guardians could not be compelled to attend any given number of Board Meetings and were free to resign at any time.

The attendance of Guardians at meetings does not appear to have been affected by any one circumstance, such as the distance they had to travel from home to meetings, their age or their status in society. It seems simply to have been a combination of individual circumstances and individual attitudes to public duty. The variation in attendance amongst clerical Guardians was as marked as for any other group. The Reverend Henry Charles Morgan, Rector of Goodrich, aged 45 in 1836, attended 53% of meetings; the Reverend Matthew Henry Jones of Goodrich House, 7%; Canon Thomas Underwood, Rector of Ross, aged 64, 2%; the Reverend Thomas Powell Symonds of Pengethley Court, 59%; the Reverend Love Robertson, Rector of Bridstow, aged 66, 57%; and the Reverend Watson Joseph Thornton, Rector of Llanwarne, aged 33, 78% of meetings. The Reverend Thornton also attended meetings of Hereford Union and later became its Chairman. It might be supposed that clergymen, despite their calling, might have many personal reasons for their intermittent attendance at Guardians' meetings: the demands of their parishes, and of their estates in the case of wealthy clergy; the fact some held benefices in different parts of the country and would have to visit them from time to time; or simply that their incomes placed limits on their activities outside their parishes. It would seem that the attendances of the Guardians of Ross Union were probably not markedly different from those of Guardians in other parts of the country.

Close reading of the Ross Union minute books for the years 1836 to 1847 gives the reader the impression that Union business was discussed and trans-acted without serious discord. It is possible, however, that the minutes were deficient in the sense that they give a sanitised version of events and the final outcomes of decision making. Committee procedures were carefully observed, motions were proposed and seconded, votes cast and results accepted. There were very few resignations during the course of a year's term of office and no dramatic departures from the Board of Guardians.

As the years passed and the Guardians became more familiar with the detail of the poor law administration, a collective body of knowledge grew, was modified and developed, and this was sustained by Guardians who served over a number of years. These men helped to bring continuity and consistency to the management of the workhouse and the Union. The skill and experience of the Union Clerk would also have been important in the way Union matters were handled and the avoidance of repetitious and time wasting procedures and possible conflict of opinion amongst the Guardians. In the first few years of the New Poor Law numerous issues were referred to officials at Somerset House for advice and guidance on how to proceed with particular problems which the Guardians had not previously encountered. As time went by, however, case law built up and the Guardians and their clerk became more familiar with their work. Consequently, fewer questions needed to be asked and fewer referrals were made and the minutes became less fulsome and less revealing.

Some Guardians served for only a year or two, just long enough, perhaps, for them to be seen to have done their duty or possibly because their personal circumstances made it difficult for them to continue. Village politics may also have played a significant part in how long Guardians held office. In some parishes, ratepayers seemed to be quite happy for the same person to serve as Guardian for many years; in others, however, where local politics were more vibrant, there was probably pressure on Guardians not to put themselves forward for election year after year without a break. Some ex-officio Guardians seemed to come and go as they pleased; perhaps they too had to give priority to other public and private commitments.

The most prominent and active Guardians of Ross Union in the first decade of its existence were Henry Chellingworth of Grendon Court, Upton Bishop, an independent farmer; Nathaniel Morgan, Quaker businessman and banker; James Wallace Richard Hall, lawyer and banker; William Cary Cocks, surgeon, dentist and chemist; Phillip Palmer, a farmer and landowner; William Bridgman senior and William Bridgman junior, gentlemen of independent means; Watson Joseph Thornton, a clergyman; and Captain Kingsmill Evans, a landowner. They were men of energy and influence in the community and were enmeshed in a complex web of business and familial relationships in which they could support each other and sustain a powerful and cohesive coalition.

An examination of the backgrounds of these men yields details of numerous connections between their families, their business affairs and those of less prominent Guardians. These connections are revealing in that they demonstrate what a powerful force they could be in swaying decisions and achieving their desired aims when they closed ranks. Sir Samuel Rush Meyrick of Goodrich Court, ex-officio Guardian as a Magistrate, was also High Sheriff of the county. His duties as High Sheriff would have been largely ceremonial, since the administrative duties were usually managed by an under-sheriff, but it would have brought him into contact with many of the most powerful men in the county who were also much involved in the poor law. His near neighbour, for example, Captain Kingsmill Evans, who was Chairman of Ross Union for eight of its first ten years of existence, lived at New Hill Court, and was Lord of the Manors of Ross and Walford. He was resident on his estate and would have been well known in the area. He had inherited his estate from his Clarke relatives and through them was related to the Hoskyns family of Harewood Park, the Kyrles of Walford and Much Marcle and the Joneses of The Cleeve,[17] also in Walford parish. Phillip Jones's daughter, Edith, was married to John Stratford Collins;[18] Collins was an elected Guardian for Ross, where he had a legal practice and counted Captain Kingsmill Evans as one of his clients.[19]

Just a mile or so from Captain Evans' house was Lincoln Hill House, the home of the Yorke family who were to become Sir Edmund Walker Head's relatives when he married Anna Maria Yorke in November 1838. It is quite possible that Sir Edmund stayed at Lincoln Hill House when he was attending the meetings of Ross Union and it would have been very easy, therefore, for him to arrange private meetings with Captain Evans if they had been thought necessary and considered appropriate.

To the north of Ross lay the parish of Foy and Perrystone Court, the home of the Cliffords, approximately five miles from Lincoln Hill House. Colonel Henry Morgan Clifford was an ex-officio Guardian of Ross Union and in August 1834 he married Catherine Harriett Yorke, a first cousin of Anna Maria Yorke, later Lady Head.[20] In April 1843, Anna Maria's brother Colonel Phillip James Yorke married Emily Clifford of Perrystone Court, who was Colonel Clifford's first cousin.[21] In 1841, Colonel Clifford's sister, Fanny Elizabeth Mary Clifford was married to James Wallace Richard Hall at St Mary's Church in Ross.[22] The marriage was solemnised by no less than the Dean of Hereford, Doctor John Merewether, and one of the witnesses was George Clive, formerly Assistant Poor Law Commissioner for Monmouth. Hall lived at Springfield House on the outskirts of Ross and had a legal practice in the town. He was a very diligent Guardian for Ross for more than a decade.

John Stratford Collins, landowner, lawyer and Worshipful Master of Freemasons,[23] was an elected Guardian for Ross and served the town's inhabitants in that capacity for many years, as did his close friend Nathaniel Morgan. Morgan's unpublished journals reveal a deeply religious and spiritual man on the one hand, but a very perceptive and astute man of business on the other. Morgan was a leading figure amongst the town's Quaker community, an energetic anti-slavery activist and a close friend of fellow reformer, the MP Joseph

Hume, who visited Morgan at his home in Ross.[24] He was active in many charities and as a mark of the respect with which he was regarded by the townspeople, shops remained closed on the day of his funeral in 1854.[25] In business he was a linen draper, a land speculator, an insurance broker and a banker. Such was the trust people had in him that during the banking crisis of 1825, ten local persons of property and social standing put a notice in the Hereford papers pledging their support to meet every demand made upon the bank of Jones and Morgan for a period of six months.[26] Whilst banks in Gloucester, Hereford and neighbouring market towns suspended business, Morgan's bank continued to trade throughout the crisis and met all investors' demands. Morgan never forgot the kindness of his supporters[27] and was no doubt pleased a few years later to find that some of them were to sit around the same table at the meetings of Ross Union Guardians. These included his brother-in-law, Thomas Taylor of Marstow; John Stratford Collins of The Whytall; the Reverend Matthew Henry Jones of Goodrich House; and Sir Hungerford Hoskyns of Harewood Park.[28]

It is clear from the examples cited that the leaders amongst Ross Union Guardians were entwined in an intricate tangle of relationships and alliances from which they could draw strength and support. They could sustain a united front in their management of poor relief and could summon claimants before them at Board meetings almost as a court of law. This amounted to almost feudal control over the lives of the poorest members of society. In the close restrictive atmosphere of the domestic politics of small rural parishes where Guardians were landowners and employers, they were all-powerful.

The Guardians of Ross Union appear to have taken their responsibilities seriously and wasted no time in taking important decisions. The first meeting was held at the Swan Inn on 25 April 1836, with Sir Edmund Walker Head in attendance.[29] At the first meeting a committee was appointed 'for the purpose of examining the workhouse accommodation in the district with a view to selecting the most eligible spot for building'.[30] The need to extend existing buildings or to build an entirely new workhouse appears to have been accepted even before all the Guardians came together for the first time. The building committee was comprised of Henry Chellingworth of Grendon Court, who was probably involved with the running of the existing workhouse in that parish; the Reverend Thomas Powell Symonds of Pengethley Court; Thomas Dowle of Bernithan Court, Llangarron; Nathaniel Morgan of Ross; and William Palmer of Bolitree Castle, Weston-under-Penyard, who was probably familiar with the circumstances of the workhouse there. The committee reported back just three days later and their decisions appear to have been simply an exercise to codify what had already been agreed in principle. The committee recommended that the three existing workhouses at Ross, Weston and Upton Bishop be used and superintended by the Workhouse Committee until the new workhouse was ready. The recommendations were accepted and the following resolution was agreed and forwarded to the Poor Law Commissioners at Somerset House:

> We the undersigned being a majority of the guardians of Ross Union convinced of the expediency of erecting such a workhouse as will enable us to put into force the rules and regulations of the Poor Law Commissioners of England and Wales have consented and do hereby consent to build a workhouse as aforesaid and borrow the necessary funds for that purpose provided the Poor Law Commissioners shall authorise us to do so on application to their Board.[31]

It is clear from the wording of this resolution that not all the Guardians saw the need for a new building or the expense which it would involve. It is very difficult to know whether the majority really represented the true picture of the Guardians' views, or whether some Guardians were persuaded or pressured into voting for the recommendations of the building committee in the days before the vote was taken. It would be very difficult for a tenant farmer to vote against the motion in open committee if his landlord was sitting at the same table and had made it clear that he expected his tenant to vote in favour. If this were to be the case then it is possible that the opposition of the dissenters was driven underground and that the seeming calm of the committee room was merely a veneer behind which the less powerful Guardians fumed in indignant, impotent silence. Looked at in another way, however, it might simply have indicated that many of the Guardians were well aware that the existing workhouse accommodation would be totally inadequate for the implementation of the New Poor Law.

The Guardians had received approval from Somerset House by the middle of May 1836, and it was decided to build the new workhouse on land attached to the existing Ross Workhouse.[32] By the end of May, plans drawn up by the Union's architect, Mr Plowman, had been accepted by the Guardians and approved by the Poor Law Commissioners and tenders for the work were being rigorously examined. It says much for the energy and the enthusiasm of the Guardians that so much had been achieved in five weeks. It is impossible to define how much this progress was assisted by Sir Edmund Walker Head, but it is clear that he probably had a great deal of personal support in the Ross area and, no doubt, from Thomas Frankland Lewis at Somerset House. After all, they both had a vested interest in seeing that the procedures for setting up the New Poor Law went well in the area where they had most personal connections. At first the construction work on the new workhouse went well, but by early 1837 the Guardians were increasingly anxious about progress, though they were assured by Mr Tristram, the builder, that the work would be complete by 31 August. But there were delays: August passed into September;

autumn passed into winter; and finally the workhouse was ready for occupation in the first week of January 1838.

The new workhouse was to become the centre of Union administration where Guardians' meetings were held in a purpose-built Board room. Prior to its completion meetings were convened in a number of different locations: the Swan Inn, which was probably deemed to be too expensive after the first few meetings; St Mary's Church vestry, which was found to be too small to accommodate full attendance; and a school, almost certainly Sir Walter Scott's School in Old Gloucester Road, since the town's British and Foreign School was not opened until September 1837.[33]

The workhouse was to be managed by a Master and Matron in a husband and wife team, assisted by a nurse, a Schoolmistress, a Porter and a baker. Outside the workhouse the Union's business was to be handled by four Relieving Officers, each with his own clearly defined area. The particular problem encountered by the Board of Guardians was that of appointing officers and servants of the Union who were reliable, trustworthy and, above all, competent to carry out their duties properly. Advertisements were duly placed in the county's newspapers for the appointment of the paid officers. It was an era when few people received training for any occupation and the Board of Guardians appear to have assumed that once officers were appointed they would know how to carry out their duties, or at least would grow into their jobs with the passing of time. This was despite the fact that under the New Poor Law, officers were required to keep detailed records, which would then be carefully examined by the Union Clerk on a weekly, monthly and quarterly basis, before he presented precise details of his findings to the Board of Guardians at every general meeting. The clerk would doubtless have been zealous in his checking of records for his own safety; he could not afford to pass records lightly because the Guardians would hold him responsible for any discrepancies which might come to light at a later date. Union accounts had to be examined by an independent auditor and regular statistical returns had to be submitted to the Poor Law Commissioners at Somerset House whenever requested. The introduction of annual audit requirements was the first mode of central control; audit changed local control into regional control.

Ross Guardians usually took swift action to investigate when salaried officers were criticised or complaints were received from those receiving or requesting relief. They seem to have been unprepared, however, for the fact that complaints would almost inevitably arise from time to time and that some officers would be guilty of misconduct. The complaints, when they came, were usually against Medical Officers, some against Relieving Officers and a few against the workhouse's Master or the Matron.

The notion that Relieving Officers might cheat paupers or be rude and abrasive to them, that Medical Officers might neglect their patients and leave

Ross Workhouse buildings in the 1960s

them unattended for days, that the Schoolmistress might be barely literate, or that the workhouse Master might be an incompetent bully, did not seem to enter the Guardians' thinking until serious complaints were received. Then they displayed shock and horror and moved swiftly, some-times just to protect them-selves, as will be seen later in the case of a Relieving Officer named Samuel Garness. It has to be remembered, however, that some of the people with whom untrained and often poorly educated officers had to contend were very difficult, ranging from persistent petty criminals to the quite seriously insane.

It was probably inevitable that the mixed general workhouse would at any one time include amongst its inmates the old, sick, infirm and senile; young single women with illegitimate children; abandoned and orphaned children; degenerates; and the respectable poor who were temporarily unemployed. In rural areas, the ebb and flow of able-bodied men and women through the work-house would have corresponded with the seasons and weather conditions and the resultant rise and fall in the availability of employment for agricultural

The Alton Road frontage of Ross Workhouse buildings in the 1980s

labourers. In every workhouse there would have been a variable group of individuals for whom any real improvement in outlook, attitude or general circumstance was unlikely, if not remote. The Assistant Commissioners were often given very large areas to supervise, sometimes several counties, and therefore were probably not able to assist workhouse officers and advise Guardians as much as was really needed, because their own lives were dominated by relentless travel around their designated area in order to attend at least some of the Guardians' meetings. Ross Union had its share of unsatisfactory officers, and the Guardians were faced with some complicated situations in the course of their duties: disruptive behaviour, neglect, murder, suicide and manslaughter.

An inquest was held at Ross Workhouse in August 1838 'to inquire into the circumstances of the death of Richard W. one of the children of the workhouse who was suffocated in the privy in the play yard'.[34] The verdict was recorded as accidental death and no doubt the matter was forgotten as quickly as possible as far as the Guardians were concerned. It returned to haunt them in 1840, however, on the death of another inmate, Dinah C.

Dinah's age was not recorded in the Union minute book but it is likely that she was in her early or middle teens. The minutes did record that she was in trouble for stealing a shilling from Mary Williams in October 1838, for which she was put in solitary confinement for ten hours and deprived of meat for two days. In June 1839 she was again confined, this time for attempting to leave the workhouse without permission and for trying to induce two other girls to join her. In August of that year the old ladies in the workhouse complained to the Chaplain that their sleep was disturbed by general commotion and bad language, and again Dinah was involved. In October 1839 the Guardians decided to return her to the care of her parents, who were not residing in the workhouse. That was probably the last they were to see of Dinah, but not the last time she was to cause them serious concern.

In March 1840 a verdict of accidental death 'from injuries received from her clothes taking *A lasting reminder of Ross Workhouse, now part of the Community Hospital. The first-floor windows were those of the boardroom*

fire'[35] was recorded at the inquest on Dinah, and later that month the Board of Guardians was informed, by a person whose name was not recorded, that Dinah had 'a short time before her death confessed that she destroyed Richard W. ... by throwing him down the privy'.[36] This led to further enquiries and it was resolved that the late Schoolmistress had been guilty of neglect, knowing but failing to inform the Board, jury and Coroner that 'the child was rickety and unable to walk from the schoolroom to the privy or to get from the floor of the privy to the seat and consequently that the child could not have fallen down the privy accidentally'.[37] Murder had been done, covered up and recorded as accidental death, and would never have been exposed but for Dinah's last minute confession. Richard W. was just two years old.[38]

Events such as these say much about the honesty and the integrity of Union officers on whom the Guardians had to depend. They also raise questions about just how aware Guardians were of happenings behind the workhouse walls or even how much they cared until events came to light which reflected on them as Guardians. It is clear from the case of the infant Richard that children were very vulnerable to intimidation and abuse. It was no doubt very difficult for Guardians to ensure that the officers of the Union were actually behaving all the time in the manner they presented when Guardians were visiting the workhouse, but it is clear that some Guardians did neglect their responsibilities and their duty of care to the poor. The Andover scandal (see chapter 9) where paupers were found to be starving is an extreme case, but does prove that some Guardians were extremely negligent in seeing that their responsibilities were met. M.A. Crowther writes:

Part of what is now a park by Ross Community Hospital that was once the workhouse gardens

Guardians could not be compelled to visit the workhouse regularly: at Andover, for example, the guardians had been almost entirely apathetic, and the master had virtually unfettered authority. The chairman of the board, the Reverend Christopher Dodson, had not visited the workhouse for five years before the scandal broke, nor had he read any of the Commissioners' regulations for three years.[39]

The mixed general workhouse became a repository for the respectable poor, the petty criminal, the prostitute, the imbecile, the lunatic, the pervert, the respectable aged, the sick and the senile. Such a mixture of characters and influences would probably have generated many fears in the public's perception of the workhouse, aided and abetted by gossip and rumour. It is surprising, therefore, to find that children were sometimes placed in the care of the workhouse at a very tender age, as the following example makes clear:

> Resolved that two of the children (Viz. William aged seven years and Elizabeth aged five years) of Thomas Powell belonging to the parish of Upton Bishop (who had a wife and five children) shall be taken into the workhouse without their parents, their mother being now before the board and consenting thereto.[40]

In the years before the New Poor Law was introduced, fair-minded Overseers in many parishes would relieve a man's poverty and allow him to keep his family together. It was the force of Utilitarianism which had brought Thomas Powell and his wife to the difficult decision of sending such young children to the workhouse. One wonders too what fears William and Elizabeth Powell experienced in the hands of officers and other inmates. A decade earlier, in 1838, fear of the workhouse had resulted in an elderly man taking his own life.

The inquest on Thomas Williams was reported to the Board of Guardians of Ross Union on 3 September 1838. The jury had brought in a verdict that 'the deceased had destroyed himself owing to the dread and horror he entertained of entering the workhouse for which he had received an order from the relieving officer, Mr Lodwidge'.[41] Thomas Williams was 85 years old and it is possible that he was severely demented; on the other hand, he may have been the innocent victim of rumour and gossip about happenings in workhouses which led his becoming disproportionately afraid and taking his own life. It is also possible that loss of self-respect – the humiliation of being dubbed a pauper – played a part in his suicide. He hanged himself with a halter in a millhouse near his lodgings in Pencoyd.[42] Resolutions passed by the Board of Guardians indicated that Thomas Williams had been in receipt of 2s and 8lbs of bread per week and that the workhouse had been offered to him because he had been given notice to quit his lodgings and had nowhere else to go. There had been no suggestion that his allowance was to be altered or withdrawn and it was further resolved 'that the Board must express their conviction that there exists no well grounded reason for entertaining a "dread and horror" of entering the workhouse'.[43] This statement seems more than a little hollow considering that it was the New Poor Law's aim that only the utterly destitute would contemplate entering the workhouse.

Relieving Officers themselves created many problems for the Boards of Guardians and often did not remain in post for more than a few months or a year or two at most. Some probably thought that the post would give them a steady income and some status in their community, but were unprepared for the demands of the job and were soon found to be inadequate, unreliable or plain dishonest. They were sometimes accused of neglect of duty, incompetence, dubious accounting, inefficiency and general indifference to the pressing needs of the poor. Some, however, were zealous to the point of folly, as indicated by the most serious case of misconduct found in the minute books of Ross Guardians, which occurred in March 1845 and resulted in the sudden and tragic death of an aged pauper.

Mary Jones was an old woman of Llangarron who had received an order to enter the workhouse from the Relieving Officer, Samuel Garness. Garness also lived at Llangarron, where in former times he had been a farmer and a publican. It was perhaps in a bid to establish or reinforce his authority as a Relieving Officer in his own parish that he seriously overreacted when Mary Jones refused to leave her home. It was alleged that Garness and unnamed others attempted to remove her by force and thus made themselves vulnerable to charges of assault. Sadly, the old lady became extremely distressed as a result of the Relieving Officer's actions and died. The Guardians made their enquiries and then, moving very swiftly in order to protect themselves:

> Ordered that the clerk (John Hawkins) be instructed professionally to undertake the prosecution of Mr Samuel Garness and the other defendants at the next Hereford Assizes and to employ such counsel to conduct the same to subpoena such witnesses and take such other steps therein as he may think fit or may be advised.[44]

Two of the most diligent of the Ross Guardians were John Stratford Collins and James Wallace Richard Hall. They were both lawyers with practices in Ross and almost certainly had a hand in the Guardians' swift legal action. They moved far more slowly, however, when Medical Officers were found guilty of misconduct or neglect. Doctors were, of course, from a different sphere of society than lowly Relieving Officers such as Samuel Garness.

Ross Union was divided into two districts for the purposes of the medical care of paupers. On receipt of an order from a Relieving Officer, Medical

Officers were required to attend pauper patients in their own homes as often as deemed necessary, until treatment was complete. One of the Medical Officers was designated to make regular visits to attend the sick in the work-house and also attend if summoned to a medical emergency by the Master. Dr George Rootes and Dr Charles Thomson were the first Medical Officers to be appointed[45] and it was not long before complaints against Dr Rootes began to vex the Guardians. The complaints were often that he neglected to call on patients to attend to their medical needs even when the urgency of the case was impressed on him by the Relieving Officer. Paupers with very serious medical conditions were left unattended for days, sometimes weeks and in one case, months. Investigations were made, the doctor was questioned, the pauper and relevant witnesses were examined and the findings of the Board were carefully minuted, but there was rarely more than a caution to the doctor. The only real argument Dr Rootes might have presented was that the area under his care was too large, that it included some very remote parishes and that the nature of the roads made speedy travelling between different patients both difficult and time-consuming. On the other hand, it might be argued that there was no excuse for leaving patients unattended for long periods of time, particularly when the Union Relieving Officer had expressed great concern about an indi-vidual pauper's condition.

In April 1837 Dr Rootes was cautioned for not having attended Thomas Davies more quickly[46] but was excused from serious complaint because there was said to be more illness than usual in the Ross area, so that both he and his assistant, Dr Aveline, had been greatly pressed by the volume of business. In November 1841 he was found guilty of great neglect in visiting his patient Sarah Nurse of Llangarron only three times over a period of several months, thus requiring the lady to walk twice a week from Llangarron to Ross, a round trip of 14 miles, to receive appropriate treatment for an ulcerated leg.[47] The following month he was cautioned again for failing to attend Ellen Wilks and Rebecca James of Goodrich,[48] and his attitude to the cases of Samuel Grundy in August 1843 and Joseph Davies in December 1843 resulted in his eventu-ally leaving the service of Ross Union.

Sarah Grundy, the wife of Samuel Grundy, went to Dr Rootes with an order for his attendance on her husband, who she said was very ill. Dr Rootes said that the patient must come to him and on being informed that Grundy's condi-tion rendered that impossible, prescribed medicine without seeing the patient. Grundy's condition worsened that night and Dr Millard of Whitchurch was called and treated him the following morning. Mr Halford, the Relieving Officer who had issued the order for attendance on Grundy, was sufficiently concerned about the man to visit Dr Rootes the same day to urge him to attend swiftly. Dr Rootes did not attend, however, until 7pm the following evening. The Board agreed that the calling of Dr Millard had been quite justified, paid his account, deducted the sum from the salary owed to Dr Rootes and once again censured his poor professional conduct.[49] In December 1843, further complaints arose against Dr Rootes when a pauper of the parish of St Weonards, Joseph Davies, died and the Guardians were sufficiently alarmed to refer the matter to the Poor Law Commissioners. Dr Rootes was not dismissed; he was allowed to resign.[50] It had taken six years of complaints before he was removed from office and even then had only happened when the Guardians of Ross Union were sufficiently concerned about the Union's reputation and their own good names to refer the case of Joseph Davies to the Poor Law Commissioners.

Dr Rootes was succeeded by Mr Wilmott, whose title suggests that he was not a doctor but a surgeon or an apothecary, but he too received a considerable amount of criticism. In September 1846, Elizabeth Beavan of Llangarron complained that Sarah Meredith, a cancer patient for whom she was caring, had not been visited by Mr Wilmott or Mr Smart, the Relieving Officer, for over two months.[51] In April 1847, Mr Wilmott neglected to respond to a call to visit Anne Powell of St Weonards for ten days[52] and in June that year Anne Scott of Goodrich had died without medical attendance although Wilmott had twice been requested to visit in the five days preceding her death.[53] In October 1847 the Minister, Churchwardens and Overseers of Tretire sent a written statement to the Board complaining about Mr Wilmott's refusal to attend Joseph Bailey's wife in a difficult labour and pointing out that Mary Anne Bailey had died. There is no record of the Union employing parish midwives and so, in the case of a very difficult labour, it was logical that the Union Medical Officer should

Ready for Christmas celebrations in Ross Workhouse in the 1930s.
The room depicted is the boardroom (courtesy of Mrs V.J. Robbins)

be requested to attend. Wilmott argued that he had not attended because he had received no order from the Relieving Officer to do so. The Board investigated the complaint and noted the following comments:

> It appears from the statement (from the minister) that no order upon Mr Wilmott to attend the case had been obtained. And the Board considering that they had no power to enter into the matter upon the question of whether Mr Wilmott acted with the humanity which a medical man might reasonably be expected to display on such an occasion and that Mr Wilmott appeared to have been legally excused from attending the patient on the ground that no order was obtained requiring his attendance the Board came to the conclusion that they could not call upon Mr Wilmott to answer the complaint.[54]

Mr Wilmott may not have been guilty of any breach in the law, but most reasonable people would be inclined to observe that he was indeed in breach of his moral duty and rightfully wonder if his taking of the Hippocratic Oath had ever been more than a mere formality. It is true that if Mr Wilmott was an apothecary he would not have been bound by the Hippocratic Oath, but even if that was the case, he appears to have escaped on a technicality.

Medical Officers were regarded by the Central Authority as servants of the Poor Law and this in itself was likely to deter doctors from working for Poor Law Unions. The Board of Ross Union had a contradictory attitude to its medical men; on the one hand they showed them a certain respect as educated professional men, but on the other, treated them as servants of the Board as far as money matters were concerned. They constantly reassessed their duties and revised their salaries in order to reduce costs. Their contracts were reviewed and readvertised on an annual basis, serving to keep them in their place and allowing the Guardians to rid themselves of troublesome officers with relative ease. One wonders why they did not use this method to dismiss Dr Rootes long before his departure. The answer was probably the difficulty they would have in replacing him. Working for the Poor Law Unions was not the most lucrative of positions for doctors, and there were few who were prepared to bury themselves in a remote rural county for very long. In addition they were paid a basic salary only just above that of the Union Clerk. The Clerk of Ross Union was paid £65 per annum[55] with all his book-keeping materials found for him: Medical Officers were paid £75 per annum[56] plus 10s for cases of midwifery, but were required to provide all medicines and medical equipment from their own resources. Also, the taint of pauperism ran right through society, and working as a Union doctor might blight a young man's future career, his income, his marriage prospects and his standing in society.

Despite the above cases, Guardians attracted most criticism over the subject of education for workhouse children, and this criticism came not from

102-year-old 'Granny' Webb at Ross Workhouse, March 1924 (courtesy of Mrs V.J. Robbins)

paupers or public but from the Poor Law Commissioners. The new Ross Workhouse was ready for occupation in early January 1838 and almost immediately the first Schoolmistress, a Mrs Griffiths, was appointed and placed in charge of the purpose-built schoolroom. She had an onerous task, very poor pay and very little personal freedom. She lived in the workhouse, took her meals with the Master and Matron and received an annual salary of £10. She was not allowed to leave the premises without the Master's permission except on two evenings a week, from 5pm to 8pm between Michaelmas and Lady Day, and from 5pm to 9pm for the other months of the year.[57] Her exact duties were not recorded but a minute made in June 1838 made it clear that the children were supposed to receive two hours' instruction per day. Whether they actually did seems highly questionable:

> Resolved that the schoolmistress be directed to walk out with the chil-dren when the weather is sufficiently fine, one hour in the morning and one hour in the evening such hours to be in lieu of those occupied in instructing them.[58]

Henry Morgan Clifford of Perrystone Court was obviously concerned about the education of the workhouse children and proposed that all the boys, unless ill, above the age of 6 should attend the Royal Victoria School in the town at a charge of 2d each per week until such time as the provision of education in the workhouse might be improved.[59] The motion was, however, withdrawn, perhaps because of opposition from some Board members on the grounds of expense. There was also concern on the part of the patrons of the Royal Victoria School about their children mixing with 'parish' children.

The problem of education in the workhouse was evidently not raised again for almost a decade; scant documentary evidence exists for the period between

July 1838 and September 1846, apart from references to the schoolroom being damp[60] and the Chaplain's ordering of religious tracts.[61] In general, public opinion was very much against the education of paupers and it was unlikely that Ross Guardians, as a whole, would have felt differently. Edwin Chadwick's plan to provide an efficient system of training for all children who came into the hands of the Poor Law administrators was abandoned. It was thought to be impracticable and also undesirable because it would confer positive benefits on the pauper class, benefits not provided for the independent poor.[62] These sentiments were raised when the matter of education came before the Board again in 1846.

The Poor Law Commission wrote to Ross Union Guardians at the beginning of September that year complaining of the insufficient education afforded to the children in the workhouse.[63] Their criticisms were based on a report received from Edward Gulsin, the Assistant Commissioner who had visited the workhouse a few weeks earlier. The Commissioners had moved swiftly on receiving Gulsin's report to request that a competent person be found to instruct the children in writing and arithmetic. The minutes of the meeting held on 17 September 1846 show that the Guardians raised a number of objections. They pointed out that the children were not in the workhouse long enough for them to learn very much; that the workhouse could not accommodate a resident Schoolmaster; that the children might benefit more than those of the independent poor; and that educating the children would be 'an unreasonable charge upon the poor rate'.[64] Only after much discussion did they finally agree to employ a Schoolmaster at a salary not exceeding £15 per annum.[65]

In April, 1848 Jelinger C. Symons, Her Majesty's Inspector of Workhouse Schools, visited Ross Workhouse and was clearly unimpressed with what he observed in the schoolroom. The Schoolmistress was still in charge and, as a minute dated 3 April 1848 indicated, the Guardians were largely unconcerned with the contents of the inspector's report:

Mr and Mrs Reginald Roff, the last
Master and Matron of Ross Workhouse
(courtesy of Mrs V.J. Robbins)

The chairman reported that, accompanied by the vice Chairman Mr C. Cocks, the Chaplain and the Clerk had met Mr Jelinger C. Symons, Her Majesty's Inspector of Workhouse Schools, at the workhouse on Monday last and that Mr Symons had examined the children in the workhouse School and made a report in the Visiting Committee's book of the result of such examination – which was read and from which it appeared that Mr Symons complained of the inefficiency of the schoolmistress and also recommended that the Board take into consideration the question of District Schools – It was determined to let the matter stand over until the expected communication from the Poor Law Commissioners founded upon Mr Symons's Report was received.[66]

The report was followed by a letter from the Poor Law Board which was minuted on 17 April 1848. It expressed great concern over the qualifications of the Schoolmistress, since 'it appeared that she was not competent to teach either writing or arithmetic'.[67] The Board was requested to call for her resignation and to appoint a competent person. Twelve years after the formation of the Union, the workhouse was still without a teacher who had an acceptable standard of education. This situation had not improved five years later, since in December 1853 the visiting Poor Law Inspector, Mr John Graves, enquired about the appointment of someone to teach writing and arithmetic. The excuse this time was lack of accommodation and lack of space to build; but the Guardians did agree, no doubt after some pressure from Somerset House, to appoint a non-resident Schoolmaster with a salary of £25 per annum. He was 'to instruct the children in reading, writing and arithmetic and the principles of the Christian Religion for three hours each day of the week'.[68] Whether the Poor Law Board took a hand in finding a Schoolmaster for Ross Union in order to prevent further prevarication is not known, but it would seem likely from an entry in the minutes dated 12 March 1855. The Poor Law Board had enquired 'whether the Guardians were satisfied as to the conduct of Mr C.H. Hughes as Schoolmaster; the Clerk was instructed to write and say that 'they were quite so ...'.[69]

The New Poor Law called for a level of professional conduct amongst its officers that was quite foreign to many of them and of which some were quite incapable. The notion of truly professional conduct had yet to evolve. Their conduct was based not on the notion of being a fair and efficient Relieving Officer or a kindly, skilful Medical Officer, but on power and the right to exercise authority over others in inferior situations. The immature use of power led men like Samuel Garness and Dr Rootes to cause numerous problems for Ross Guardians, but other problems they encountered were essentially general day-to-day difficulties relating to inadequate buildings, poor facilities and difficult paupers.

6   Poor Law and Anti-Poor Law in Hereford

In the 1830s the cathedral city of Hereford resembled a large market town with a clerical aristocracy. Its trade was rooted in agriculture: it supplied the needs of those who owned, managed or tilled the land. The apparent insignificance of a rural town, however, belied some of its clerical and political connections. The Hon. Edward Grey, for example, the brother of Earl Grey, the Whig Prime Minister who held power between 1830 and 1834, became Dean of Hereford in 1831 and Bishop of Hereford in 1832, and continued to hold office until his death in 1837. He was made bishop by his brother in an apparent act of nepotism which served two very good purposes as far as the family was concerned; the cleric gained rapid advancement in the Church hierarchy and the Prime Minister gained a reliable Whig bishop in the House of Lords.[1] Hereford may have 'preserved a Barchester-like air of serenity',[2] but it is more than likely that behind the mask of polite manners and social graces there were as many tensions, misunderstandings, plots and counter plots, and as much advantage seeking, as in Barchester itself.

In 1832 Bishop Grey's place as Dean was filled by Dr John Merewether of Queen's College, Oxford. Dr Merewether was ordained in 1820 at the age of 23 and became chaplain to the Duchess of Clarence, later Queen Adelaide, in 1824. In 1828, the Lord Chancellor presented him with the living of New Radnor,[3] very close to the Lewis family stronghold of Harpton Court. It is curious that a seemingly promising young clergyman, so early in his career chaplain to a duchess and later a queen, should have been 'rewarded' with a living so far from the sphere of court and in such a rural county. He was, however, a man of energy and as well as being the incumbent of New Radnor, he was also Vicar of Madley and, within four years, Dean of Hereford at the age of 35. It would seem, too, that he was an aggrieved man, a man who felt he had been betrayed by false promises. Owen Chadwick has written:

> Dr Merewether, the Dean of Hereford, who was promised a bishopric by the dying King William IV, and was politically suitable, since he organ-ised the Tory party at Hereford elections, reminded Peel of the royal

promise and said that a bishopric would be most congenial to his feelings. Peel replied that he considered the king's intention to lay no obligation upon him and that his principles precluded him from attaching
weight to any considerations but those of professional character.[4]

It is not difficult to understand that there would have been tensions in the
cathedral close in the City of Hereford, where the bishop was a Whig and
brother of a Whig Prime Minister and the Dean was a decided Tory activist
who at the same time felt that he ought to be Bishop. It is clear from his
personal correspondence that Sir George Cornewall Lewis did not like Dr
Merewether at all; he seems to have had little respect for him as a person, a
clergyman or a political adversary. Writing to Sir Edmund Walker Head in
April, 1850 he commented candidly, and not a little unkindly, that 'the Dean of
Hereford, much to the relief of New Radnor, has lately died'.[5] This comment,
voiced in a letter to an old and trusted friend, was probably truly felt and says
as much about Lewis as it does about the Dean. In the same letter Lewis went
on to say: 'Many people wish Gilbert [his brother] to become a candidate, but
he prefers remaining as he is, and has no wish to become a Church dignitary.
The Deanery of Hereford is not very tempting: £1000 a year with a house in
ruins, and a cathedral to subscribe to.'[6]

The duties of the Dean of Hereford included care of the cathedral church,
the chained library archives, almshouses and other properties, and the vicars
choral, and the conduct of choral services. Head and Lewis no doubt thought
that these were the right and proper duties for a Dean and that he should not stray
into being a political activist, especially not a Tory one. Whatever some might
have thought of him as a clergyman, a church dignitary and a man, however,
Dr Merewether had endeavoured to mount an urgent restoration of the cathedral, which was in very poor structural condition. It is clear that he made large
personal contributions to the restoration, since the work came to an abrupt halt
at the time of his death in 1850. This is substantiated by comments made in the
General Board of Health Report compiled on the condition of Hereford City
in 1853, in what was probably an oblique criticism of the Church and the use
of diocesan revenues. It stated that the cathedral was in a very poor state of
repair and the central tower was likely to fall. It also confirmed that a major
restoration had been embarked upon by Dean Merewether in 1842, but that the
work had been suspended since his death for want of funds. This was, indeed,
condemnation of the clerical community, for the report also pointed out that
many of the houses and a large proportion of the land in the city belonged to
the cathedral. This was perhaps intended to suggest that the Dean and Chapter
and the Prebendaries had drawn incomes from city rents and tithes and paid
scant attention to the cathedral church and its structural maintenance for many
decades.

Bishop Grey, who was described by Owen Chadwick as 'not eminent'[7] in his profession, died in 1837, and was followed by another Whig, Dr Thomas Musgrave. He was Bishop of Hereford until 1847, when he became Archbishop of York. There is no record of Bishop Grey attending the meetings of the Hereford Poor Law Guardians, but the Dean, Dr Merewether, did attend meetings and also, in his capacity as Vicar of Madley, the meetings of Dore Union. Dore Guardians treated him with considerable respect in asking his advice when assessing the workhouse properties available to the Union whilst new buildings were being planned and erected. At a meeting held on 11 August 1837, it was resolved:

> That the Dean of Hereford be requested to give the Board the advantage of his suggestions as to the arrangements respecting Madley Workhouse the necessary repairs and fixtures as well as the Rent to be paid by the Board of Guardians and that the subject be considered at the next meeting.[8]

The Guardians of Dore Union were probably exercising courtesy and caution for very good reasons: national politics, parochial politics, and cathedral politics. Dore Union was heavily influenced, if not dominated, by the Clives of Whitfield Court in the parish of Treville. The first Chairman was Edward Bolton Clive, Member of Parliament for Hereford, who, despite his parliamentary duties, often attended Guardians' meetings. His son, Colonel Edward Clive, also sat as an ex-officio Guardian, as did his son-in-law, Dr Henry Wetherell, who was also the Archdeacon of Hereford. Edward Bolton Clive was followed as Chairman by his son and heir the Reverend Archer Clive, who was also a Prebendary of Hereford Cathedral. The Clives were Whigs and would have been well aware of Dr Merewether's political views and, from within the cathedral walls, would also have known that he was not an easy colleague with whom to communicate. Although he believed himself to have been promised a bishopric he had been passed over on two occasions when the see of Hereford became vacant, seemingly because of his politics; he might well feel aggrieved.

The Church of England was a major landowner in Herefordshire. Some of the clergy were very rich estate owners in their own right, many clergymen were involved in public affairs as members of the Magistracy, and many were involved with the implementation of the New Poor Law. The clergy had been administrators in the relief of poverty at parish level before the advent of the 1834 Act. Taking into account a parish priest's duty of care to the poor, it was perhaps seen as fitting and compatible with his calling for him to be alert to the effects which the new legislation might have on the well-being of his flock. After 1834, however, the whole complexion of the administration of poor relief changed; parish politics became Union politics, and Union politics became national politics. Many may have questioned whether it was appropriate for clergymen to become so deeply enmeshed in the politics of the New Poor Law, but if they were really diligent in their duty of care it was difficult for them not to become embroiled in politics on some occasions. In Herefordshire, not only the humble parish priests, but also high ranking churchmen involved themselves in the New Poor Law, which raises the question of whether the new Act was a greater political issue than the seeming peace and tranquillity of the county would suggest. Anne Digby has written that:

> Clerical supporters of the New Poor Law stressed that it was the law of the land and that its provisions were not intended to punish the poor, while clerical opponents of the 1834 act emphasised that it was against the law of God and oppressed the poor.[9]

The dilemma which clergymen faced arose from the fact that once the relief of the poor was centralised under the Poor Law Commissioners, poor law affairs became a matter of national politics in a way they had never been before, and priests had to decide whether they were for or against the new legislation. Many must have had troubled consciences as they considered their position and which of their numerous roles they placed first; landowner, employer, justice, ratepayer or guardian of the flock. Some, however, did speak out quite unequivocally and the Reverend T.B. Morris, Rector of Shelfanger in Norfolk, was just such a man. He made complaints to Guiltcross Guardians about their inhumane administration of the New Poor Law and also preached against it from his pulpit. He stated his opinion very clearly in 1836 when he wrote:

> I consider the Poor Law Amendment Act to be harsh and unjust in its operation, impolitic in its consequence, immoral in its tendency, and unchristian in its principles.[10]

The City of Hereford had its caring clergymen too. On 18 December 1832, Ross businessman Nathaniel Morgan wrote of the death of a good friend, the Reverend Henry Gipps, in his journal: 'Died today a most Pious Clergyman at Hereford who devoted his time and considerable wealth to promote the Happiness of man – greatly lamented by all who knew him – in his 47th year'.[11] He had been Vicar of St Peter's and Rector of St Owen's, both parishes within the city, and was followed in 1833 by the Reverend John Venn. Venn was the son and grandson of evangelical preachers and probably journeyed to Herefordshire well aware that innovation and reform would be necessary. When he arrived he found Hereford amidst a rural decline in a remote part of England, cut off by poor communications. He was forced to complete his

33-hour journey to the city by arriving in a local conveyance known as the 'fishcart'. It was a contrast to the prosperous village of Pinner, in Middlesex, where he had been vicar for three years.[12]

The general condition of the city had probably not improved very much even 20 years later, for the Board of Health Report of 1853 painted a gloomy picture. Argument appears to have revolved round the issue of who should pay for city improvements and whether the costs were really justifiable, and while such debates continued, little changed despite the obvious need for improvement.

John Venn was an energetic man and he soon began to establish organisations to aid the poor and help them improve their lot; self-help was central to his thinking. He set up St Peter's Literary Institute, which provided a reading room and lending library for working men, and also arranged lectures on a variety of subjects, some given by Venn himself.[13] He formed the Hereford Friendly Society to encourage people to save against illness and hardship, and, in 1838, the Hereford Missionary Society, which worked amongst the poor and the sick.

Having arrived in Hereford in 1833 Venn would have had the opportunity to judge the condition of the poor before and after the implementation of the Poor Law Amendment Act of 1834 and, while he sustained his views on self help, between 1838 and 1841 he had a change of heart and expressed great concern about the general condition of the city's poor. The new workhouse in Kennel Lane was opened in 1838 and, in November 1837, when the appointment of officers was proceeding, John Venn wrote a long letter to the Guardians of Hereford Union which began as follows:

> As the minister of the Parish in which the workhouse is locally situated,
> I naturally feel interested in the arrangements that may be made for the
> spiritual instruction of its inmates; and I would venture respectfully to
> submit to the Board what I conceive to be the most desirable plan.[14]

The Poor Law Commission's expectation was that the clergyman of the parish in which the workhouse stood would make arrangements for the religious life of the workhouse. Venn was clearly of the opinion that this pattern of thinking would be adopted in Hereford and his plan contained a large amount of detail concerning the remuneration agreed for the workhouse Chaplain, £50 per annum, but he went on to point out that no man could consider such work without other income or employment. He suggested that the Poor Law Guardians of Hereford should appoint him as Chaplain and he would appoint a curate to officiate at the workhouse and help him with the numerous poor in his parishes of St Peter and St Owen. At that time he might well have believed the opinion expressed by the Commission, influenced by Utilitarians like Edwin

Chadwick, that only the most feckless of able-bodied men and women would end up in the workhouse and that the deserving poor would be well treated. In his letter he went on to make known his views on idleness and vice:

> It is of course impossible to foretell what the average number of inmates may be, but at times the number will doubtless be very considerable, and amongst them there will be a large proportion of old and infirm and children, and occasionally a great many able-bodied people. The field therefore will be a very important one in a ministerial point of view, and require no small proportion of a Minister's time to be devoted to it. The number of sick and infirm will need a great deal of individual instruction and consolation and the children ought frequently to be catechised and the able-bodied will chiefly be such as have brought themselves there by imprudence and idleness and vice and will only remain there for a short time, it will be most important that when there the opportunity (seldom perhaps offered to their own Parish Minister thro' their irregular habits) should be improved with the utmost diligence.[15]

John Venn's views as expressed in his letter to the Hereford Guardians clearly lend weight to the argument that the new workhouse system imposed an Anglican morality on workhouse inmates. If they did not attend church regularly and remained, therefore, largely out of the reach of their own parish minister, then they should be worked on and improved with the 'utmost diligence' while they were a captive congregation. This cannot be seen in any way but as a means of social control. It might be argued that this is what the Poor Law Commission envisaged when it assumed that the minister of the parish in which the workhouse stood would arrange the religious teaching for its inmates. The self-improvement of the poor which was so widely advocated was to be coupled with the imposed improvement of regular living habits and religious teaching in the closed world of the workhouse. It was the imposition of middle class views: inmates were not free to choose. Venn's letter also suggests that he considered the deterrent aspect of the workhouse to be appropriate. It might be said that his Utilitarian opinions were in line with those of the Poor Law Commission, but for some reason not recorded, not to the liking of the Board of Guardians. Venn's advice was ignored and the Reverend Albert Jones was appointed instead.

In 1837 Venn obviously believed that the New Poor Law would be good for the poor; those who were not culpable in their own distress would be cared for and those who were culpable would be deterred by the 'Workhouse Test'. He had not considered the possibility that the 'Workhouse Test' might be applied so harshly that the deserving poor might be turned away hungry and in desperate need of shelter. His illusions were soon to be shattered and as the New Poor Law was implemented he became more and more concerned about the city's poor. In February 1841 he called a public meeting to discuss the situation. He was supported by the recently arrived Bishop Thomas Musgrave, Dean John Merewether and the Mayor, F.L. Bodenham, and in that august company addressed some of the most influential men in the city.

> Every inhabitant of this city must have perceived and mourned over the sad state of our poor. There are many who entirely depend on what they can get by importunate begging, and a display of wretchedness; whilst numbers of a far more respectable character are suffering in patient silence, the greatest distress.[16]

If the poor of Hereford were indeed reduced to such a wretched situation, the logical deduction must be that either the new legislation was unequal to the task of caring justly for the poor, or it was being applied too zealously.

Later that year, Venn started the Hereford Society for Aiding the Industrious.[17] It distributed soup, sold subsidised coal, provided low interest loans from £1 to £10, ran a savings bank, and purchased 28 acres of land for allotments, available at low rents.[18] Later in 1847,[19] the society purchased land and built a mill to enable the poor to benefit from the efforts of their gleaning by having their grain ground cheaply. The need for these self-help activities and much charitable giving in the city during the first decade of the New Poor Law raises serious questions about its implementation within Hereford Union, its general management and the attitudes of the Guardians. It might also be argued, however, that the poor law was intended to deter the poor from becoming malingerers and that the self-help groups and the charitable giving were, in fact, incidental to it and merely the response of a Christian society accepting its duty of care to the poor. There were many societies such as the one started by John Venn throughout the country, but many were short-lived and the poor did not always benefit from their struggle to be thrifty when difficult circumstances arose. Anne Digby has written:

> Nationally, there was a growth in the number of friendly societies after 1834. This had pleased the administrators of the New Poor Law, who attributed it to the stricter regulation of relief which had encouraged the labourer to be more independent, to develop foresight and to provide for future contingencies. But labourers resented the practice of the boards of guardians, who followed a ruling of the Poor Law Commission in 1840 that no preferential treatment should be given to members of benefit clubs, and who deducted from the standard poor relief allowances to the sick and aged the sums that the recipient had already received from his friendly society. The thrifty felt that they were penalized, since even if they had not made contributions to a benefit club their total income would still have been the same.[20]

John Venn drew attention to the wretched condition of the poor of Hereford, but Mr George Wythen Baxter of Eaton Place, St Martin's, criticised Hereford Union directly. In 1841 he published his *Book of Bastiles* which contained, together with many lurid pages about workhouse malpractices throughout the country, his own petition to Parliament that called for the New Poor Law to be abolished and replaced with a more humane system. In this petition, presented to Parliament by T.S. Duncombe MP, he made many claims about the effects of the New Poor Law in Herefordshire and while it is possible that some of these claims were exaggerated, it provides clear evidence that there was a lively anti-Poor Law campaign and that the claims were based on real concerns. He stated:

> That your petitioner has narrowly watched the working of the New Poor Law system in his own county, Herefordshire, and has found the same to be cruel, and expensive almost beyond endurance, both to the poor and the ratepayers ... In the City of Hereford, the householders, who formerly, under the old system, were rated at 4s per rate, are now paying 9s 7d; and many farmers in the county have publicly declared their inability to keep on their farms and pay such exorbitant poor-rates ... Instances of bastardy now happen to an extent unprecedented under the Old Law; sheep stealing is greatly on the increase ... and incendiarism, formerly almost unknown in this county, is at present of frequent occurrence ... again, the serious and unnatural offence of child murder is constantly being committed in this county; for scarcely has an assize been held since the introduction of the New Poor Law, but what there have been trials for infanticide; and at this very time there are two unfortunate females to be tried for that heinous offence.[21]

Baxter's petition was followed, on 7 March 1841, by a letter to T.S. Duncombe from Captain Thomas Bennett, Vice-Chairman of Hereford Board of Guardians, in which he refuted Baxter's claims and said that all of his statements were '... wicked, malicious, and malignant falsehoods, and that they are merely got up ... for the purpose of bringing the Poor Law Act into disrepute, and annoying the Government'.[22] Baxter was indeed a Tory, and the Whig government was then not in a strong position. Indeed, Lord Melbourne, the Whig Prime Minister, resigned at the end of August.

Whatever disquiet they may have felt amongst themselves, the Guardians of Hereford Union replied confidently with a counter petition which was presented by Mr Edward Bolton Clive, MP and which answered all Baxter's accusations and quietly dismissed them. Indeed, the final paragraph of their petition firmly expressed their resolution to fulfil their duties:

Your petitioners have respectfully to assure your Honourable House that they are resolved to persevere, with impartiality and firmness, and without fear, favour, or affection, in the arduous and unpopular task of relieving destitution, of detecting imposition, of discouraging profligacy and raising the moral character, and physical condition of the lower orders. Through good report and evil report, your Petitioners will continue to execute the duties entrusted to them, in the fullest confidence that the enlightened and reflecting portion of the community will not be swayed by vague accusations or unfounded statements.[23]

This does not sound like the petition of a Board of Guardians in a defensive or over-nervous state. It suggests that they were confident in what they were doing and would continue in the same manner. It might also be argued that the very fact that these men were willing to stand as Guardians meant that they were in broad agreement with the new legislation. The comments about raising the moral character and condition of the 'lower orders' reinforce the notion of an imposed middle class morality. The petition was signed by the Chairman, the Reverend Watson Joseph Thornton.

The publication of Baxter's book came at the same time as the introduction of Venn's society for aiding the industrious. This may have been purely coincidental, but it is possible that the two men met and discussed poor law matters, though as yet no evidence that they were acquainted has been discovered. Whether they worked together or not, in their own way they were both demonstrating against the New Poor Law. Baxter openly opposed the new system, while Venn attempted to make up for its alleged shortcomings.

The analysis of Guardians' attendance at Ross Union Board was greatly assisted by the manner in which the clerks kept their records. At Hereford, the clerks kept less detailed records than their counterparts at Ross, with the result that the collation of names and dates provided less detailed and less reliable material. It is clear, however, that Hereford Union Guardians rarely served for more than two or three years and many served only for one. They obviously did not have the same level of commitment as the Guardians at Ross where, it will be recalled, some Guardians served continuously for 10 or 12 years.

The contrast between the two Unions in terms of Guardians' years of service was probably attributable to a number of factors. Ross Union had a group of about a dozen Guardians who were prominent members of local society, while Hereford Union Guardians appear to have received less leadership from their Guardians of independent wealth. It is difficult to know which Union was the more representative in this respect, since it would appear that other historians have not given any particular emphasis to the issue of leadership amongst Guardians. Ross Guardians were often related, closely connected by virtue of their social standing or, at the very least, well known to each other, but Hereford Guardians changed frequently and were perhaps on less familiar terms. Ross Union Board was left to get on with its work; Hereford Union Board faced persistent and orchestrated opposition, not least by political accusations from George Baxter and veiled criticisms from John Venn. It is not surprising that under such circumstances, some Guardians who had no real appetite for public duty and politics lacked staying power. Guardians from city parishes may have also found that it was not at all advantageous for the health and prosperity of their own business affairs to be too closely connected with a Board of Guardians which was generally unpopular and perceived to be harsh to the poor. Watson Joseph Thornton, however, did more than his duty and obviously did have an appetite for public affairs. He was an elected Guardian for Ross Union without a break from 1836 to 1848; and an elected Guardian for Hereford Union in April 1837, vice-Chairman the following year and Chairman of Hereford Union from 1839 to 1847.

The Guardians of Hereford Union met for the first time on 14 April 1836. Of those present there were 50 elected Guardians and 14 ex-officio Guardians, of whom four were clergymen. Of the elected Guardians 22 were farmers, six could not be traced through the 1841 census, tithe map apportionments or trade directories, and others included a brewer, a painter, a wool merchant, a corn merchant, a timber merchant, some gentlemen of independent means, a surveyor, a seedsman, a surgeon, a glover, an attorney, a wheelwright and an innkeeper. After this initial meeting, however, it was very rare for there to be such a large attendance except in April, at the first meeting after the annual election of Guardians. The usual attendance was less than half the full number and often less than a third. The reasons for this are difficult to deduce, partly because of the nature of the clerk's record keeping, but it is possible that there was a considerable amount of factional thinking amongst the members of the Board and therefore a lack of cohesion, which in turn perhaps induced apathy. At Ross there was a strong group of ex-officio and independent Guardians who were the driving force of the Board's enthusiasm and momentum; this seems to have been lacking on the Hereford Board.

There were in the city two existing workhouses which the Guardians decided to use until a new workhouse for the accommodation of 300 paupers could be built. The workhouse in All Saints parish was in future to be used for all able-bodied males and the workhouse in St John's parish would be used for all other classes of pauper. There seems to have been tacit agreement from the outset that it would be necessary to build a new workhouse in order to segregate the different classes of pauper as required by the new Act. In the meantime the work of the Union went on, and by the third week in May three Relieving Officers and three Medical Officers had been appointed and commenced their duties. In June, Sir Edmund Walker Head made a point of seeing the Relieving Officers in order to impress upon them the need for accuracy in describing and classifying paupers and in all their duties.[24] Indeed, the keeping and inspecting of records was taken very seriously from the outset of the Union's existence. At a meeting held on 14 July 1836 it was resolved that at each meeting, after matters arising from the previous meeting had been dealt with, three Guardians were to be deputed to examine the books and accounts of the Master, the Relieving Officers and the Union Treasurer, while the meeting continued.[25] The following week it was ordered that the Medical Officers provide details of the patients they had seen since the beginning of the Union and in future present their books for inspection at the weekly Board meetings.[26] It was clear that Hereford Union was to be run on strict Utilitarian lines and that parsimony was a guiding principle.

This parsimony was soon shown in a number of instances. In October 1836 Elizabeth Powell of Withington parish was advanced the sum of 14s for the purchase of a coffin for her husband's burial, but the sum was to be considered as a loan.[27] In the following month, Relieving Officer Charles Lucy was empowered to give Matthew Morgan 10s towards the costs of his daughter's funeral on condition that on receipt of the money he handed over his daughter's clothes.[28] This appears rather heartless, but every effort was made to keep Union costs to an absolute minimum, however severe or insensitive such demands might appear. Overseers who were tardy in paying parish contributions to the Union were quickly reminded and warned of legal action if they did not comply. The minutes show that numerous orders were made to force Overseers to apply to the Magistrates for the apprehension of husbands and sometimes wives who had deserted their families and left them chargeable to the parish. John Lloyd, for example, was apprehended and sent to Hereford gaol for three months for deserting his family in November 1836.[29] Orders were also made against children for not maintaining their elderly parents. In November 1836 a summons was procured to compel John Davies, who was living at Staunton (whether Staunton on Wye or Staunton on Arrow is not recorded), to contribute to the maintenance of his father, who belonged to the parish of Kenchester.[30]

The largest number of orders, however, was in respect of illegitimate children and the Guardians' attempts to compel putative fathers to provide for their maintenance. The minutes often show that the Union Clerk, Nicholas Lanwarne, was instructed to investigate the circumstances of the birth of a child being maintained with its mother in the workhouse. His investigations sometimes resulted in an affiliation order being made against the father of the child, but on other occasions it was clear that the girl had no idea who the father might have been and it would therefore be decided that the matter was not worth pursuing. On some occasions, however, the clerk's investigations could rebound to everyone's embarrassment. A minute dated 14 October 1843 states:

Ann Bailey applied for relief in the right of her illegitimate child charge-able to All Saints and she with her child were ordered into the workhouse and it appearing that John Hall a clerk in the office of the clerk to the union was charged with being the putative father, the clerk was directed to request Mr Pritchard the attorney to examine into the case and if suffi-cient proof to apply to the magistrates for an order of maintenance.[31]

The register of births in Hereford Workhouse has survived for the period 1838 to 1856 and indicates that the workhouse contained a core of the city's low life. There were 309 births registered in this period and of these 10% were legitimate and 90% were illegitimate. Of the 277 illegitimate births, 168 were marked as 'first bastard', 64 were marked 'second bastard', and the remainder as 'third, fourth, fifth or sixth bastard' and sometimes followed by the doctor's note 'girl on the town'.[32] This indicates that while there were children born to the respectable poor who were in the workhouse, the main problems were illegitimate births and concerns about respectable women having to be housed with prostitutes. In July 1839, the Chairman proposed that at the next meeting the Guardians should debate the possibility of 'separating prostitutes and mothers of base children from other women of better character'.[33] Their fears were well founded, for later that year it was found necessary to provide a larger ward for women suffering from venereal disease because the one in use was already full,[34] and they identified the source of the problem as an 'infa-mous house in Bowsey Lane'. The minute book records that:

The Committee of the Poor Law Guardians ... beg ... to lay before the Magistrates the copy of a resolution ... relative to the case of a pauper child of only fourteen years of age, who was yesterday received into the Workhouse in a state of utter destitution and afflicted with the venereal disease, in the hope that the Magistrates may be induced to take some means to put down the infamous house kept by Diana Fuller in Bowsey Lane in this city, and others of similar description and as an additional inducement to this being done, the Committee beg permission to state that very lately there were no less than eleven venereal cases of young Girls in the Union House at one time, some of whom were belonging to distant parishes not connected with this union and brought into the House for Relief to the great Expense of the City and inconvenience to the house several had been living with the woman Fuller before alluded to ... The Committee direct that a copy of this Resolution be laid before the City Magistrates in court upon Monday next. 14 December 1839.[35]

Later, Captain Thomas Bennett, the Chairman, reported that he laid the resolution before the Magistrates himself and that 'they had promised to take measures for the suppression of the Nuisances'.[36] The outcome of the actions of the Magistrates was not recorded in the Guardians' minutes, but the report itself gives an indication of their attitudes and concerns as Guardians. The fact that at the time of the report there were 11 young girls in the workhouse who were infected with venereal disease caused considerable expense to the Union and practical problems within the workhouse in segregating the girls from other paupers. In fairness to the Guardians, they could simply have sent those girls from parishes not contained within the boundaries of Hereford Union straight back to their place of settlement, but they did not. They saw that the girls were given medical treatment, treatment they may well not have received if they had been sent home and tried to hide their symptoms from their family. This was perhaps an acceptance that not all paupers who found themselves in the workhouse were entirely culpable in their distress.

It is likely that the infamous Diana Fuller lured young girls to her house in Bowsey Lane, girls who came from distant parishes which made contact with home difficult, introduced them to prostitution, and abandoned them as soon as they were infected, pregnant or both. Caroline Beavan, the girl referred to in the Guardians' resolution, had been living in Fuller's house for some time and was only 14 when she was admitted to the workhouse. This was corruption at an early age. Women with low moral standards were considered by the Poor Law Guardians to be extremely dangerous because of the corrupting influence they might have on young girls in the workhouse, and it was this, as much as the risk of spreading infection, that necessitated their segregation from respectable women and young girls. The future for girls such as Caroline Beavan was indeed very bleak once they were released from the workhouse or decided to leave of their own accord. They were unlikely to be employed as domestic servants for fear of their influence on other servants, and were likely to fall into a life of prostitution.

The punishment books for Hereford Union Workhouse have not survived, but the entries in the Guardians' minute books suggest that discipline and the general behaviour of the paupers in the workhouse was a problem. Some problems may have arisen as inmates simply reacted against their incarceration. The attempts of the Guardians to improve the 'lower orders' resulted in the imposition of an alien way of life, an imposed morality and the application of various punishments. These varied from reduction of food rations to the wearing of the 'disgrace' dress, segregation, confinement, birching and flogging. The majority of the recorded incidents took place in 1838 and 1839 with a gradual trailing off in the 1840s.

In June 1838 James Davies broke out of the workhouse and returned drunk, for which he was placed in the refractory ward.[37] Later that month Mary Godsall, aged 15, had her diet stopped for 48 hours 'for neglecting to work and general bad conduct'.[38] In September that year she was confined for four hours 'for working with negligence' and so was Ellen Thomas, a young woman of 22 years.[39] In October, Ann Pritchard had her food reduced 'for repeatedly doing her work in a very improper and negligent manner'.[40] The following month she was placed on half rations for three days for stealing workhouse bread and 3d from another pauper.[41] In January 1839 Joseph Beeks, Francis Griffiths, Thomas Williams and Thomas Symons were put in the refractory ward for fighting, Thomas Pritchard had his diet stopped for 24 hours 'for being idle' and George James was punished in the same manner 'for working with negligence'.[42] At the beginning of May, Mary Godsall was confined on two successive days for 'behaving in a disorderly manner',[43] and a few days later she was confined for four hours, put on half rations and also reprimanded by the Board of Guardians for refusing to do her work.[44] On 22 May, Godsall and four other females were sent to the town gaol for one month's hard labour for striking the Workhouse Porter.[45] In July, Ann Pritchard, probably a prostitute, was charged with using indecent language and was ordered to be kept away from the other women.[46] In August, two boys of 13, Thomas Prosser and John Williams, absconded from the workhouse and were later confined in the refractory ward; and John Williams also had his diet reduced for using improper language.[47] A few days later, Mary Godsall was confined and placed on half rations again for having absconded and for having enticed Eliza Williams to go with her.[48] For one pauper, however, the workhouse was preferable to the employment found for him in the community, for in September 1839 it was reported to the Board that John Llewellyn had returned to the workhouse from his employment and it was ordered that he be employed in breaking stone for two hours per day until the circumstances surrounding his leaving his master had been investigated.[49]

The number of punishments being imposed in the workhouse must have given rise to some concern amongst the Guardians and perhaps the feeling that they should take more direct control of discipline. The Chairman, the Reverend Thornton, moved that:

> No punishment to be inflicted unless at least three of the committee be present. All punishments to be entered in the Book. All persons to be brought before the committee before being punished, instead of before the Board afterwards as now ordered.[50]

The Reverend Thornton also moved that 'the Punishment Book be laid on the Board Table every Wednesday at 11 o'clock'[51] and later it was made clear that the new arrangements for the administration of punishments should not be construed as restricting the punishment powers of the Master.[52] It is clear that there was general concern about the need for paupers to be made to conform to workhouse rules and to learn to adopt a lifestyle their 'betters' considered appropriate for them. It is evident, however, that some of the paupers with whom they had to deal were very awkward characters. In September 1839 the

Master complained that Ephraim Watkins repeatedly left the workhouse for short periods of time and returned drunk and for this Watkins was cautioned by the Board;[53] but it was the case of the defiant Elizabeth Lawrence that must have caused the Guardians and the workhouse officers particular annoyance.

Elizabeth Lawrence, a single woman aged 28, had deserted her two children, leaving them chargeable to the parish of Burghill and in the care of the workhouse. She had refused to take them from the workhouse and for this she had been sent by the Magistrates to Hereford Gaol to serve a sentence of one month's hard labour. On her release from the gaol she was received into the workhouse and boasted that the hard labour she had been given was in fact sewing and knitting. She also stated that she would rather be in gaol than in the workhouse. This infuriated the Master, William Preece, and he made representation to the Guardians to inform the Magistrates that their sentence of hard labour had not been obeyed by the superintendent of the gaol. Once back in the workhouse she was repeatedly ordered, against regulations, to break stone, but she steadfastly refused. She also refused to care for her children and when ordered to go to the nursery to feed one of them on a diet ordered by the Workhouse Medical Officer, she told the Master what he might do with 'that stuff' in no uncertain terms. Further punishments were inflicted through confinement and amendments to her diet, but all to no avail, and she still refused to break stone. A few days later a report was received which stated that Elizabeth Lawrence had not been put to hard labour whilst in gaol on the 'directions of the Medical Attendant'.[54] The Guardians and the workhouse officers must have felt utterly defeated in their attempts to punish and reform her. She was obviously a strong-minded young woman and not easily frightened by officials. She was clearly in error in not caring for her children and therefore seen as in need of correction, but there was little the Guardians or the workhouse officers could do with such a person. By her own admission she preferred the gaol to the workhouse, probably considering it better to be incarcerated in the town gaol without having to care for her children than to be imprisoned in the workhouse with them. She may also have agreed with others who thought that the food in the town gaol was much better than that provided in the workhouse.

The large number of punishments inflicted on the inmates of the workhouse during 1839 raises questions as to whether the Guardians were being too zealous in their application of the New Poor Law. On the other hand it might be argued that the workhouse population at that time consisted of a hard core of very difficult and dissolute paupers who had lived very wayward and idle lives under the Old Poor Law and were now reacting predictably to rigid discipline and the imposition of a morality they neither accepted nor understood. As time went on, however, the Guardians and officers in the workhouse may have become more proficient in their management of paupers and, as a result, found less need to impose punishments on them. It is clear, however, that the work-house Visiting Committee did not spare the rod in punishing inmates when it was deemed necessary and 1840 began with their ordering that James Evans be punished 'with a birch rod on the bare breech for breaking the schoolroom windows',[55] and that John Bishop receive 12 stripes 'on the bare breech for improper behaviour in Chapel during Divine Service'.[56]

The language used in the minute books is interesting in that it conveys the notion of the prison. In March 1840 Police Constable William Preece was paid £5 for the apprehension of Thomas James who had 'escaped'[57] from the work-house, and in July that year, Mary Davies was punished for 'breaking out' of the workhouse. The minute states that:

> The Master reported the following punishment – Mary Davies of St Martins had on the punishment dress at 3 different meals for absenting herself from Chapel and breaking out of the house through the Board Room Window and going into the town on Sunday last in the after-noon and returned at 9 o'clock the same evening to look for her supper – ordered 12 hours confinement on Bread and Water.[58]

In November 1842 the management of difficult paupers, particularly women of bad character, was still causing problems but these were gradually being overcome through the construction of additional buildings. A minute from that month reads as follows:

> The pauper Offence Book showed the following punishments. John Wheatstone's Bread stopped for 48 hours for repeatedly going into the

The staff of Hereford Workhouse in the early 1900s. (Hereford City Library)

Garden and conversing with female paupers of bad Character in the new building – Ann Gisborne admonished for conveying bread from John Wheatstone to a female pauper and Harriett Parry, 24 hours solitary confinement and short diet, for refusing and neglecting to do the work ordered by the cook and the nurse.[59]

The Guardians of Hereford Union clearly took the notion of 'moral improvement' of the 'lower orders' very seriously and discipline in the workhouse was imposed firmly and consistently. One wonders, however, if the same had always been the case in the school and whether the Schoolmaster was given consistent support by the Master and the Guardians. In March 1840 the Board expressed the view that the Schoolmaster was 'inadequate to the discharge of the duties of his office'[60] and he was given notice to leave on 13 May 1840. The teacher was in an alien atmosphere and mixing with the type of characters with whom he would not normally associate: the children, for their part, were in an equally alien position and it was perhaps inevitable that there would be serious confrontations. This unfortunate Schoolmaster's successor also experienced some difficult times as the following minute of December 1843 indicates:

The Master reported that eight of the boys in the workhouse had behaved themselves improperly towards the schoolmaster by kicking him and throwing dirty water in his face – They were severally had before the Board and informed by the Chairman that three of them would be flogged twice and the remaining five once, for the above offence.[61]

The Poor Law Commission laid down strict rules about the use of corporal punishment in the workhouse: only boys under the age of 14 could be punished in this manner and the punishment was supposed to be administered under specified conditions. The punishments noted in the minute books conform for the most part with the regulations, apart from an entry made in July 1838, when the Master presented the Guardians with the following report:

Mary Collins aged 6 and Mary Roberts aged 6 had three slaps in the open hand with a small birch rod for going to sleep in the chapel during divine service on Sunday. It is often the case that one half of the children are sleeping during divine service and if the master is not allowed to make use of some slight and mild punishment on such occasions as those there will be no attention whatever from this class in a very short time.[62]

One wonders why so many children should sleep through the service in the chapel; perhaps it was due to lack of sleep, under-feeding, the length of the service, the manner of its delivery by the Reverend Albert Jones or a combination of all of these. Whatever the answer might have been, it was against regulations for small girls to be punished in this way, if indeed punishment was appropriate at all. Despite the fact that the law had been infringed, the Guardians' response went unrecorded. It is possible that they turned a blind eye to the incident because at that time the discipline in the schoolroom was poor. The Master went on to say in his report that if he could not be allowed to chastise the children in this manner when he considered it to be necessary, there would soon be no order at all. He continued:

> Almost every hour in the day there is fighting, throwing stones, falling out, breaking windows, biting one another and often cursing swearing and telling lies, and except some mode of slight punishment is authorised by Board all other discipline is out of the question.[63]

It is evident from a case cited by Frank Crompton that the corporal punishment of girls was not restricted to Hereford Workhouse. As late as 1859 the Schoolmistress at Worcester continued to correct girls with taps on the hand with a small stick, despite having been cautioned not to do so on a previous occasion, because she considered it 'part of her ordinary discipline' and stated that 'she scarcely considered such correction to be corporal punishment'.[64] One wonders how many punishments went unrecorded in the new workhouses despite the regulations which were intended to protect the inmates and control the actions of officers. Hereford Union minutes show that the Guardians and officers had some very difficult paupers to contend with, particularly young women of dubious character, but the records do suggest that the punishments inflicted on them were generally within the law, and in the case of serious misbehaviour the pauper was always taken before the Magistrates.

The weekly checking of the Master's account books as well as the records of the Relieving Officers prevented the abuse of power on the part of officers and as a result, between the years 1834 and 1847 only one Relieving Officer was found to be inefficient and dishonest and decided to resign. Similarly, the records of the Medical Officers were checked each week and as a result there were fewer complaints about these men in Hereford Union than there were in the substantially smaller Union of Ross.

In 1839 the Poor Law Commissioners wrote that 'the workhouse is not intended to serve any penal or remunerary purpose; and ought not to be used for punishing the dissolute or rewarding the well-conducted pauper'.[65] If this was indeed the official view of the Commissioners, then the notion of social control of paupers and the improvement of the 'lower orders' stemmed from the opinions of the Guardians of individual Boards and the social make-up of those Boards was all-important in the general implementation of the New Poor Law.

7   Welsh Border Unions – Kington

In 1835, Pigot's *National Commercial Directory* described Kington as an 'ancient and respectable market town',[1] well built and consisting of 'two spacious streets'.[2] It had once been host to 'a considerable clothing trade'[3] and although that had been lost, some of the town's inhabitants were still employed in glovemaking, but in much smaller numbers than in former times. By 1835, it was said that 'the concern of the greatest magnitude at present conducted here is an iron-foundry, which together with the manufacture of nails, employs many hands'.[4] Almost all other employment in the area would have been linked with agriculture.

Kington Union was composed of almost equal numbers of parishes from Radnorshire and Herefordshire. This might be explained in part by the location of Kington close to the Welsh border and also by the influence of Thomas Frankland Lewis, whose family estate was just a few miles distant in Radnorshire. It was the duty of the Assistant Poor Law Commissioners to combine parishes to form Unions of a manageable size, and they usually consulted local landowners before drawing up their final plans. In the case of Kington Union, Sir Edmund Walker Head is unlikely to have proceeded in any other manner and would almost certainly have been at great pains not to upset the Lewises.

As a local landed magnate, and in his capacity as the Chairman of the Poor Law Commission at Somerset House, Thomas Frankland Lewis would have had a particular interest, if not concern, in seeing that Kington Union got off to a good start and was seen to be managed well. He would, however, have been faced with a particular dichotomy. As a politician and an important figure in poor law affairs he would have wanted to see the 'Workhouse Test' applied firmly in order to avoid undue criticism from political adversaries, but as a local landowner in the Kington area, he may have wished to be perceived as being humane and not guilty of applying it too harshly. In the first few months of Kington Union's existence he attended the meetings of the Guardians quite frequently. He probably felt he should be seen to be supporting the New Poor Law in the area that included his own estate and may also have wanted to see

the proceedings at Guardians' meetings in general and in Kington in particular. If he did make any contributions to discussions his comments were not
recorded, but it is highly likely that amongst the Guardians there was a regular
attender who acted as his spokesman: mentioned by no one, but heard and
understood by all.

The first recorded meeting of the Kington Guardians took place at a posting
inn, the King's Head, on Friday 26 August 1836.[5] There were 24 Guardians
present, mainly farmers, but also a clergyman and two glove manufacturers.
Among the 13 ex-officio Guardians present were: Thomas Frankland Lewis;
Edmund Watkins Cheese of Ridgebourne House, a local solicitor; John
Cheese of Mill Farm, Clerk to the Kington Railway Company; Peter Rickards
Mynors of Evenjobb, Radnorshire and Treago Castle, Herefordshire; Samuel
Beavan, Esquire; James Davies of Moor Court, Pembridge; William Unett of
Bollingham Chapel; John Whittaker of Newcastle Court, Radnor; Sir William
Cockburn of New Radnor; and the Right Honourable Earl of Oxford, Lord
Harley. There were also three clergymen: the Reverend George Coke of Lower
Moor, Eardisley, Rector of Aylton; the Reverend John Bissell, Vicar of Titley;
and the Reverend Maurice James, Rector of Pembridge. Also present was Sir
Edmund Walker Head.

The decisions taken on 26 August 1836 suggest that Sir Edmund had
prepared the ground well in order to arrange matters as he wished. James
Davies was elected Chairman; Edmund Watkins Cheese, vice-Chairman;
Mr Benjamin Bodenham was appointed as Union Clerk; and Mr Thomas
Oliver as Treasurer.[6] These elections and appointments were of considerable significance in a small town; they concentrated power in the hands of a
small number of influential men. Edmund Cheese and Benjamin Bodenham
were attorneys at Upper Cross, Kington; and James Davies, Edmund Cheese
and Thomas Oliver were directors of the Kington and Radnorshire Bank.[7]
Bodenham was also the fire insurance agent for Atlas as was Oliver with
the Royal Exchange. There were, of course, business benefits for some as a
result of unpaid work as a Guardian. A man might be Guardian for one Union
and paid legal advisor or Treasurer to a contiguous one or, if he was not so
involved, such a post might become the source of income through his business partner. As well as keeping their eyes open for good business opportunities, however, some of these men were almost certainly making a political
point too. The New Poor Law had resulted from Whig legislation and, despite
their support for Kington Union, a published list of those attending the
Herefordshire Conservative Dinner at the Shire Hall in Hereford in October
1836 included: Sir William Cockburn, John Cheese, Peter Rickards Mynors,
James Davies and Edmund Watkins Cheese, all Guardians of Kington Union.
It is quite likely that they were intent on seeing that the local Whigs did
not have everything their own way in the administration of poor relief. On

the other hand, leading Whigs might have thought it politic to have these influential gentlemen as members of the Board of Guardians rather than as a powerful group orchestrating opposition outside it.

Kington was untypical of the other Herefordshire Unions in that so many of its parishes lay in an adjoining county. Having had some experience of Welsh Unions, Sir Edmund Walker Head was sceptical about their Guardians' ability to run Union affairs and also doubted their interest in public affairs and public duty. He made this point strongly when writing to the Poor Law Commissioners, saying that: 'The zeal for business and the readiness to engage in the management of an union is much more lax in Wales than in England.'[8] He continued by stating: 'That consequently if there is any accumulation of pauper cases or union business, such as must meet us at the outset of an union, it is utterly impossible to prevail on the farmers to apply themselves to it.'[9] Hence he promoted non-farming businessmen as Guardians and attempted to make Kington Union as English as possible.

His low opinion of the Welsh was shared by his friends George Clive and George Cornewall Lewis and confirmed by their candid remarks in private letters. In April 1837 Head wrote to George Cornewall Lewis and quoted from a letter which he had received from George Clive whilst Clive was attending to his duties as Assistant Commissioner for Monmouthshire. Clive is quoted as saying that he wished 'that the devil would fly away with this miserable race of Celtic savages'.[10] Head appeared to concur with these sentiments, adding the caveat, however, that Wales begins just beyond New Radnor, meaning, presumably, just beyond the Lewis estate. Head ended his letter by saying that 'the gradual action of the Boards of Guardians, railroads and other opportunities for intercourse, may civilise them in about three centuries'.[11] Writing to Head from Malta in June 1837 George Cornewall Lewis wrote

Rt. Hon. Sir Thomas Frankland Lewis, drawn by Eden Upton Eddis

Harpton, the Lewis family home outside New Radnor, as photographed by W.H. 'Billy' McKaig in the early 1900s. The lawn in front of the house is set out for croquet

that '...George Clive is, I have no doubt, quite right in his opinion of the intelligence of the Welsh. And how that intelligence is to be raised, while they retain their villainous Celtic language, is not easy to see.'[12] He continued by saying that what Head had 'said in a former letter about the cowardice and timidity of the Welsh is, I suspect true of all ignorant and borne communities. It prevails here to a remarkable degree.'[13]

One wonders whether Sir Edmund harboured similar worries about the Guardians of Kington Union. His successor in 1840, William Day, was clearly unimpressed when he complained about the lack of cleanliness in workhouses. He described their beds as 'dungheaps and everything else in keeping',[14] and added that 'from Kington to Cardigan and Haverfordwest they were all alike'.[15] Indeed, he had dismissed the Masters of two Welsh workhouses for disguising filthy beds by placing clean sheets over the dirty ones in anticipation of the Assistant Commissioner's arrival.

In order to assess the workings of Kington Union and the diligence of the Guardians and their paid officers, however, it is necessary to put into context the task which faced them in August 1836. Some clues to the management of Kington's poor relief are provided by the town's return which formed part of the Poor Law Report of 1834. The mode of poor relief in Kington in 1834 was in stark contrast to that envisaged when the Union was formed in 1836. The town's workhouse had been closed because a majority of the ratepayers believed that it would be cheaper to relieve the poor in their own homes. Since 1820 their poor relief had been managed through a Select Vestry and this was thought to have been generally beneficial to the town's inhabitants. It is possible that this really meant the inhabitants who paid rates, but it may also have been acknowledged that the poor were happier in their own homes than in a workhouse and that not maintaining a workhouse both released more of the poor rate directly to the poor and reduced the rates. The town was divided into four townships, each with its own Overseer, who was usually a farmer. It was his job to collect the rates which had been set by the four Overseers and the Churchwardens and sanctioned by two of the Magistrates. The system demonstrates clearly the very parochial nature of the Old Poor Law.

Those who claimed relief were usually known to the Overseers, and each case was assessed on the basis of need and the claimant's character. Investigations were sometimes made to decide whether adult children could support aged parents, but these investigations were often not started or abandoned because of the difficulty in proving an individual's ability to pay. It was readily admitted that agricultural labourers could just about support themselves and their families on a diet of bread, bacon, potatoes and tea with an income of £20 per year, but could save nothing against the possibility of difficult days ahead. It also showed that poor labourers would have little chance of providing support for their parents in old age. Craftsmen earning £30 per year might, it was thought, with economy save a little money for the future and their wages were generally sufficient to keep artisans off the poor rates and out of the workhouse. The men most likely to claim poor relief in aid of wages were agricultural labourers and, because of the depressed state of the trade in 1834, the town's glovers. Agricultural labourers could not always supplement their family income with help from their wives and children because the mixed nature of the farming in the area could only provide women and children with employment in stone picking and seasonal work such as haymaking. Those receiving relief in 1834 were listed as '50 males above 50 years of age, 30 above 10, about 100 under 10; 46 females above 50, 80 above 10, about 80 under 10; chiefly glovers and farmers' labourers'.[16] The transition from the Old Poor Law to the New Poor Law was, in fairness to the Board of Guardians, managed in a fairly gentle manner, in that they did not make sweeping changes, and continued to show paupers at least some compassion. They continued to provide additional coal during severe weather, gave allowances of turf for fuel and continued to pay cottage rents. It was clear, however, that all this was to end, for at that first meeting of the Guardians in August 1836 the decision was taken to build a new workhouse.[17] Just before Christmas the Commissioners approved a proposal for a building that would accommodate 170 paupers[18] and in March 1837 they approved the purchase of land for that purpose.[19] Kington's old workhouse had been closed down because it was deemed cheaper not to use it, yet the new one was to be built in the interests of economy. One wonders who worried most:

ratepayers about their pockets or paupers who remembered the old work-house and feared incarceration. It was, however, one of the basic tenets of the New Poor Law that paupers of different classes should be segregated, and in most of the old workhouses the limitations of the buildings made that quite impossible.

As the implementation of the New Poor Law began to take effect on the lives of the poor of Kington Union, the results soon showed how inappropriate the legislation was with respect to remote rural areas such as those along the Welsh Border. This point is best illustrated by the issues surrounding the parish payment of pauper cottage rents. This method of supporting labourers on the edge of poverty had been widely used under the Old Poor Law in the area, but was not to be encouraged under the New Poor Law. At a meeting held in January 1837, just five months after Kington Union was formed, it was resolved 'that although this Board consider it desirable to abolish the custom of paying Rents for the cottages of Paupers yet it is not expedient if not impossible to effect such abolition Immediately'.[20] Many of the rural poor simply could not pay rent for their cottages and feed and clothe themselves and the Union was faced with paying subsidies or forcing people into the workhouse.

In August 1839 a pauper of Kington, one Thomas Cowdell, had all his household goods distrained for non-payment of rent and, having nowhere else to live, he and his family were received into the workhouse. It being the beginning of the harvest, however, Cowdell had good employment prospects and he and his family also had the opportunity to gain much from gleaning. He was caught in a trap; he could stay in the workhouse and remain unemployed and kept by the parish, or he could take advantage of the available harvest work and live in a cottage devoid of furniture and the basic articles of domesticity until he could earn enough to buy them. Ironically, the unfortunate Cowdell would have been seen by the Central Authority as 'undeserving', despite his wish to help himself; this again demonstrates the inadequate nature of the new legislation in marginal cases. Cowdell does not appear to have been a malingerer and must have thought that the world was against him; he wanted to work but his circumstances seemed to make it impossible for him to do so. After due consideration the Guardians, no doubt sensibly thinking about costs, decided it would be expedient as 'a case of sudden necessity'[21] to grant Cowdell a loan of £1 'to enable him to purchase necessities such as bedding ... to enable him to furnish a house and provide for his family by his own exertions, he being anxious to leave the house'.[22] This seemed to be a sensible, practical solution to the problem, particularly since the assistance provided was in the form of a loan and not a grant.

The Poor Law Commissioners were not impressed. Rules were to be followed to the letter and this caused many problems until Edwin Chadwick and the trenchant Utilitarians surrounding him began to lose favour and regulations became less rigid. The Commissioners pointed out that:

> ... although the loan is evidently illegal the Commissioners will not cause it to be disallowed, in full confidence that the Guardians will not repeat it, especially as the practice of immediately redeeming goods distrained for rent has a direct tendency to multiply proceedings on the part of the landlords against labourers in the hope of thus extorting relief.[23]

This seems to point to the folly of a Utilitarian ideology that would have preferred Cowdell and his family to remain in the workhouse, rather than risk the possibility that the man might gain relief to which he was not entitled or his landlord his unpaid rent by devious manipulation of the poor law system. This was the same accusation which was made against the Speenhamland system of providing relief under the Old Poor Law. Yet abuse of the system there certainly was, for in July 1838 the clerk to Kington Union was directed to write to Mr John Davies of the parish of Gladestry concerning his labourer's wages and the poor man's apparent need to ask for assistance from the Union. The circumstances certainly point to manipulation of the labourer to redeem money spent on rates or, at the very least, extreme parsimony:

> The Board of Guardians of the Kington Union beg leave to inform Mr Davies that a person of the name of William Griffiths his labourer has applied to the Board for relief and on investigating the case they find that the man has his house and garden rent free worth one shilling a week, the setting of five bushels of potatoes worth 9d per week, the milk of a small cow worth about 1/6 a week and three shillings in money making altogether only 6/3d. The Board think it their duty to call this subject to Mr Davies's notice as at the present price of Flour it is quite impossible for a family to live on such a sum and the Poor Law Amendment Act does not admit of relief being given in aid of wages.[24]

In other circumstances, however, where there was no hint of manipulation by employers and landlords, the Kington Guardians made awards of shoes and clothing, paid rents and granted numerous loans between 5s and 25s as the following instances illustrate. In January 1837 Mary Pugh was given 5s for her journey to Hereford Infirmary[25] and Mary Jones, a poor girl of Huntington parish, was given 30s for the purchase of clothes to go out to service. The clothes were, however, not to be given to her until she had procured a place.[26] In February 1837 Mary Evans was given shoes valued at 5s 6d to enable her to go into service,[27] and later that year the Guardians agreed to continue to pay the cottage rent of James Galliers, who had become totally disabled as the result of an accident.[28] Cases such as these would have been scrutinised by the

Assistant Poor Law Commissioner in order to emphasise the need to adhere to rules and regulations. All relief provided by the Union came with considerable loss of dignity for the poor and this is neatly illustrated by a letter received from Sir Edmund Walker Head in which he reminded the Clerk to Kington Union to ensure that the Relieving Officers adhered strictly to section eight of their duties, 'by duly affixing on the doors of the parish churches the lists of paupers relieved during the previous quarter'.[29] The deserving poor and the undeserving poor were all as one; they were just paupers. Their feelings and personal dignity were of no concern.

The placing of pauper lists on church doors was in one sense an element of social control; it proclaimed to the whole community the names of those who were dependent on parish relief and put paupers in their place at the bottom of society. It emphasised accountability and society's control over the labouring classes. It was an example to all that to be a pauper, for whatever reason, was shameful. When a man sought a little help from the Union in order to stand on his own feet and provide for his family himself, as Cowdell did, his efforts to assist himself and the Guardians' efforts to help him were thwarted by bureaucratic intervention from Somerset House. On the one hand the Guardians were charged with care of the poor; on the other, they were faced with a law and regulations which probably seemed to them quite unworkable in their particular area and circumstance. Practical, economic solutions to problems of basic necessity were, despite the New Poor Law's emphasis on economy, hindered by Utilitarian ideology and dogma and the imposition of an Anglican morality. It is quite clear that in some instances moral correction took precedence over the relief of poverty. This is illustrated in the case of a young woman referred to only as 'A.B.' in the Guardians' letter seeking advice from the Poor Law Commissioners in January 1838:

> A.B. has a bastard child on allowance of 1/- a week. She is not a strong young woman but is in a situation in a farm house on wages of £3 a year and from her capabilities never likely to obtain larger wages. The sum she now earns is only sufficient to keep herself in clothes and necessities. Now that the workhouse is nearly ready the Board of Guardians is employed in revising the lists and this and similar cases present considerable difficulty for if the mothers are forced into the House they will be inmates there for life. The Board of Guardians hope to be speedily favoured with the direction of the Commissioners whether it is imperative on them to order all such cases into the house or whether they are at liberty to use their discretion.[30]

The reply was swift in arriving and was signed by Edwin Chadwick. He stated that the out relief for the child in question was not prohibited as regulations stood at present but suggested that the Guardians of Kington Union should give full consideration to the following points made by the Commissioners:

> They wish the Board of Guardians to consider first that the general interests of morality and economy (as distinguished from the apparent interest of the individual parish in this case) require a strict adherence to principle in bastardy cases of recent occurrence. Secondly that the permanent residence of the mother in the workhouse is not found by experience to ensue from the application of the test. Thirdly that it must necessarily be the duty of the Commissioners at no distant period to issue peremptory orders bearing on these cases and therefore it is highly expedient that the Board of Guardians should at once act in the same mode as the law will hereafter require them to do.[31]

The Guardians of Kington were probably quite right in their judgement that girls such as A.B. would have remained in the workhouse for the rest of their lives, despite Chadwick's indication to the contrary, and would therefore become a permanent drain on the rates of their parishes. This being the case, the agenda of the Poor Law Commission can only be seen as a firm intention to impose an upper class morality on all such unfortunate girls and to punish them for their lewdness or their folly. If Kington Guardians had been allowed to maintain A.B.'s child on out relief it would have cost 52s per year, but by taking the girl into the workhouse her maintenance would have been added to Union expenditure potentially for the rest of her life.

Anne Digby has pointed out that there were often three types of unmarried mothers in Norfolk workhouses:

> The brazen woman, one with as many as five bastards; the occasional idiot mother, one of whom had three children; and the unfortunate girl who was expecting her first child and who now paid a heavy price for her previous behaviour.[32]

This was much the same as the pattern revealed by analysis of the birth register of Hereford Union and described in the previous chapter. Here the Principle of National Uniformity and notions of morality appear to clash: on the one hand the intention of the Poor Law Commissioners was that all unmarried mothers should only receive assistance by entering the workhouse which clearly provided a uniform approach throughout the kingdom, but that same uniform approach meant that unmarried mothers of very different character would usually end up sharing accommodation, something that prevailing morality would have considered inappropriate. The limitations on accommodation did not always allow for women of good character to be separated from prostitutes. A young woman such as A.B. in Kington who had one illegitimate child might eventually have got married if maintained on a combination of earnings and out relief for her child; in the workhouse she was perhaps more likely to fall under the dangerous influence of women who were prostitutes and petty criminals. In addition, little discrimination was made between girls expecting their first baby and notorious women who had produced numerous bastards; they were all seen as immoral. Frank Crompton has written:

> Immoral females were considered to be a very dangerous influence on girl paupers, with unchaste women thought most dangerous of all. Immorality was believed to be proven in any woman who mothered a bastard, although interestingly the bastard itself, in the isolation of the workhouse children's ward, was not discriminated against. This probably demonstrated that it was contact with immorality, not heredity, that was thought to be the danger.[33]

The support of illegitimate children was a vexed and sensitive issue. Under the Old Poor Law it was easy for an unmarried mother to accuse any man of being the father of her child.[34] If she made the charge on oath before a Magistrate, the Magistrate could commit the man until he either agreed to support the child or appeared before the Quarter Sessions to contest the case. Edwin Chadwick's report of 1834, however, declared that 'a bastard will be what Providence appears to have ordained that it should be, a burden on its mother, and where she cannot maintain it on her parents'.[35] This was opposed by the anti-poor law campaigners as an affront to womanhood and a licence for men to behave licentiously, irresponsibly and without punishment. The problem was that paternity was so difficult to prove that some fathers escaped without incurring any liability, while others were sometimes made chargeable in spite of the fact that their paternity was in doubt. This did not stop the Boards of Guardians from attempting to secure affiliation orders against putative fathers and, as previously mentioned, this action was frequently undertaken by the Clerk to Hereford Union, Nicholas Lanwarne.

In Kington Union minutes there are very few references to the pursuit of putative fathers and when this did occur, it was usually to secure the fulfilment of a bond already in place, as in the following example. In October 1836 the Board of Guardians decided to pursue John Watkins, a farmer from Lyonshall, for the fulfilment of his bond to indemnify the Overseers against support of his bastard child born to Mary Morris.[36] Similarly, only one reference to grandparents being required to support their grandchildren was noted between 1834 and 1848. In July 1840 the Board ordered the Relieving Officer and the Overseers of the parish of Brilley to 'proceed against Mrs Eleanor Jones to compel her to contribute towards the support of Henry Jones, Thomas

Jones, Frederick Jones and Caroline Jones paupers of the parish of Brilley aforesaid and the grandchildren of the said Eleanor Jones'.[37] It is perhaps not surprising that there were few cases of grandparents being required to support their grandchildren, because in cases where parents sought relief, the grandparents were unlikely to be in any position to assist. Eleanor Jones was perhaps unusual in being able to contribute to the maintenance of her grandchildren.

The low incidence of cases might appear strange, but may illustrate the Guardians' reluctance to make such charges unless they were very sure that the grandparents really had the funds available. In 1832, however, in answer to the Poor Law Commission's enquiry, the Overseers and Churchwardens of Kington stated that 100 boys and 80 girls under the age of 10 were being supported by the parish.[38] It is almost certain that some of those children would be orphans, some deserted and some members of large families whose parents could not support them without assistance. There may, however, be a clue to the apparently low number of cases against putative fathers who were pursued for the maintenance of their bastards in the detail of the register of baptisms for Kington Parish Church. In most parish registers the baptism of an illegitimate child recorded only the child's name and the mother's name, and occasionally the child's surname is different from the mother's, presumably indicating the father's surname. The entries in Kington parish register are, however, rather different. In 1832 a new register was started and by 1851, 1,200 baptisms had been recorded, of which 87 or 7.2% referred to illegitimate children. Of particular interest is the fact that of those 87 entries, 26 baptisms or 30% recorded the name of just the mother, but 61 baptisms or 70% recorded the names of both parents. This might suggest that the parish priest was exerting his influence with respect to public morals and also putting pressure on unmarried mothers to name the fathers of their children. If this was indeed the case, it would have been easier for the parish Overseers to take putative fathers before the courts in order to extract maintenance for their bastards and, as a result, ease the pressure on the ratepayers' pockets.

There is probably little doubt that some of the young women in question had been seduced on the promise of marriage; some, however, had probably had a number of sexual partners, some of whom may have been already married. Girls such as these would no doubt have accused the man they thought most able and most likely to pay for her child and his folly. It was very easy for a girl to accuse a man of being the father of her child; while it was difficult for her to prove his guilt, it was equally difficult for him to prove his innocence. An analysis of the Kington marriage registers[39] covering the period from 1832 to 1855 shows that of the 61 unmarried couples noted in the register of baptisms, only three of these couples had married at Kington parish church by 1855, though some of the fathers had married other women.

This perhaps suggests that fathering bastards was considered to be more of a crime against the parish and its ratepayers than a crime against morality. The advent of the New Poor Law, however, was to herald a change of attitude amongst the upper classes and this point was neatly illustrated by M.A. Crowther when she stated that:

> Sexual standards cannot be tabulated like wheat prices, but rather than the moral standards of the poor having declined after 1795, it is likely that the standards of the upper classes hardened. Traditional village habits, including the anticipation of marriage, became opprobrious.[40]

The upper classes' perception of lower class morality appears to have been in direct ratio to the costs they bore as ratepayers. The 1851 Census Report[41] for the 12 months to 30 March 1851 recorded that in England and Wales there were just over 42,000 illegitimate births, approximately 6.9% of the total of 615,865, and whilst acknowledging the imperfections of the report, this suggested that the illegitimacy rate for Kington was probably in line with the national average.

The influence of men such as the Reverend Henry William Maddock, Vicar of Kington, may have been significant in imposing moral responsibility on the inhabitants of the town. He was presented with the living by the Bishop of Hereford in February 1835,[42] the Bishop then being Bishop Edward Grey, brother of Earl Grey who had been Prime Minister from 1830 to 1834. The Bishop may have chosen Maddock because he saw him as an energetic man who would impose his moral authority as a clergyman on the town's inhabitants, and he certainly appears to have played an active part in public affairs. In 1836 he was elected as a Guardian for Kington Union[43] and a year later he was listed as an ex-officio Guardian.[44] This indicated that he had also become a Magistrate for the session of 1843.[45] As a Guardian he pressed successfully for the appointment of a workhouse Chaplain, for the purchase of Bibles and prayer books, and, for services of divine worship to be held in the workhouse dining room each Sunday.[46] As a result of his proposal, in 1838 the Reverend John Randall, who was Vicar of Lyonshall in the patronage of the Bishop of Hereford, was appointed Chaplain at a salary of £25 per annum.[47] In 1846 the Reverend Randall resigned and was followed by Maddock himself at the same salary.[48] Maddock was therefore able to exert his influence on the public as a Poor Law Guardian, as workhouse Chaplain, as a Magistrate and as a parish priest.

The roles assumed by an energetic clergyman such as the Reverend Maddock almost certainly created overlapping circles of influence and responsibility which at times must have caused conflicts of interest for him to overcome. As a Magistrate he had a duty to punish vice and wickedness; as a Poor Law

Guardian he had a responsibility to administer poor relief according to law and regulation; as a workhouse Chaplain he was charged with concern for the inmates' general comfort as well as their spiritual needs; and as a parish priest he had a duty of care to all his parishioners who might need his help, rich and poor alike. In such a position it is clear that, wittingly or unwittingly, he might quite reasonably be seen as an instrument of social control in which justice, the state and the Established Church were brought together very neatly.

In her survey of sermons preached in the Church of England in the middle of the 19th century, Jenifer Hart has suggested that some clergymen explained the hierarchical structures of society by pronouncing them 'to be the order of nature'[49] while other clergymen declared them to be 'the creation of Divine Providence'.[50] Either way, the teaching proclaimed them to be under God's control and direction and therefore beyond alteration or criticism. This being so, it would seem that man should be content with his lot, whatever that lot might be. This must have been a difficult lesson for the inmates of workhouses and strongly at odds with the Victorian notions of 'self help' and 'self improvement'. One wonders, however, considering their lack of education, whether the pauperised poor really understood the middle class notions of religion which were presented to them or whether they merely adopted a fatalistic attitude to their lot in life and accepted that they could do little to change it. In sermons for workhouses 'inmates are assured that God intends to make them rich, not merely hereafter but now, by offering them pardon for sin and much else'.[51] The notion that God would pardon them for sin, perhaps the sin of bringing themselves to the workhouse by their own misdoings, suggests social control through implied guilt. Some would undoubtedly have brought themselves to the workhouse by their own foolishness and misbehaviour, but others were merely the victims of life's tragedies and misfortunes and were probably not culpable at all. The message of many sermons, however, was quite clear and Jenifer Hart makes the point very succinctly:

> One should not find fault with distinctions of rank, because they are dispensations of God's providence. Each class must move in its own sphere. Again and again people are told that they must do their duty in that state of life in which it hath pleased God to place them, labouring faithfully with contentment. Children should be taught to be satisfied with any, even the humblest lot, and discharge their duties with contented acquiescence. Any attempt to banish social distinctions would be a rebellion against the appointment of God, for it was God and not the higher orders of society who placed people in the rank they hold.[52]

Thus it would appear that the lower classes should work to keep themselves independent of parish or Union assistance, but not attempt to improve their station in life. This brings to mind the saying drilled into so many children of the Victorian age: 'God bless the lord and all his relations, and let them keep us in our proper stations'. Despite their duty of care to the poor, the clergy appeared to be an important 'interface' between the landowning elite and the lower orders and certainly played an important part in exercising social control.

8   Welsh Border Unions – Dore

The nodal point of Dore Union was the village of Abbeydore, from which it derived its name. Abbeydore stands on the west bank of the River Dore, which flows through the Golden Valley; in the west of the county. In the 19th century it was a remote district of widely scattered settlements with very small populations. The inhabitants of Dore Union derived their income and their living almost exclusively from the land, as labourers, smallholders, tenant farmers, or landlords.

The first Chairman of Dore Union was Edward Bolton Clive[1] and in many ways he was the ideal person for that role. His involvement in the Poor Law at Westminster and locally in Herefordshire provided him with numerous formal and informal contacts, not to mention his friendship with the Lewises. He lived a long and productive life, managing his own considerable estates and participating fully in public and political affairs; he was still an MP for Hereford when he died at the age of 80 in July 1845. In 1790, he had married Harriet,[2] the daughter of Andrew, Lord Archer of Umberslade in Warwickshire and had had four children: Edward, Archer, George and Harriet. Edward, the son, was a colonel in the Grenadier Guards,[3] but sat as a Magistrate[4] and as a Guardian for Dore Union[5] when he was resident at Whitfield. He perhaps had in mind his eventual inheritance of the family estates and the role he would then assume, but he died unmarried, despite interests and opportunities, in April 1845[6] just three months before his father. The Clive estates therefore passed to the second son, Archer. Archer had been to Harrow and Oxford and, despite his father's declared aversion to clergymen,[7] had entered the church. It is not clear why Archer's father thought so poorly of his chosen profession, but his choice did not appear to disturb a happy relationship between father and son. The dowry which Archer's mother brought to her marriage had included the advowson of Solihill in Warwickshire,[8] and he became the incumbent there as soon as the living became vacant in 1829. In his diaries he referred to his work as a Poor Law Guardian at Solihull and its connections with his work as a parish priest, and his comments will be explored below. After the death of his father he left Solihull and moved his family to Whitfield and took up the pursuits of the landed gentleman, while at the same time continuing his duties as Chancellor of the Choir and Prebendary of Hereford Cathedral.

His younger brother George Clive was a barrister, the first Assistant Poor Law Commissioner for Monmouthshire and in the 1850s and 1860s, MP for Hereford like his father before him. In 1865 he purchased Perrystone Court, the former home of William Clifford, Edward's closest friend since their youth, and made it his permanent home. The Clive and Clifford families remained on close and friendly terms for many years, and Archer and Caroline Clive often visited Perrystone after they had made their home at Whitfield.

Harriet Clive married the Reverend Doctor Henry Wetherell, Archdeacon of Hereford, who also sat as a Guardian of Dore Union. Despite Edward Bolton Clive's aversion to clergymen, the clergy were to be prominent as Guardians: these included the Reverend Henry Lee Warner, a large land-owner, who lived at Tyberton Court; Doctor John Merewether, the Dean of Hereford; Archdeacon Wetherell; and in 1848, Archer Clive.

The Dore Union was the last to be formed in Herefordshire. The reason for the delay in forming Dore Union is not clear; it may simply have been over-looked because it was so small, but there may also be a clue to be found in the ownership of land, in particular the estate of the Scudamores of Kentchurch Court.

The Scudamores had held lands and lived in the parishes along the Welsh Border for over 500 years and still held lordships there in the 1830s. The owner of Kentchurch Court at that time was Colonel John Scudamore, whose family had a close friendship with the Clives of Whitfield Court, which was situated just seven miles away. 'Colonel and Mrs Scudamore lived much abroad but when they were at home hardly a day passed without somebody from Whitfield going to Kentchurch or vice versa.'[9] If this were the case and the Scudamores happened to be abroad in 1836 when the boundaries of either Herefordshire Union were being settled, it would have been quite possible for the Clives and the Lewises to delay the legal settlement and shape of Dore Union until Colonel Scudamore was available for discussion with the Assistant Commissioner, Sir Edmund Walker Head. Although no clear evidence has been discovered, all the circumstances suggest that this might have been the case. Dore Union was composed of 27 parishes in Herefordshire and two in Monmouthshire, namely Grosmont and Llangua, both parishes contiguous with Kentchurch. As principal landowners in the area it is more than likely that the Scudamores and the Clives included Grosmont and Llangua in Dore Union so that their influence over Poor Law affairs amongst his own tenants, employees and villagers would not be diluted. This hypothesis is further supported when it is recalled that the Assistant Commissioner charged with the settlement of Monmouthshire Unions was George Clive, whose opinions of the Welsh and their ability to run a Union have already been noted. It will also be recalled that Sir Edmund Walker Head agreed absolutely with George Clive's opinion and it would, therefore, perhaps be expected that the two men would collaborate, if not conspire, in defining Union boundaries to the satisfaction of Colonel Scudamore. They would be guaranteed the support of Edward Bolton Clive, and no doubt that of Thomas Frankland Lewis. Powerful landowners could often arrange Union boundaries to suit their own interests; the result was perhaps a variable mixture of old fashioned 18th century paternalism and 19th century Utilitarian social control.

One wonders what concerns were uppermost in Sir Edmund's mind as he cast his eye over its Guardians as they gathered for their first meeting in the convivial surroundings of the Red Lion at Abbeydore on 11 April 1837. A room had been hired for this and future meetings at the cost of 2s per meeting or 2s 6d with a fire.[10] Perhaps Sir Edmund was a little disappointed that the first meeting of the Dore Union should begin with a poor attendance, for just six of the ex-officio Guardians and 22 elected Guardians were present; ten of the 29 parishes in Dore Union failed to provide a Guardian. The poor attendance may have resulted from the fact that Dore Union was small and 'closed' in nature and the landowning influence and its power well known to all. On the other hand, the reason could simply have been the geographical spread and location of the Union. Some parishes may also have been concerned about the potential cost to the ratepayers or have felt unable to argue against the large landowners.

The lack of enthusiasm for the New Poor law in areas such as Kington and Abbeydore should have sent a clear message to politicians, Poor Law Commissioners and Assistant Commissioners alike that the new legislation was totally inappropriate for some parts of England and Wales. It was of course not the message they wished to hear. It was easier to blame the failure of the New Poor Law on lack of leadership from landowners, farmers and the clergy and in some cases they may have had a point.

At the commencement of the first meeting of Dore Guardians, Edward Bolton Clive was elected Chairman and Mr Thomas Hughes, Vice Chairman. Here was, perhaps, a little political expediency in that Thomas Hughes was one of the two elected Guardians for Grosmont, one of the Monmouthshire parishes. There may have been some resentment that Grosmont and Llangua had been included in a Herefordshire Union. It was also resolved 'that in consequence of the Parliamentary duties of the Chairman frequently requiring his absence it is expedient that a second Vice Chairman be appointed,'[11] and Mr Francis Hamp was duly elected. The following month Mr Hamp resigned the post,[12] almost certainly because one of the sites that the Guardians were considering to purchase on which to build a new workhouse belonged to him. In June the Union Clerk entered into the minute book that Mr Hamp's land had been purchased for £2,000[13] and that the plans for the new building had been approved,[14] Mr Hamp becoming one of the ten Guardians who were elected to form the building committee.[15] A Mr Crickmay was appointed as Clerk of Works at one guinea per week.[16]

Whilst the building proceeded, the administration of Dore Union had to be established, existing parish properties had to be assessed for their suit-ability as temporary accommodation for paupers, and Union officers had to be appointed for the day to day management of union affairs. In order to cover the widespread area three Relieving Officers were appointed: John Price for the Clodock District; John Farr for the Kentchurch District; and Thomas Bigelstone for the Madley District.[17] It was probably for this same reason of the distances which had to be covered that the Union was divided into two medical districts: Madley, and Clodock with Kentchurch. Henry James was appointed Medical Officer for the Madley District with a salary of £60 per annum plus 10s for each midwifery case, and a Mr Lane was appointed to the Clodock and Kentchurch District with a salary of £125 per annum plus 10s for midwifery cases.[18] The parishes of Madley and Kentchurch had their own existing poor houses and after they had been re-equipped with neces-sary fittings, utensils and linen, they were used to segregate male and female paupers until the new workhouse at Abbeydore was ready for occupation and the proper classification of paupers as prescribed by the New Poor Law could be effected. This is made clear in a minute referring to one James Pritchard in October 1837.[19] Pritchard had been ill and in receipt of 1s per week for two weeks on top of his usual allowance but when the fortnight was up he was to remove himself to the poor house at Kentchurch while his wife and chil-dren remained at the poor house at Madley. The classification of paupers was regarded as the most important facet of the New Poor Law and the Central Authority was at pains to see that the relevant rules and regulations were adhered to without hindrance from parsimonious Guardians who might try to avoid what they deemed to be unnecessary expenditure.

In the years before the advent of the New Poor Law the parishes of Kentchurch and Madley had administered poor relief through Select Vestries,[20] but neither of these parishes made submissions to the Poor Law Commission's questionnaire in 1832, so it is not possible to comprehend fully how well their vestries were run or what the ratepayers thought of their administration. At the beginning of Dore Union its affairs were run in a very similar way to a Select Vestry. The minutes almost suggest that Relieving Officers referred claims from paupers to the Board of Guardians for approval rather than taking decisions for themselves; or, perhaps they were simply bypassed by paupers who applied directly to the Board in the way they had applied to the vestry. Although rules required that pauper claims for relief should be routed through Relieving Officers, perhaps for a while everything carried on as before. In this remote area, where communications were difficult, it would have taken some weeks, perhaps months, before the routines of the New Poor Law were completely understood. Whichever way applications were made, paupers' needs were assessed and individual grants were made; the early Union minutes include lists of paupers relieved as illustrated by the following examples. In July 1837 some paupers were assisted to help them through periods of illness: James Price was given 1s in cash and 1s in bread per week for four weeks; John Morris 3s to 4s in cash and 2s in bread per week for four weeks; John Gwatkin 4s in cash and 1s in bread per week for two weeks.[21] The following month's awards suggest, however, that the Medical Officers were beginning to make recommendations on the basis of clinical need without reference to the Board. William Philpots and David Price were each provided with a truss, presumably to help them to continue to work and earn their living.[22] In the weeks that followed, lists indicate that from five to 15 individuals usually sought help, and the details of the assistance given were recorded next to their names. These awards ranged from cash and bread allowances in times of temporary sickness to the Board's agreement to pay for the hire of a room at 1s per week for the reception of a male pauper suffering from venereal disease.[23] This unfortunate man would no doubt have been considered to be a very dangerous risk to the health and morals of the other paupers, to be kept out of the workhouse at all costs. At the beginning of the New Poor Law there were no set procedures for dealing with particular cases, which sometimes led to rather harsh treatment for some paupers. Marginal cases should have been dealt with by the Assistant Poor Law Commissioners, but they had a very heavy workload and it is likely that Guardians sometimes decided to make their own decisions in order to get though the cases and Poor Law business before them. In some ways the Board of Guardians demonstrated common sense and kindness, but they were also capable of insensitivity and petty spitefulness, as the following examples illustrate.

In May 1837 it was resolved that the allowance paid to the mother of Harriet Watkins, a bastard child of Vowchurch parish, should be stopped and also that the mother should deliver the child to the Relieving Officer, presumably so that she could be sent to the workhouse while enquiries were made about the putative father.[24] This was a curious action to take because women with illegitimate children were supposed only to be relieved in the workhouse. It might be supposed, therefore, that at this early point in the Union's working the Guardians were unaware of the legal strictures placed upon them, or perhaps they merely chose to disregard them if they felt so inclined. Alternatively, perhaps the mother was in employment and able to support herself but not the child. Then again, if the Guardians knew the name of the child's father it may simply have been a ploy on their part to put pressure on him to maintain his child. Whatever the true facts of the case, it was a very unkind and unfeeling action to split up mother and child and send the child to a workhouse miles from home.

In March the following year the clerk was instructed to write to Hereford Union stating that Dore Union would undertake to pay the funeral expenses of Mary Sykes, aged 98, if she might be permitted to live with her granddaughter in the parish of Clehonger.[25] At one level this might appear to be an act of kindness; at another level it may simply have been about costs and the settling of accounts. It also illustrates the widely held belief that children, or in this case grandchildren, should support their elders in their old age where it was at all possible.

In August that year the Guardians passed a resolution which can only be seen as extremely petty and spiteful. It was resolved 'that the Relieving Officers ascertain whether any paupers in this Union keep dogs either their own or other persons and that the weekly pay of such paupers be stopped until the dogs are made away with'.[26] The logic of such a resolution is difficult to see; the savings the Board would make by destroying paupers' dogs was unlikely to be significant, because paupers would not feed to dogs food which they could eat themselves. At first sight this action just seems like extreme parsimony, but there may have been other reasons. Dogs might be used for poaching and while some landlords might turn a blind eye to a poor man's poaching the odd rabbit or the occasional pheasant, many would not. Most of Dore Union's Guardians were landlords or farmers, and there might be in this petty resolution an attempt by one or two landlords to curb the activities of certain well known poachers. In rural areas the names of those men regularly involved in poaching were usually well known, but complex ties and allegiances amongst the people in remote communities made it difficult for such men to be apprehended unless caught red-handed by a gamekeeper. The labouring classes would almost certainly unite against the estate owner in sustained silence.

If Guardians appear sometimes guilty of harsh judgements and mean decisions, it should be remembered, in mitigation of their actions, that the minutes often do not make the reader party to the reasons for their decisions. They were also feeling their way with a new system of poor relief which imposed on those who administered it a great measure of accountability; parish autonomy had never before been subjected to such scrutiny and audit by a central authority. On the one hand they wished to exert and maintain their own independence; on the other, they did not wish to fall foul of the Poor Law Commission. It had legal powers which had not previously existed and would, if necessary, use them. It was likely that in these circumstances a Board of Guardians would sometimes appear harsh and insensitive, and also make mistakes. Parish Overseers were in an even more unenviable position: they could be summoned before the Board of Guardians to explain their actions or before the Magistrates to explain alleged neglect of duty. There was also an annual audit carried out by an independent outside auditor, and a man such as Nicholas Lanwarne at the Hereford Union would not compromise the presentation of his accounts by avoiding asking parish Overseers difficult and uncomfortable questions. Looking at the minutes of Dore Union over a period of 12 years from 1837 to 1849 it is not difficult to see why so many Overseers held office unwillingly. The Overseer's lot was not a happy one and he often held office on a rota basis, returning every few years.

On 7 December 1838 Dore Union Guardians resolved 'that John Broad, the Overseer of Madley, should be summoned before the next meeting of the Magistrates to explain his neglecting his duty in the care of Mary Ann Thomas who was with her dead child lying destitute in a Barn in the said parish'[27] for five days without receiving relief, although Broad had been informed of the woman's circumstances. It is not known whether this was a mature woman with a grown child or a young girl with a newly born illegitimate child, and nothing more was recorded in the minutes. Complaints of this nature against Overseers were rare in minutes books; complaints were usually made by Overseers, Churchwardens and parish priests because Relieving Officers or Medical Officers had not attended cases reported to them.

When Overseers were charged with neglect of duty it was not usually in connection with tragic cases such as that of Mary Ann Thomas, but for neglecting to pay parish poor rates to the Dore Union Treasurer. In the period from 1837 to 1849 there were numerous occasions when the Overseers were threatened with court action if payment was not forthcoming within a given time, usually two weeks. Some parishes appear to have been notorious: Treville, Wormbridge, Thruxton, Orcop, Longtown, Kenderchurch, St Margarets, St Devereux, Abbeydore and Madley often paid up just in time to avoid court appearances, but on a few occasions Overseers were fined sums ranging from 5s to £5 for neglect of duty. Proceedings could, however, become very complicated when Guardians did bring Overseers to court, because of the numerous roles which some men filled. The Abbeydore Magistrates met at the Red Lion and in many cases were the same men who met there as Poor Law Guardians. Their numerous roles and connections could cause some embarrassment and this is clearly illustrated by the case of a Mr Howard who was the Overseer of Madley.

In April 1841 Mr Howard appeared before Abbeydore Magistrates for the non-payment of parish funds to Dore Union after a warrant had been signed to distrain Mr Howard's own personal possessions, but had not yet been served. Howard appeared before the Board of Guardians to plead for more time. He had paid £9 on account and asked for two more weeks in which to pay the remaining £20.[28] His request was granted and, since the matter was not mentioned again, it may be safely assumed that Howard kept his word. It must have appeared a strange set of circumstances to Howard: men wearing Guardians' hats asked Magistrates to bring him to court; then, on another day, in the same room, some of the same men, wearing Magistrates' hats this time, heard his case and issued a distress warrant; and a few days later in the same room the same men, again wearing Guardians' hats, mitigated the sentence and held back the distress warrant to allow him more time to pay. This seems a very unjust waste of the man's time, particularly if his failure to pay had been caused by ratepayers' reluctance to hand over their money rather than his neglect of duty in attempting to collect it. One wonders where Dr John Merewether, Dean of Hereford, stood in this case; he was a Guardian of Dore Union, Vicar of Madley and Chairman of Madley Select Vestry.[29] Overseers such as Howard no doubt thought themselves to be in an unenviable position. Once elected they could be fined if they refused to hold office yet carried out all of their duties unpaid and could have their goods distrained for not paying the parish rates due to the Guardians. Most Overseers were farmers or tradesmen, so there was a limit to how much time they could spend on collecting rates, particularly from farmers who held small hill farms on the slopes of the Black Mountains. In the case of Dore Union, separate rate collectors were not appointed until the middle of the 1840s, which meant that until that date Overseers had to also physically collect the rates. The non-payment of funds was a constant problem and a cause of much correspondence between Guardians and Treasurer.

The Treasurer of Dore Union was Nathaniel Morgan, Guardian of Ross Union, a banker and businessman.[30] One of his banking partners, Francis Hamp of Bacton Villa in the village of the same name, was a Guardian of Dore Union from 1837 to his death in 1849. He was Chairman of the Board for some years after Edward Bolton Clive, and it was the same Francis Hamp who sold the piece of land on which the new workhouse was built. He was a man of considerable wealth; the tithe map apportionment for Bacton shows that he owned over 900 acres of land in that parish alone. At the time of Hamp's death on 26 March 1849, Nathaniel Morgan visited him in the company of John Stratford Collins, Guardian of Ross, whom he described as 'our friend and solicitor'. He confided to his journal that he estimated Hamp's estate as being worth between £150,000 and £200,000 and also remarked that 'I much regret my partner did not do the good he might have done to the poor and needy he ought to have done while living in this much distressed country and which I often wished him to do for many reasons'.[31] Although Morgan was clearly distressed by his friend's passing, he did not flinch from observing what he obviously thought to be a neglect of care for the poor by a man who was very wealthy. The many personal and business connections between Guardians in the same and neighbouring Unions sometimes created business opportunities of great benefit but also brought into sharp focus possible conflicts of interest.

The connections between Nathaniel Morgan and Francis Hamp were a case in point and one wonders whether Hamp left the Board room when Dore Union Guardians discussed banking correspondence from Morgan, or whether he was part of those discussions. The minutes do not make this clear, but they do make clear Morgan's concern about the state of Dore Union's bank account.

In October 1841, Nathaniel Morgan wrote to the Guardians about their account, which was £240 overdrawn, stating that since he was precluded from charging interest unless there was an average credit in hand of £400 over the course of a year, it did not suit him to continue the account. The Guardians' response was merely to put pressure on Overseers to pays outstanding funds quickly and to direct the Clerk to explain the difficulties the Union regularly encountered.[32] In September 1842, Morgan wrote again indicating that he would like the account 'in a more favourable state'[33] and in May 1843, he requested that the overdraft of £300 be 'immediately reduced'.[34] In December 1847 he told the Poor Law Board that the account was again overdrawn and that cheques would be dishonoured until the account was in credit.[35] Morgan's pressure on the Dore Guardians to keep their account in credit was tolerated while his banking partner, Francis Hamp, was alive and attending Board meetings, but less than a month after his death the Guardians tried to have Morgan dismissed as their Treasurer. This move, however, rebounded on them and brought their sorry financial affairs under the spotlight of the Central Authority. On 20 April 1849 the clerk minuted that the Poor Law Board declined to

Dore Workhouse, since converted into housing, photographed in 2008

dismiss Mr Morgan as Treasurer of Dore Union on account of his refusal to clear cheques against an overdrawn account. They also requested to know the precise 'state of the account at present'.[36]

Enterprising men like Nathaniel Morgan and Francis Hamp were quick to grasp the business opportunities provided by the New Poor Law and so were numerous shopkeepers and merchants, who saw the possibility of good profits to be made from supplying goods and services to the newly formed Unions. New workhouses were being built, paupers had to be fed and clothed and someone had to supply all the provisions the workhouse needed. Some were honest traders, but some tried to pass off shoddy goods as top quality.

It was not just businessmen who benefited from the establishment of the Poor Law Unions. A new class of minor officials, such as Relieving Officers, was created, providing new employment opportunities and status for a wider spectrum of the population. A reasonably literate man who could read, write and cast simple accounts could be in receipt of a steady income as a Relieving Officer for many years if he was diligent and did not cheat paupers of their rightful allowances. Inevitably, some were fair and honest men whilst others were inadequate or plainly dishonest. Curiously, the cheats often seemed naively unaware that they would ultimately be brought to account and be required to explain their actions. In the countryside where everyone knew everyone, however, they were soon found out. In the past the Magistrates had rarely carried out minute inspections of Overseers' accounts and perhaps they assumed that the same would be true of Relieving Officers' accounts under the new system. Village accounts might have been settled with nods and winks and a tankard of ale at the local coaching inn without too many questions being asked, but everything was changing and under the New Poor Law, accounts were administered very efficiently.

During the transition from parish autonomy to Union authority all men had to change their thinking. The men born in the 1790s and the early 1800s who were now to take charge of the New Poor Law had been brought up in an age when privilege and helping sons, younger brothers, nephews or cousins into lucrative positions was seen not as unfair nepotism, but as a family duty. The idea of regular audit and accountability to a Central Authority was an alien notion with which they had to wrestle and come to terms. As the process of transition ensued some officers found themselves and their misdoings entangled in a web of checks and balances which evolved as the new system became established. There was a continuous flow of information between the local Guardians and the Commissioners at Somerset House and questions were asked; questions which could not be ignored or answered with nods and winks and set aside with tankards of ale. Some officers were dismissed, others were just 'allowed' to resign. Kington and Dore Unions had their fair share of these but their departure rarely ended in prison or even court appearances. Counsel often declared that the evidence was insufficient to secure a conviction and it would be less expensive to recover deficits in their accounts by claiming redress from the men who had stood surety for them when they were first appointed. At Somerset House, however, the Central Authority maintained a 'black list' and once an officer had been dismissed from one Union, it was assured that his employment would never be sanctioned in another one.

At a higher level men with legal training could do very well for themselves by accumulating numerous posts, none more so than Nicholas Lanwarne. A solicitor, he was appointed as clerk of Hereford Union from its beginning in 1836. In July 1837 he was appointed as the solicitor to Dore Union[37] and in October that year he accepted the position as auditor as well, at a salary of 16 guineas a year.[38] In November 1842 he resigned as auditor[39] and became clerk to Dore Union with a salary of £70 per Year[40] whilst continuing in his post as clerk to Hereford Union. He was clearly a very able man and a very well organised one. The minutes of Dore Union had been kept more than satisfactorily before Lanwarne's appointment, but after his arrival they exhibit much greater precision than before. He indexed the minutes very carefully so that information could be located very quickly; he was a busy man and did not wish to waste valuable time looking through pages and pages of minutes unnecessarily. Indeed, Lanwarne used his time most profitably, making money whenever the opportunity presented itself. In October 1841 he presented Dore Union Guardians with two accounts totalling £78 18s 11d for conducting the 1841 census in his capacity as Superintendent Registrar for Hereford. For the registration of births, marriages and deaths as required by the legislation of 1836, Dore Union had been added to Hereford Union at the suggestion of the Registrar General. It was not clear why this arrangement was made, but it may simply have been that there was a dearth of suitably educated men who were willing and able to perform the precise duties which were required. In the 1830s and 1840s much reforming legislation was passed and men like Nicholas Lanwarne were very favourably placed to earn substantial incomes by enacting it at local level and attending to all the necessary documentation. Nicholas Lanwarne was in the right place at the right time.

In the early years of the New Poor Law, 1836-1840, the minutes of the Guardians' meetings reveal a considerable amount of detail about their particular concerns and how they thought about paupers and poor relief. As Guardians and their clerks became more familiar with routine matters, however, the minutes became briefer and much less detailed and, as a result, less revealing. By looking at a sequence of events over several years, however, it is still possible to capture a glimpse of life in the workhouse and the tensions amongst the minor officers who were almost as incarcerated as the paupers. The Master was all-powerful and the Nurse, the Porter, the Schoolmistress or Schoolmaster could not leave the workhouse other than at prescribed times without his express permission. If he used his power wisely, there would be few problems, but if he was a bully, many problems might ensue, resulting in frequent changes of staff. The staff who seemed to change most frequently were the Schoolmistresses and in this respect the Unions of Kington and Dore were no different. They were different, however, in their attitude to pauper education.

In April 1838 Kington Union appointed Thomas Scandrett as the workhouse Porter[41] and at the end of that month he was directed to take the boys and girls in the workhouse to Kington National School every morning and afternoon, and the Union paid the school 1d per child per week for their education.[42] In the following month, however, there was an outbreak of typhus fever in the workhouse; attendance at school was suspended and the children were directed to read under the supervision of the Porter.[43] As a result of this temporary measure, the Porter was deemed competent to teach the children and was employed as Schoolmaster and Porter at a combined salary of £20 per year.[44] This arrangement seems to have been continued for over two years, since the subject of education was not mentioned again until September 1841 when a Guardian, John Whittaker of New Court, proposed that a Schoolmistress be appointed, presumably to save money, because the terms of her employment were extremely parsimonious. She was to teach from 9am until noon, from 2pm until 4pm and, at her own discretion, from 7pm to 8pm for the older boys whose lessons were interrupted whilst learning a trade. In addition she was to teach the girls knitting, needlework and spinning, and all for the princely sum of £10 per annum plus her food and lodgings.[45] This was a very low salary indeed, but perhaps not so very unusual. In her study of rural Norfolk Anne Digby has stated that in the early years of the New Poor Law, annual salaries ranged from £15 to £35 for a Schoolmaster and £10 to £20 for a Schoolmistress, plus board and lodging.[46] She has also pointed out that Norfolk Boards of Guardians endeavoured to follow the Old Poor Law practice of employing a pauper at a notional 'salary' to act as workhouse schoolteacher.[47] The Kington Guardians were, however, intent on the children being trained for work; for some time the girls had been trained to make straw bonnets and a tailor and a shoemaker had been employed to teach boys their trade.

Shortly after Mr Whittaker's proposal, a Schoolmistress was appointed and her conditions of employment were laid down very carefully, with a hint of past trouble and trouble yet to come. It was clearly stated that the Schoolmistress was to have the Porter's lodge entirely for her own use and that no one but the Schoolmistress was to have control over the children, except the Chaplain.[48] Normally the Master and the Matron of the workhouse were above the Schoolmistress in the workhouse hierarchy, so this statement hints at previous conflicts between staff, suggesting that there had been interference from either the Master or his wife, the Matron. Schoolteachers were in a curious position in the workhouse setting; they were probably better educated than either the Master or his wife, but were definitely inferior in terms of status.

In November 1841, a Miss Mary Woolf was appointed as Schoolmistress,[49] and six months later the Chaplain was requested by the Board to provide them with a special report on 'the advancement of the children and the general conduct and management of the school'.[50] The Chaplain's report has not survived, but it is likely that it was not very favourable because the following month Miss Woolf resigned.[51] It is possible that Jelinger C. Symons, Her Majesty's Inspector of Workhouse Schools, who lived in Herefordshire, was consulted in this case, but, if so, his report is not extant. A few weeks after Miss Woolf's resignation, however, her mother wrote to the Board complaining about her daughter's treatment at the workhouse:

> Gentlemen,
> I am in deep distress on account of my poor daughter who is quite out of her mind perhaps I ought to come to see you personally to request you will have an investigation of the cause of her affliction but I cannot leave her it will not be safe to do so but I trouble you with this Note to say that I believe she has been very ill treated at the Union House and has been threatened and taunted that she will go to Prison and to be transported for some fault she has committed which has so prayed on her mind that her intellect has quite gone if the Gentlemen will please call an investigation I believe that there will be evidence to show that she has not been treated properly by persons in the employ of the Board.[52]

The Board did carry out an investigation but resolved, on 25 June 1842, that the charges made against the Matron, Mrs Tringham, were quite unfounded.[53] Just two weeks later, on 9 July, Elisabeth Matilda Coniam was appointed as the new Schoolmistress.[54] This was a very quick appointment and one wonders whether Mary Woolf's life was made difficult in order to make room for another, but then Elisabeth Coniam left in December 1844[55] and in February 1845 Mrs Mary Matilda Farrell was appointed,[56] only to resign in June because she found it too arduous having to walk the boys to and from the National School twice a day. Shortly afterwards, however, she regretted having tendered her resignation and asked the Board if she might rescind it. The Board considered the matter and resolved that she could keep her post, that she would no longer have to walk the boys to school, and that the 'matron would not interfere with her in her school duties'.[57] Just a few months later, at the beginning of December that year, however, Mrs Farrell resigned again without giving a reason, or at least no reason was recorded.[58] Anne Digby has expressed the view that the rapid turnover of workhouse teachers resulted from the low salaries offered by many Guardians and 'the unappealing conditions of service in the workhouse and the lack of prior training of many workhouse teachers which made them unequal to the demands made upon them'.[59] It would certainly appear that the rapid succession of Schoolmistresses at Kington Workhouse was caused by a number of circumstances: low salary, low status, onerous duties, an unpleasant working atmosphere and, perhaps, a spiteful and interfering Matron. The boys continued to attend the National School run by the Reverend W. Jones Thomas[60] but there was no mention of a replacement teacher in the workhouse until August 1846, when Mr Edward Lewis was appointed Porter and Schoolmaster at 2s 6d per week on a month's trial, which was to be increased to 4s per week if appointed permanently and also backdated.[61] By that time, Mr Tringham, the Master of Kington Workhouse, had died and William and Ann Bishop had been appointed as the new Master and Matron.[62]

The attitude of Kington Guardians towards the education of pauper children seemed to vary between reasonable and minimal provision, depending on the balance of opinion amongst the Board members. It should perhaps be remembered that many farmers were hardly literate themselves and therefore saw no point in educating pauper children. They probably resented the notion that paupers might become more educated than they were themselves, with the added sting that they had paid for their education. At times all the Kington Workhouse children attended the National School, at others just the boys attended, and sometimes none of them attended. Schoolmistresses at the workhouse came and went, sometimes teaching all the children, sometimes just the girls. Men holding the joint posts of Schoolmaster and Porter fared little better than the Schoolmistresses. It was more than likely that most of those appointed were quite incapable of teaching, though some may have provided industrial training. A woman who could instruct the girls in spinning and the making of straw bonnets might be described as a Schoolmistress, and similarly a Porter who had been taught a trade which he could pass on to the boys in the workhouse might be described as a Schoolmaster. It was training such as bonnet-making and shoe-making that many of the Guardians from farming circles saw as education: not reading, writing and arithmetic. It was for this reason that they failed lamentably to support efficient Schoolmasters and Schoolmistresses when they did manage to find them.

The attitudes of Norfolk farmers on the other side of England were very much the same as those in Herefordshire, in that they were sympathetic to spending money on training pauper children if it was likely to reduce their dependence on the rates in the long term. Anne Digby has pointed out that there was also hostility amongst farmer Guardians to the notion of having maps in the workhouse schoolrooms because geographical knowledge might lead later to migration from the area and therefore reduce the reserve of labour which they found useful during harvest. 'Moreover, an academic education for the pauper child could conflict with the idea of the New Poor Law as a means of social discipline for the poor.'[63] It is difficult to see attitudes such as these as anything more than Utilitarian notions of social control. Farmer Guardians were intent on making the New Poor Law work, but only in as far as it did not interfere with their own interests and the availability of an ample reserve of labour when they wanted it. At Kington the farmer Guardians appear to have reacted very largely like their counterparts in Norfolk. Compared with the educational provision at Dore Union Workhouse, however, that provided at Kington made Kington Guardians appear very forward-thinking in their attitude to education.

Although Dore Union was operating from April 1837, the first mention of education in the minutes of Guardians' meetings occurred two years later in May 1839, when they agreed that a pauper named James Garnett should be employed to assist in the education of the children in the workhouse. It is not clear at this point whether he was assisting another teacher or whether he was in charge of the children and their education himself. In February 1840 he was referred to as the 'Schoolmaster' but his status was still not clear.[64] In the 1841 census the Schoolmistress at the workhouse was recorded as one Susan Cross, aged 20, but her real status was suspect for she featured in the Guardians' minutes on several occasions with reference to the illegitimate children she had produced. Central regulations were ambivalent about education at that time and, while it was quite common for a pauper to be deputed to carry out the duties of a Schoolmistress unpaid, the Central Authority did not approve of such arrangements. Even if using paupers as Schoolmistresses had been approved, it was unlikely that Susan Cross would have been looked on favourably in that capacity. A Schoolmistress with bastards was hardly a good example to the girls in the workhouse. The Guardians may have considered it expedient that in the official census the workhouse should not appear to be without a Schoolmistress, but in January 1843 'the clerk was directed to request the Chaplain to report next Board day whether he considers the pauper who officiates in the workhouse as schoolmistress is capable of instructing the children'.[65] Although the Chaplain's comments were not recorded in the Guardians' minutes, it was clear that his report was not favourable, because they decided to advertise for a Schoolmistress. This was hardly surprising, for as the mother of bastards Susan Cross would have been viewed as dangerous to the morals of the other paupers, particularly the children, and a Chaplain could not countenance such an influence. Having heard the Chaplain's report the Guardians elected to advertise for a Schoolmistress at the salary of £15 per annum and, receiving no applications for this unattractive salary, decided to readvertise the position at £20 per annum.[66] A few weeks later a Mrs Wright was appointed.[67] Nothing more was mentioned about Mrs Wright, but in a report of his inspection of Dore Union Workhouse in January 1847, Mr John Graves stated that a 'good resident Schoolmaster or Schoolmistress would be desirable'.[68]

In March of that year Harriet Sparks was appointed as Schoolmistress[69] and the Poor Law Commissioners approved her appointment, having first requested to know whether she was a Protestant or a Dissenter.[70] Her religious denomination was not recorded, but it was likely that she was Church of England, considering the strength of the clergy on Dore Union Board. Later that month the Chaplain reported to the Board that the new Schoolmistress was very attentive to her duties and that the children were improving, but that there was a need for slates, pens and testaments.[71] In November it was agreed that the Schoolmistress would benefit from additional training and the Guardians agreed to appoint a substitute teacher during her absence. It was anticipated, too, that on her return Harriet Sparks would have an increase in salary.[72] Here was perhaps the first really positive step the Guardians had taken to provide a reasonable standard of education for the workhouse children. In early 1848, however, the workhouse was inspected again and this time the report said that the children were rather backward and that none of them could add a sum of any kind. The inspector, John Graves, agreed though that things would improve when the regular teacher returned from her training.[73] In May 1848 Harriet Sparks returned to her duties, but she resigned less than a year later in January 1849,[74] for as a teacher with training, more attractive teaching opportunities outside the workhouse system would have been open to her. In March that year Mr John Griffiths was appointed as Master and Schoolmaster at £30 per annum and his wife as Matron at £20 per annum.[75] This was perhaps an unusual arrangement, but nevertheless it was a logical and practical solution to bringing an element of consistency to education in the workhouse.

Dore Union Workhouse was sometimes sparsely populated as is shown in the census returns. At the time of the 1841 census it was occupied by: the Master, his wife, the Schoolmistress and the cook; 12 male paupers above the age of 20; nine females above the age of 20; ten boys between six months and nine years; and eight girls between nine months and 14 years. In total there were 39 paupers: 21 adults and 18 children. Combining the posts of Schoolmaster and Master (whose wife would be the Matron) also overcame the problem of trying to find a single person of either sex who would be prepared to bury themselves in the remote countryside of the Welsh Border without transport and access to the nearest town. It would have been a very dreary life, resident in the workhouse with little chance of recreation or opportunity to meet other people.

Attendance at Dore Union meetings was never very fulsome unless the Guardians thought there would be discussion of a particularly sensitive issue or if they were specifically requested to attend. In May 1841 such a request was sent out for a meeting at which the continuing complaints for neglect of duty against the Relieving Officer, John Farr, were to be discussed.[76] Similar problems were evident at Kington. In March 1839 it was recorded by the Clerk that since only two Guardians attended the last meeting, it was not possible to transact any of the Union's business.[77] In the following spring, he noted that decisions had been delayed because of the 'unavoidable absence of a large proportion of the guardians at Knighton Fair',[78] Knighton being an important hiring fair. As late as May 1847, it was recorded that there were no Guardians elected for the parishes of Lyonshall, Eardisley, Glascwm and Newchurch and the Guardians from the previous year had refused to serve in office again.[79]

Many of the inhabitants of Dore and Kington Unions lived in very remote spots, which tended to deter farmer Guardians from travelling long distances to attend meetings. Distance must have been a particularly serious problem during winter months and also at busy times in the farming year, notably during lambing, haymaking or harvest.

In his study of the Rebecca Riots David Williams stated that:

> The Poor Law Amendment Act was the outcome of the reforming passion of Edwin Chadwick. He regarded pauperism as a problem in administration only, and not in social responsibility.[80]

Chadwick failed to see that legislation which was essentially designed to solve an urban problem did not work when applied to remote rural areas where the nature of poverty was different. No doubt the Clives and the Lewises did not use their influence in their own areas to enforce the New Poor Law to the letter because they could soon see that it was impossible and that compromise or modification was essential. Any deviation from the law, however, Chadwick saw as betrayal of reform. Relations between Edwin Chadwick and Thomas Frankland Lewis were never good, largely because of Chadwick's bitterness at not being appointed a Commissioner when the first appointments were made and then at being passed over when vacancies arose as Commissioners resigned to take up other posts, but also because he sought to modify Chadwick's uncompromising rigidity in Poor Law affairs.[81] No doubt Lewis understood that the topography of the Welsh Border unions of Dore and Kington created huge impediments to efficient Poor Law administration and that the easing of regulations was the only way in which the New Poor Law was likely to work satisfactorily.

Anthony Brundage has argued that Edwin Chadwick really did believe that men of property were the safest element to whom local administrative power could be entrusted, that their power on Poor Law Boards would be assured through the plural voting system – additional votes allocated to individuals in accordance with their land and property holdings – and that their authority would be further enhanced because men of property also served as Magistrates.[82] At the same time, he also anticipated that the discretionary powers of Boards of Guardians would be severely limited. 'With a strong central authority mandating the use of the Workhouse Test to the able-bodied and their families, the system would be largely self-acting.'[83] He was equally aware, however, that his superiors and local Magnates sitting on Boards of Guardians would seek to water down 'the principles of 1834' when political expediency required them to do so.[84] The Whigs embraced government reform, but not at any price.

The Whigs were both a party and a tradition. Their beliefs did not constitute a rigid ideology, but rather a loosely held set of principles, not all of which would be endorsed by every Whig. If there was a core belief held by all, it was a commitment to liberty, as that concept had been developed by Fox and others during the long period of political and intellectual repression that began in the 1790s.[85]

In conclusion, it is difficult to see why wealthy and influential men would give long-term personal support to the running of a remote rural Union such as Dore Union when in most cases they appeared to get little out of it. They must have had either a strong sense of public and moral duty or strong political motivation to see the swift implementation of Poor Law reform. It might be argued, however, that by taking the administration into their own hands they could hinder the onset of excessive central government control and defend liberty at the same time. As powerful local magnates, men such as the Clives could thwart Edwin Chadwick and the ideologues who surrounded and supported him in his drive for centralisation, by asserting their independence in their own localities. In this way they could sustain their own local power and also defend the poor against the envisaged harshness of the New Poor Law. The Central Authority at Somerset House needed the landowners for the local administration of poor relief: it could not entirely control them. The formation of Boards of Guardians created a powerful local power base, and the men who sat on such Boards were not afraid to use that power.

9 Workhouse Scandals –
Andover and Leominster

In July 1846, John Besley, a pauper inmate of Leominster Union Workhouse, wrote a letter to the Poor Law Commissioners at Somerset House in which he made complaints against the Master and the Matron, Thomas and Elizabeth Woolley, complaints which in effect amounted to accusations of cruelty, neglect and fraud. This was a bold and perhaps rash step to take because in writing directly to the Commissioners, he raised doubts about the probity of the Guardians and their efficiency as a Board, and also risked placing himself in danger by provoking anger and spite in Mr and Mrs Woolley. As far as the Commissioners were concerned, Besley's letter could hardly have arrived at a worse time, because in 1845, Sir George Cornewall Lewis, then the Chief Poor Law Commissioner, was in the unenviable position of having to answer questions before a Parliamentary Select Committee about the effectiveness of the Poor Law Commission in the wake of the scandal of Andover Workhouse, where paupers had been discovered almost at the point of starvation. The repercussions of the Select Committee enquiry rumbled on well into 1846 and although the problems discovered at Leominster were by no means on the same scale as those at Andover, there were similarities.

Workhouse Masters sought to retain the good opinion of their Board of Guardians in support of their position and personal authority and in return it was usual for Boards of Guardians to support the Master against pauper complaints. The Leominster complaint was to show similarities between Andover and Leominster in that both Boards seem to have had undue confidence in and regard for their Workhouse Masters, a confidence which perhaps allowed them to absolve themselves of some of their responsibilities towards their pauper charges. The concentration of power in the hands of Magistrates, Guardians and workhouse officers meant that paupers had little redress against abuse, for few were literate enough to write directly to the Poor Law Commissioners. In cases where paupers were able to write to their own Board of Guardians or threaten to write directly to the Commissioners, as in the case of John Besley at Leominster, the outcome was neither fair nor just. But first the earlier case at Andover must be considered. Ian Anstruther's concise account of events in *The Scandal of the Andover Workhouse* makes sobering reading for anyone, even those readers who might be inclined to dismiss reports of workhouse cruelties as greatly exaggerated stories.

The Master of the workhouse there was a Scotsman named Colin McDougal. He had served in the artillery as a sergeant-major and fought at the Battle of Waterloo, was a firm disciplinarian, efficient in applying rules and regulations to the letter, and ran the workhouse on military lines. He was assisted by his equally efficient and formidable wife, as well as his teenage children, Elizabeth and Joseph, Elizabeth teaching the girls and Joseph the boys. The McDougals presided over a cruel regime in which cuffing, slapping and verbal abuse were commonplace and almost routine, while harsher punishments were inflicted for the most trivial of reasons. A pauper might have his already meagre rations halved for several days or be locked in the dark and eerie dead house (mortuary) overnight simply for speaking at the wrong moment. The Chairman of the Andover Board of Guardians, the Reverend Christopher Dodson, however, would not have a word said against Colin McDougal despite revelations of cruelty and misconduct.

The scandal came to light when one of the Guardians, a farmer called Hugh Mundy, became alarmed by rumours of pauper starvation circulating in the town and decided to investigate. One of the tasks given to workhouse inmates at that time was the crushing of animal bones for fertiliser, bones collected from the kitchens of the gentry, butchers' shops, slaughter houses and hunt kennels. At Andover, it was alleged that paupers were so hungry that in their distress they were driven to eat gristle and bone marrow from the bones they were given to crush, in order to supplement their inadequate diet, and Hugh Mundy's investigations found the allegations to be true. At the commencement of the New Poor Law the Central Authority had provided Boards of Guardians with a choice of several workhouse dietaries of varying quality. The Andover Guardians had chosen the cheapest of these and continued to use it even after it was officially withdrawn by Somerset House as inadequate. The situation was made worse by the fact that for his own benefit, McDougal gave the paupers short weight, thus reducing rations still further, even to the point of drastically watering down the children's milk and ignoring the Medical Officer's orders for additional rations for the sick and for nursing mothers. It was hardly surprising that the paupers were driven to eat almost anything they could find, including meat residues on animal bones and scraps put out for the pigs and chickens.

It seemed unbelievable that a man who inflicted harsh punishments on paupers, abused them with cuffs and shouts, allowed the children to be caned, fought with his wife, visited taverns and returned to the workhouse drunk every Saturday night, did not question the morality or legality of paupers' starvation rations, and took liberties with female paupers, should have been so well thought of by a clergyman who had a duty of care to the poor both as a clergyman and as a Poor Law Guardian. At the enquiry into the running of the workhouse, one Elizabeth Hutchins, a pauper in the workhouse, gave evidence that she had often had sexual intercourse with the Master because her children were starving and that was the only way she could get extra food for them. This raises many questions about the Guardians' ignorance about or indifference towards the running of the workhouse and about the judgement of the Chairman. It also raises questions about the Reverend Dodson's fitness to be a Poor Law Guardian and, even more seriously, his fitness to be a clergyman. After the scandal he continued as Chairman of Andover Workhouse for many years because no one else would take the position, and through his influence Colin McDougal was allowed to resign from his post, meaning that he would not be blacklisted at Somerset House and was free to seek employment as Master of a workhouse in another part of the country.

Andover may have been an extreme case, but while it was clearly in the interest of the Central Authority to believe this, it would be naive to think that similar cases did not exist elsewhere. The Andover Workhouse visiting committee had been criminally neglectful in their duty of care to the inmates and it is to be hoped that the huge publicity which surrounded the scandal may have induced other Boards of Guardians to look more closely at the running of their own workhouses and to question just how much they could trust the officers whom they had appointed. The Andover Workhouse scandal provided the anti-Poor Law campaigners with much ammunition. It was as the reverberations of the case rolled on that John Besley's letter of complaint about the Master and Matron of Leominster Workhouse arrived at Somerset House. It is impossible to know whether the arrival of Besley's letter was carefully timed, but, if he had been able to read newspaper reports of the Andover Scandal, it may have been so.

Thomas Woolley's name first appeared in the Leominster Vestry Minutes in April 1821, when he examined the vestry accounts.[1] He performed the same task in 1822 for which he was paid 10s 6d[2] and in December 1824 he became Vestry Clerk.[3] He held the post without a break from 1824 until 1855,[4] when he was 76 or 77 years old. In addition to being Vestry Clerk, Thomas Woolley was also Workhouse Master, under the Old Poor Law as well as the New Poor Law, from 1818 until his enforced retirement in the autumn of 1850.[5] The fact that he had held these positions for so many years meant that considerable power and influence over poor relief and the lives of applicants had been vested in one man for a generation and more. This was particularly significant because in 1825 Leominster became a Select Vestry, which gave the parish ratepayers the right to appoint a paid Assistant Overseer of the Poor or a Vestry Committee to manage poor relief. It meant also that paupers who had been denied relief by the Select Vestry could no longer appeal to a Magistrate to overturn the decision. He would almost certainly have been placed in a strong position to offer advice to the Overseers of the Poor and the Board of Guardians, and thus to influence decisions about who should or should not be given assistance. At a time when a man's character, or his character as perceived by the ratepayers, contributed greatly to his success in obtaining relief, Woolley's knowledge of pauper families was probably invaluable to the Leominster Select Vestry and to its Poor Law Guardians.

Leominster had possessed a poorhouse or workhouse from the 1730s and unlike other Unions in the county, and indeed the country, it did not borrow funds to build a new workhouse after 1834, but merely adapted existing buildings. This was unusual because the new Boards of Guardians were encouraged by the Poor Law Commission to build new and imposing workhouses of a prison-like appearance, both to add to the deterrent effect and to facilitate the segregation of different classes of pauper. The Leominster Guardians chose the cheap option. In 1739, Priory House and Green had been rented by the Overseers of the Poor as a 'school of industry' for the benefit of the poor of the Borough of Leominster; in 1797 they were leased from Countess Conyngsby for use as a workhouse; and in 1826, a year after the creation of the Select Vestry, they were purchased by Leominster Corporation, who in turn sold them to the Union Guardians in 1837 for £745.[6] Although amendments and alterations were made to the buildings, they were never really adequate for use as a workhouse and as late as 1855, Assistant Poor Law Commissioner John Graves wrote in the visitors' book as follows:

> The workhouse, on my inspection this morning was in a fair state of cleanliness and order. The schoolroom is not sufficiently large for the average number of children in the school. The present vagrant ward is also insufficient. The laundry and workhouse are too small. I concur with the recommendation of the visiting committee dated 18th April, 1855 that, if possible, some additional land should be taken by the guardians.[7]

Somewhat surprisingly, the Guardians' minute books for the Leominster Union during the period 1834-1852 have not survived, and information regarding John Besley's complaint can only be derived from the letter books which hold the correspondence which passed between Leominster Union Guardians and the Poor Law Commission. These letter books contain no hint of any serious problem at Leominster Workhouse until October 1845, when John Besley made his accusations. These raised suspicions about the behaviour of the Woolleys, and also the question of whether the Guardians' confidence in the couple had been misplaced and indeed whether they had been complacent about the running of the workhouse. Specifically, they suggested that the Woolleys may have been misappropriating workhouse food for their own sons outside the workhouse, and had perhaps been using Union property for their own purposes for many years. Little is known about John Besley except that prior to his admission to the workhouse he had been employed in several large country houses, the last of which was Shobdon Court, where he served as butler or under-butler to Lord Bateman. Whilst in the workhouse, he exchanged letters with his brother who lived near Taunton. He was unusual in being a literate pauper with the confidence and the ability to compose as well-drafted a letter as some Union Clerks. He wrote as follows:

> I can swear they have rob'd the inmates of hundreds of pounds of bread, cheese, beef and that there is not a meal but we are wronged of and the House has been like a hotel all summer – a greater hypocrit and liar never put on a pair of shoes – a lad Davies was put in Prison because he returned his cheese it was so little and again for picking up a few crumbs from under the table after supper – next day he had only half allowance. She told him if he spoke another word he would go in again, this was all malice for speaking out about stinking meat with maggots in it and short allowances.[8]

John Besley also described the abuse of a blind and sick pauper who, finding that a meal disagreed with him, asked if he could have bread in place of it. A

Leominster Workhouse, since converted into housing, photographed in 2008

plate and spoon were thrown at him and one assumes that he could not avoid them because of his blindness. He was given a little bread and water for supper and nothing more until dinner the next day. Besley complained, too, about his own treatment whilst sick. It would appear that he was asthmatic and was in a ward where the rain came through the roof onto the bed. He claimed that he should have been put in the infirmary ward, but the workhouse doctor did not consider it necessary. It would no doubt have been part of the control system that the doctor would have resisted any suggestions from a pauper; paupers had to know their place.

During cold snowy weather Besley claimed that he had asked the Matron for more coal for the fire but had been refused. He also claimed that one of the women in the workhouse had asked him to request more coal, but begged him not to mention her name for fear of being put on half-rations. Besley said he would complain to the Guardians but the woman replied that 'It would be of no use as they were all combined together, Magistrates, Guardians, Doctor – and you dare not call your soul your own'. To this Besley added: 'he found it to be true'. He made other accusations about the conduct of the Woolleys, but one further example illustrates the range of alleged abuses. Besley observed that Mr Woolley's sons, and sometimes his grandsons, carried as many as 12 or 14 heavy baskets from the workhouse. If this was so, it is possible that Mr and Mrs Woolley were supplying their sons with provisions from the work-house at the expense of the pauper inmates.

The Commissioners at Somerset House wrote to the Leominster Board of Guardians, enclosing a copy of Besley's letter, and asked them to investigate his accusations. The Guardians did not immediately dismiss Besley's letter, but called both Master and Matron before them to hear it read out. It was signed not only by Besley, but by two other male paupers, and four more men added their marks. Mr and Mrs Woolley either answered the accusa-tions or countered them with accusations of their own about Besley's behav-iour. They stated that the baskets that were carried from the workhouse each week contained their sons' laundry, which Mrs Woolley did for them. It was admitted, too, that sometimes they were given vegetables from the garden which Mr Woolley tended himself. They claimed that John Besley was a diffi-cult pauper and attempted to erode his case and question his morality by stating that he took 'improper liberties' with the female paupers. The Woolleys clearly anticipated a visit from an inspector from Somerset House, and in the days and weeks which followed the reading of Besley's letter prepared to defend themselves by bringing forward paupers who would give statements which supported their position. Charles Gardener, an inmate of four years, and Joseph Howell, an inmate of nine years, both declared that they had no complaints about the workhouse.[9] Milborough Preece accused John Besley of taking 'improper liberties' with her and stated that she had 'kicked his shins well',[10] and Mary Davies, who had acted as cook and nurse for five years, alleged that Besley had behaved improperly towards her when, owing to illness, he had been allowed to remain in bed while the other paupers were at prayer.[11] It is questionable just how much the testimony of these paupers should have been believed; it is quite possible that they were telling the truth, but it is equally possible that they had been bribed or bullied into making their statements. They were, after all, extremely vulnerable as paupers and might have been very nervous about reprisals from the Master and Matron if they refused to co-operate in discrediting Besley. The vulnerability of paupers in workhouses must have meant that in cases such as Besley's the outcome was always likely to favour workhouse officers.

Three of the Leominster Guardians visited the workhouse in the company of the Union Clerk, Mr T. W. Davies, to carry out investigations. The Guardians were Mr Southall, a draper in the town, Mr Newman, also a draper and a local Magistrate, and Edward Evans of Eyton Hall, a local landowner. During the Guardians' examination, Besley attempted to justify his accusations about goods being removed from the workhouse by Mr Woolley's sons by relating one particular incident. On the occasion in question the Master's sons had been carrying 'things' from the workhouse and had used 'rough language' to the workhouse Porter for having locked the door. Later, the Porter's keys were found outside on the grass and he was alleged to have said that it was best not to say anything about the mystery since only the Master's sons were left in the workhouse and they could have had them.[12] Besley stated that the Union Clerk dismissed the story of the keys by saying that 'they could not hear that now', and shortly afterwards he was placed in solitary confinement. Besley claimed that he 'was locked up until three o'clock. It was with difficulty I got my dinner untill I said I would let the Commissioners know of it.' He alleged later that Mr and Mrs Woolley had threatened him and the other paupers who had signed the letter that they would be punished if they wrote again. Besley declared, however, that he would write again as he 'could not have justice'. It was likely that after that encounter the Woolleys decided to take legal advice because the clerk from the office of Mr Hammond, a lawyer, visited the workhouse. It was shortly after this that Mr Woolley denied John Besley access to any writing materials.

At the beginning of November 1846, the Poor Law Commissioners requested copies of the minutes of the Guardians' meetings and were clearly taking Besley's case seriously. On 15 December 1846 Assistant Poor Law Commissioner John Graves was dispatched to inspect Leominster Workhouse. Strangely, his report was dated 31 May 1847, almost six months after the date of his visit, but it does appear that he was thorough in his inspection. He also managed to defuse a very complicated situation and avert more potentially damaging publicity, which was clearly part of his duty. The Commissioners would no doubt have been concerned not to let the matter become public if it could be avoided, particularly so soon after the scandal at Andover Workhouse.

In his report to the Poor Law Commissioners John Graves made a point of the fact that Thomas Woolley had been the Master of Leominster Workhouse for 32 years and that the Guardians thought highly of him and his wife and 'desire their continuance in office'.[13] Reliable and efficient Workhouse Masters were difficult to find and since Thomas Woolley had been well regarded for so long, the Guardians were unlikely to make any hasty decisions about his position. Indeed, Edward Evans of Eyton Hall, one of the Guardians who had visited the workhouse to examine John Besley, was determined to support the Woolleys. He believed that the accusations against them were all lies and that Besley and his followers 'were a set of villains'.[14] Graves, however, was less than enthusiastic in his comments:

> On the whole, it appears to me that Mrs Woolley ought not to be removed and that there is scarcely sufficient reason to remove Mr Woolley, on the ground that he is unfit or incompetent to perform the duties of his office, or that he has refused or wilfully neglected to obey and carry into effect any of the rules orders regulations or bye laws.[15]

Graves had chosen his words very carefully; they were not critical, but neither were they full of praise. They fell short of admonishing the Woolleys, but were sufficiently restrained to ensure that they could not be perceived as any form of recommendation. He was sitting on the fence in order to prevent provoking an inflamed response from either party which might become public. His role was to smooth things over and prevent more damaging publicity for the Poor Law Commission. He was equally careful in his comments about John Besley: critical but not condemnatory. He provided the Guardians with a simple solution to a difficult problem, an expedient which allowed them to rid themselves of Besley without losing face. He reported that:

> John Besley, from his previous habits, is unlike the ordinary inmates of a workhouse in an Agricultural district and had contributed much to spread discontent among his companions. Most of the Guardians seemed to be of the opinion that his assertions were not to be believed. I stated to the Board that I thought it would be better to allow him out-door relief if the Guardians were of the opinion that he was not able bodied.[16]

In his report John Graves exonerated Thomas and Elizabeth Woolley but rebuked them for several relatively trivial matters, including the washing of their sons' laundry in the workhouse, supplying them with vegetables from the workhouse garden, and brewing beer on Union premises. They were strongly supported by the Leominster Guardians and were allowed to continue in office until the autumn of 1850. The Guardians would have continued to employ Mrs Woolley after that, at a salary of £25 per annum, but it was felt that Mr Woolley's infirmity and increasing deafness meant that he 'was unable to maintain that order and discipline essential for making the workhouse a local test of destitution'.[17] At the Guardians' meeting held on 19 July 1850 the Clerk was requested to inform Mr Woolley 'that the Board are under the necessity of calling upon him to retire from his situation as master of the workhouse at the end of three months from this time'.[18] In the 1851 census for Leominster, Mr and Mrs Woolley were recorded as living at 36 Broad Street, next door to one of their sons and his family. Mr Woolley was then 73 and his wife 71 years old.

It was quite possible that Thomas and Elizabeth Woolley were an honest couple who had served the Poor Law in Leominster very well for many years and justly deserved the Guardians' good opinion of them. John Besley was an educated man who was perhaps embittered by his situation and sought to amuse himself by making much of minor abuses in the workhouse. He might have been a trouble-maker and, as described by the Guardian Edward Evans, 'a villain', but it is surprising that an educated man would take the risk of making serious accusations against the Woolleys in writing, if there was no truth in them. He had intimated that it was well known that Mr Woolley had been £400 short in his accounts under the 'Old Law'[19] and would surely have realised the seriousness of such an accusation. If it were proved to be unfounded, legal action for libel might follow and serious consequences ensue as a result. He also claimed that the Master and Matron kept very late hours, particularly after Leominster Races, and perhaps this is what he meant when he said that the workhouse had been 'like an hotel all summer'.

If there was indeed nothing to hide, then the Master and Matron, the Union Clerk and several of the Leominster Guardians went to extraordinary lengths to silence John Besley. After the investigating Guardians and the Union Clerk had examined Besley, he was placed in solitary confinement, presumably while they interviewed other paupers and in the hope that such confinement might bring about a change of attitude. He also claimed that he was threatened by the Woolleys that if he wrote any more letters he would be punished and later, as has been seen, he was denied writing materials. He intimated, too, that some letters from his brother in Somerset had not arrived, and hinted that they had been withheld or suppressed. If he had received the letters, he would have wanted to answer them and it would then have been very difficult for Mr Woolley to deny him materials to do so.

If Mr and Mrs Woolley were as virtuous as the Guardians seemed to consider them to be, one wonders why they did not just ignore Besley's accusations. If they were sure they could be easily refuted, it is curious that they took the measures they did. It is possible, however, that there was a further dimension to the investigation carried out at Leominster Workhouse. It occurred at a difficult time for the Poor Law Commissioners, a time when, as has been noted, the Parliamentary Select Committee set up to investigate the Andover Workhouse Scandal was still working, and the Commissioners would obviously have been anxious not to be faced with more lurid revelations about workhouse abuses. It was more than likely that, being a literate man, Besley was aware of the proceedings of the Select Committee and timed the arrival of his letter carefully, in order to cause the maximum disquiet for the Leominster Guardians and the Central Authority at Somerset House. He might also have been aware of local connections with the Poor Law Commission. At that time the Chairman of the Poor Law Commission was George Cornewall Lewis and his friend Sir Edmund Walker Head was a full Commissioner. It would have been particularly difficult for them to have to answer for a scandal in Herefordshire, a county where they both had so many social and political connections.

George Cornewall Lewis was appointed as the Chief Poor Law Commissioner at the end of January 1839 and remained in that post until 2 August 1847. The timing of his departure was significant: the Poor Law Board Act which replaced the Poor Law Commission with a Board (see below) received the Royal Assent on 23 July 1847. This Act did not come into force until December 1847, but during the months from July to December, the Commissioners were able to dispose of most of the impending cases and arrange the handover of power to the Poor Law Board. On 4 August 1847 George Cornewall Lewis was elected MP for Herefordshire and subsequently held a number of ministerial posts until his election defeat in 1852. Sir. Edmund Walker Head had been appointed a full Commissioner in November 1841 and he too remained in office until 1847, when he was appointed Governor of New Brunswick, later becoming Governor General of Canada. These positions were, however, still in the future and throughout the Andover Scandal and the subsequent Parliamentary Select Committee of Enquiry, they were both Poor Law Commissioners and subject to many criticisms. George Cornewall Lewis was clearly very unhappy about his own situation and poured out his feelings to his friend George Grote in a letter dated 27 January 1847:

> It has been my great object to prevent the attacks of the last session from being used as a means of destroying the central office, and subverting the existing administration of the law ... To be exposed to the insults of all the refuse of the House of Commons without the power of defending oneself, and to have one's chief opponent as the secretary of the board of which one is a member, without the power of dismissing him, is a position nothing but necessity can render tolerable, and which I only submit to for the present because I have no alternative.[20]

The 'chief opponent' he referred to was Edwin Chadwick, with whom working relations had always been difficult. The difficulties began with Chadwick's feeling that he had been ill-used because he had been passed over for an appointment as a Poor Law Commissioner; blue blood was required and his rank and status were seen as an obstacle to such an appointment. S.E. Finer, Chadwick's biographer in 1952, made the point very neatly:

> When, therefore, Chadwick's name came up at the Cabinet table, there was a frosty silence ... 'It was considered that his station in society was not as would have made it fit that he should be made one of the Commissioners.' The Cabinet passed on to the next business.[21]

This was a poor beginning for a new experiment in the centralised control of the Poor Law, for it led to internal dissension at Somerset House which went on for years and did enormous damage to the development of a smooth and consistent administration of relief. Indeed, Finer made the point that: 'The personal hostility between Chadwick and Thomas Frankland Lewis (George Cornewall Lewis's father) began to wreck the administration of the new law from the very outset.'[22] That mutual distrust never went away and was sustained when George Cornewall Lewis followed his father as Chief Poor Law Commissioner in 1839. By 1840, Chadwick had become 'completely estranged from his superiors, and frequently sniped at them for their backsliding from the "principles of 1834"'.[23] He objected when they made substantial concessions to the granting of outdoor relief by withdrawing the Consolidated Order of 1842 and replacing it with a General Order. This order allowed six exceptions to the prohibition of outdoor relief and since different orders were in force in different parts of the country, it made nonsense of the Principle of National Uniformity. Finer encapsulated the differences of policy between Edwin Chadwick and George Cornewall Lewis when he stated that:

> Lewis was eager to bow to the public, Chadwick was determined to thwart it. Where the Consolidated Order operated Lewis continually tried to modify it, but Chadwick maintained it: and where it did not operate Lewis tried to ban it and Chadwick to get it adopted.[24]

Finer also made the point that George Cornewall Lewis seemed to be totally unable to appreciate the connection between the law and its administrative machinery. Finer accepted that:

> It was possible to defend his policy of relaxing the modes of granting relief, but never his indifference to the apparatus of central control. He regarded reductions in his staff of Assistant Commissioners with indifference. He never grasped the importance of centralized and 'adminis-

trative' audit. He brought no support at all to Chadwick's defence of the machinery of administration.[25]

Lewis seemed to be unaware that his indifference to administration was, to some extent, a contributory factor in the failures of the Commission and the criticisms levelled at it. The fundamental differences between Lewis and Chadwick were, however, those of class and of each man's loyalty to the 'principles of 1834'. On the one hand Lewis viewed Chadwick as a social inferior who had ambitions above his station; on the other hand, Chadwick felt betrayed by the false promises of politicians and in particular Lewis's readiness to bow to public opinion at the expense of the Principle of National Uniformity, merely for the sake of political expediency. In his zeal for the New Poor Law and his determination to hold fast to the 'principles of 1834', it was easy to portray Chadwick as the harsh villain of the new, unfeeling and cruel law; a man unable to bend and show any notion of kindness or humanity towards paupers. Indeed, when the Parliamentary Select Committee set up to enquire into the Andover Scandal revealed the antagonistic relations between the Poor Law Commissioners and Chadwick, he was very vulnerable to being made a scapegoat for all the Commission's problems. George Cornewall Lewis had many influential relatives from whom he might expect assistance. In 1844 he had married Lady Teresa Lister, widow of Sir Thomas Henry Lister and daughter of the Honourable George Villiers, the third son of Thomas Villiers, the first Earl of Clarendon, which gave him powerful allies in the Whig Cabinet formed in July 1846. Lord John Russell, the Prime Minister, was Lewis's brother-in-law; the Earl of Minto, the Lord Privy Seal, was Russell's father-in-law; and the Earl of Clarendon, President of the Board of Trade,

Statue of
George Cornewall Lewis
in bronze by
Baron Carlo Marochetti
in front of Hereford's Shire Hall

was also Lewis's brother-in-law. Edwin Chadwick had no such powerful elite on whom he could call for assistance.

The Andover Scandal and the Commissioners' handling of it, coupled with general criticism of the New Poor Law, was a very convenient stick with which to beat the government. John Walter, a Tory MP for Berkshire and owner of *The Times*, sustained an unrelenting attack on the New Poor Law. He hated the very idea of workhouses and feared the absolute power of the Central Commission, against which there would be no appeal.

Indeed the fear of centralism appears to have been powerful. During the Andover Enquiry, Walter had reported on proceedings every day and, as pointed out by Ian Anstruther, he was of the opinion that:

> To use the poor in a cruel experiment to prove that poverty was caused by idleness: to treat them as though they had broken the law, just because they were out of work; to lock them up like convicted criminals, just because they were destitute and hungry, separating husbands and wives and children, and even impounding their simplest possessions; he considered an act of truly monstrous wickedness.[26]

The New Poor Law was an experiment: the first centralised control of poor relief. The intention was to stamp out pauperism, but at the heart of the system there appears to have been confusion about the difference between poverty and pauperism, and it was this confusion which almost certainly led to the harsh treatment of paupers and the excessive level of cruelty which became almost routine at Andover Workhouse. The notion that all poverty was the result of wanton idleness and therefore really pauperism, seems to have prevailed in the minds of some Guardians and workhouse officers. It was arguably the attitude of the Central Authority which caused this idea, for there seem to have been very few Utilitarian zealots on Boards of Guardians. They well understood that poverty had many causes: idleness, old age, sickness, large families, inadequate wages and unemployment. Pauperism, on the other hand, suggested a contentment to live on parish relief, either in aid of wages or in total, whatever economic conditions prevailed. What the Commission and the Guardians really feared was eleemosynary relief; that is, relief which engendered the anticipation of more relief, perhaps from one generation to the next, and a contentment to be dependent on alms. Poverty might become pauperism through circumstances but not necessarily through deliberate intent. That distinction, however, was not always recognised. It was the point that John Walter was making: that poverty was not necessarily the result of idleness. The deterrent effect of the 'Workhouse Test' was cruel when applied sternly, because it failed to make any distinction between pauperism and genuine poverty. In the first few years after 1834 it was assumed that all paupers were culpable in their own destitution, but within a decade there was a softening in public attitudes, probably as a result of the publicity surrounding serious cases of workhouse abuse. It became recognised that children, the old, the sick and, at times of high unemployment, the able-bodied, were not culpable in their own distress and should be treated less severely than once considered appropriate.

It is arguable that the reformers of 1834 never intended that the poor should be treated harshly or punished for their poverty, but merely insisted that the distinction between the genuinely needy and the malingerer was one that needed to be made by everyone. The point was made very neatly by Gertrude Himmelfarb in her lengthy study of poverty when she stated that:

> Introducing the Bill in the House of Commons, Lord Althorp, Chancellor of the Exchequer, admitted that it violated the economic law that required everyone to 'provide his own subsistence by his own labour'. But he went on to defend it as fulfilling a higher law, the religious and human duty to support those who were 'really helpless, and really unable to provide for themselves'. While some of the reformers may have been less interested in helping those who really needed relief than in deterring and punishing those who did not, there is no doubt that the report (and the law) appealed to many who sincerely wanted to do both.[27]

At the time of the Andover Enquiry the Poor Law Commissioners found themselves caught up in a maelstrom of conflicting and changing opinions. The fact that Chadwick was permanent secretary to the Poor Law Commission made his criticisms all the more damning and irksome. In those circumstances it was not surprising that George Cornewall Lewis should have felt as he did when he poured out his frustrations to his friend George Grote. His strong feelings arose not only from the fact that John Graves had been hastily despatched to investigate alleged abuses at Leominster Workhouse. The criticisms and insults he had to face in the Commons as a result of what he saw as Chadwick's betrayal were even more distressing than the possibility that John James might discover another Andover situation so close to home in Leominster. It was possible, perhaps likely, that having satisfied himself that nothing on the scale of the abuse at Andover Workhouse had occurred at Leominster, Graves was content to report back verbally to his superiors at Somerset House and let his written report wait until the ensuing clamour and criticism of the New Poor Law had died down, hence the almost six-month delay in its submission.

The Select Committee of Enquiry into the Andover Workhouse scandal was held in public, with a dozen Andover paupers appearing in the House of Commons to give their evidence in person, as well as McDougal, Dodson, other Andover Guardians and inhabitants. The problems of Andover were examined and extended to include the general workings of the Poor Law Commission and this scrutiny revealed so much of the poisonous atmosphere which had pervaded the administration from the very beginning that the Commission's fate was sealed; it was replaced by the Poor Law Board. Ian Anstruther summarised its demise very neatly:

> Thus, in July, 1847 after a reign of thirteen years, the Poor Law Commission finally expired, hounded to death by public opinion – by the outrage felt by ordinary people against a dictatorial junta whose powers to oppress the starving poor had been used with heartless, doctrinal severity – for whom, luckily, the owner of *The Times* had become the champion and dedicated spokesman.[28]

One wonders if the change from Commission to Board was very much for the better as far as the paupers were concerned. It is more than likely that the only real changes that took place involved improved administrative systems, because the Commission had been reviled for its administrative inefficiency. The Poor Law Board did have the confidence of being permanent, confidence not allowed to the Poor Law Commission. Initially the latter was given a life of five years, and as a result of criticisms about the treatment of paupers, its powers were renewed annually thereafter. The Commissioners were therefore in a precarious political position through their short existence.

It will probably never be known whether the inmates of Leominster Workhouse who supported John Besley's letter of complaint suffered vindictive reprisals at the hands of Mr and Mrs Woolley, for if they did, such reprisals would not have been recorded. It is not clear, either, what became of John Besley, but it is likely that the Guardians took the advice of John Graves and gave him outdoor relief. This could have been done quite easily on the grounds that his asthma justified his exclusion from the class of pauper described as 'able-bodied', but in the absence of some of Leominster Union's minute books it is not possible to prove this. What is clear is that by 1851 he had disappeared; a search of the 1851 census revealed that he was no longer an inmate of Leominster Workhouse, a resident of Leominster or, indeed, living in Herefordshire. There might be a clue to his fate, however in the parish register for Shobdon, because the burial of a John 'Beasley', aged 50, was recorded in 1850.[29] This would make sense because having been turned out of the Leominster Workhouse John Besley would have been returned to the parish in which he last had settlement and no doubt it was convenient, as far as the Leominster Guardians were concerned, to have him out of the town.

Thomas and Elizabeth Woolley continued in office until the autumn of 1850. Their last year as Master and Matron of Leominster Workhouse was, however, a difficult one because there were enquiries into the deaths of two small children: Alfred Page, who died aged six weeks in January, and Benjamin Morgan, who died aged about 5 in October. On 17 January 1850, Mr Watling, the workhouse Medical Officer, wrote in the Indoor Medical Relief Book that an inquest should be held on the infant child of Ann Page 'who died at the workhouse from supposed ill treatment on the part of the mother'.[30] The Visiting Committee investigated and Mr Watling gave an explanation of his concern, but oddly, his comments were not recorded, unlike the details provided by other officers including Mrs Pritchard, the midwife, Ann Wall, the nurse, and several female paupers.

Mrs Pritchard said that she had been present at the birth of the child and commented that the mother was frightened and that the child was sickly and distressed. Ann Wall said that the child was healthy when he was born, 'but soon began to dwindle away'.[31] This was Ann Page's first child and as a very young mother she could not initially suckle him. Two other paupers, Martha Tomkins and Martha Smith, had had to wake her from heavy sleep at night when the baby cried to be fed and had often suckled him themselves. No one had ever seen the mother treat the baby roughly but she had spoken harshly to him when he had cried in the night. This may have been regarded as culpable neglect and given rise to Mr Watling's comment in the Indoor Medical Relief Book. It is more likely, however, that the girl's age and her mental and physical health were the most important factors in the baby's death. If the girl was only 16 or 17 years old and had carried a child to full-term on workhouse rations, she was probably severely undernourished and physically exhausted. It might be argued, though, that if 'less eligibility' applied, her condition might have been no different outside the workhouse. The Visiting Committee concluded 'that there is no ground for a coroner's inquest as suggested by Mr Watling, but some degree of blame attaches to the mother of the child for neglect and also to the nurse for not communicating the state of the child to the Medical Officer'.[32] The blame had gone as far down the workhouse hierarchy as it could go; it was common for nurses to be blamed. They were often paupers themselves and therefore in an invidious position. Ann and Alfred Page could be seen as victims of circumstance, and seem to have derived more help from other paupers than from the workhouse officers employed to care for them.

In October 1850, just before Thomas and Elizabeth Woolley relinquished their positions as Master and Matron of Leominster Workhouse, Benjamin Morgan died and a formal inquest was held. The proceedings were presided over by the Deputy Coroner, one Henry Thomas Fluck, who conducted a very thorough enquiry. Benjamin Morgan had been admitted to Leominster Workhouse on 6 March 1849. He was an illegitimate child who had either been deserted or orphaned, because there was no mention of his natural parents. He had been, therefore, a member of arguably the most vulnerable class of pauper in the workhouse; he was alone and entirely the responsibility of the workhouse officers. The inquest revealed that he was always of a weak constitution, appearing to suffer acutely from digestive difficulties and bowel problems, and had been confined to the infirmary ward on several occasions. Hannah Twigg, the Schoolmistress, was blamed for the boy's decline because it was suggested that she sometimes gave his food to the other children. It may simply have been the case, however, that at times the boy could not eat his food and she had given it to the other children, who were only too ready to eat it, so that it would not be wasted. She was not actually admonished for allegedly depriving the boy of his food, but she was blamed for not reporting his condition to the Medical Officer. She had, however, discussed Benjamin's digestive problems with the Matron and as a result of their talks, his diet was amended and he was fed on milk, sago, rice and arrowroot. It was, though, too little too late, because the child died of 'wasting'. It was indeed strange that neither Hannah Twigg nor Elizabeth Woolley thought it necessary to draw Benjamin Morgan's worsening condition to the attention of the workhouse Medical Officer.

It would be easy to blame the two women for neglecting Benjamin, and they justly deserve some blame, but some of the jurors were of the opinion that the Medical Officer was also culpable. The boy had been confined to the infirmary ward on several occasions and was known to be a sickly child and that being so, the Medical Officer, from his routine visits to the workhouse, ought to have been aware of the child's delicate health and weak constitution. It was possible, of course, that it was thought that the death of such a child was inevitable; he was, after all, illegitimate and a pauper, of 'tainted stock' and therefore inherently weak and unlikely to survive. The verdict was 'natural causes'. There was heavy criticism of the workhouse Schoolmistress, Hannah Twigg, as well as the Visiting Committee, but no real blame was levelled at the Matron. Benjamin Morgan may have died of natural causes, but the circumstances surrounding his care, decline and death suggested neglect – neglect in which several workhouse officers were culpable. The main blame, however, was placed firmly on Hannah Twigg. The Guardians of Leominster Union however confirmed their confidence in the Schoolmistress, but she resigned a few weeks later. Once again the blame had travelled down the hierarchy as far as it could go, but at least the Coroner indicated that the Visiting Committee were also 'open to censure',[33] a point reinforced by Poor Law Inspector, Edward Hurst, when he visited the workhouse some time later. He informed them they must be vigilant, 'especially with regard to children'.[34]

One might wonder where the Chaplain of Leominster Workhouse was during the enquiries into child deaths and the Besley affair. The letter books containing the correspondence between the Poor Law Commission and the Leominster Guardians show that a Reverend J. Bartlett was appointed

Chaplain in March 1842,[35] with a salary of £25 per annum, and that the Reverend Charles Walter Robinson was appointed at the same salary in January 1846,[36] but it seems almost certain that in the problematic year of 1850, the Union did not have a Chaplain and that there was considerable opposition to making a new appointment. The Guardians' minutes recorded that they were still refusing to appoint a Chaplain as late as June 1853,[37] probably on the grounds of expense, as in that same month the Guardians wrote to the Poor Law Board to ask if it would sanction the appointment of a Chaplain who was paid by private subscription, rather than one who was paid a salary by the Guardians.[38] The Poor Law Board replied that it would not be happy to sanction such an arrangement, but that it would approve an appointment in which the Chaplain received a low salary, because a small salary would still place the Chaplain under the authority of the Guardians.[39] This point was very important, because it would affect the Central Authority's system of control. If the Chaplain were to be paid by anyone other than the Guardians, the Central Authority would lose control and in the hierarchy of the Poor Law, the status of the Chaplain was considered to be very important. The Guardians' refusal to appoint a Chaplain had led to the resignation of one of their own number, the Reverend Charles Edward Evans of Eyton Lodge, Curate Perpetual of Lucton and son of Edward Evans of Eyton Hall. The Reverend Evans had been a Guardian for several years and at the time of his resignation he was Vice-Chairman of the Board. Despite the Guardians' entreaties he refused to return; and the Guardians continued to refuse to appoint a Chaplain.

If there had been a diligent Chaplain making regular visits to the workhouse to conduct services and also making impromptu calls, he would have been aware of the general condition of the paupers and in particular he might have been alerted to the problems of inadequate child care which led to the deaths of Alfred Page and Benjamin Morgan. Since there was no Chaplain at that crucial time, the Leominster Guardians would have only known about the running of the workhouse from written reports and from what they were told by the Master and other officers. Prior knowledge of the imminent arrival of the Visiting Committee would have meant that plans could be made in readiness for their inspection. One wonders why the Leominster Guardians were so strongly against the appointment of a Chaplain and indeed why the Central Authority had not applied some pressure to the Board for an appointment to be made. It is clear from the minutes of 1853 that parsimony was one reason for their obdurate attitude, but there might have been another reason, namely religious dissent. Two of the Guardians involved in the examination of John Besley, Mr Southall and Mr Newman, were almost certainly related and members of two prominent Quaker families in the town. It was also possible that a number of the other Guardians were from nonconformist backgrounds and that the Reverend Evans was confronted with resistance which emanated from fear of proselytism and deep-seated antagonism towards the payment of church rates.

The Churchwardens of a parish church were free to levy a church rate on the owners and occupiers of property for the maintenance of the church building, the graveyard and the boundary wall, irrespective of their religious beliefs. At Leominster, however, the church rate seems to have been a particular problem, because the Churchwardens were often obstructed in their collection of it by nonconformists who felt it to be unjust. Some who were entitled to attend vestry meetings as parish ratepayers in the general sense took the opportunity to oppose the spending of church rate revenues and rather than pay the rate, preferred to have their possessions distrained for unpaid charges. Quaker John Southall, a draper, and his brother Samuel, a grocer, both Leominster Union Guardians, were all too familiar with having goods distrained. Remaining true to their convictions caused considerable distress – the humiliation of having personal possessions removed for public sale in pursuit of a legal obligation which was manifestly unjust. One such occasion was described by Hannah Southall, John Southall's wife, in a letter to their son, John Tertius, in August 1838.[40] She stated:

> We have at length had the long expected seizure for church rates, and it proved quite as trying, or more so, than I had expected. They came last week on market day. The Superintendent of the police with one of his men entered the house, producing the warrant, and then proceeded to perform his office. They first took a round mahogany table out of the counting house. Next four of the parlour chairs which were in that room and then they ... walked into the kitchen and seized my nice copper stew pan and the small round table which the servants need in the evenings. Altogether amounting in value to about four pounds –

a sum which she considered to be more than the warrant demanded. Samuel Southall also had goods taken that day, and so did other members of the Society of Friends, and quite probably members of other dissenting groups too. The distraint of goods for non-payment of church rate, tithes and militia duty appears to have occurred quite frequently and if there happened to be a significant number of nonconformist Guardians on the Leominster Board, their presence was almost certainly a factor in the sustained opposition to appointing a new Union Chaplain. The full truth, of course, is unlikely ever to be known, but in the face of overwhelming resistance, perhaps the Reverend Evans felt that resigning as a Poor Law Guardian was the only way he could really make a point. Taking into account the events and enquiries of 1850, however, it is surprising that the Leominster Guardians still failed to see that the appointment of a diligent Chaplain might act as a safeguard against possible problems in the future. When problems did arise, the approaches adopted for their effective management differed depending on the Poor Law Authority involved. The Central Authority tried to avoid damaging publicity, clarified legal points for the Board of Guardians concerned, and attempted to smooth things over. The Besley case was a clear example of this. Left to their own enquiries, Boards of Guardians generally adopted a position of apportioning blame and pushing that blame as far down the poor law hierarchy as it would go, as in the case of Benjamin Morgan.

It is almost certainly true to say that the abuses at Leominster were far less serious and cruel than those at Andover, but in both workhouses the problems arose for the same reasons: that too much power over the lives of paupers was concentrated into too few hands for too many years. The Reverend Christopher Dodson, who thought so much of Colin McDougal, was Chairman of Andover Union from 1836 until the end of his days in 1876. Edward Evans of Eyton Hall, whose support for Thomas and Elizabeth Woolley never seemed to waver, was Chairman of Leominster Union from 1836 until his retirement in 1852. The concentration of power in the hands of men who were landowners, employers, Magistrates, clergymen and Poor Law Guardians, meant that they were a force against which the poor could never contend. It is ironic that men whose role in the administration of poor relief was supposedly to act as defenders and protectors of the poor should preside over such iniquities as those suffered by the paupers at Leominster and especially those at Andover and, at the same time, be styled 'Poor Law Guardians'.

Gertrude Himmelfarb makes the point, however, that after the middle of the 19th century, as the political ideology which underpinned the New Poor Law began to change, so did the Poor Law itself. In the conclusion to her study of poverty she states that:

> As poverty – the normal poverty of the normal working classes – became less onerous and less problematic, the idea of poverty became normalized and 'moralized'. The stigma that had attached to poverty in the aftermath of the New Poor Law and in the turmoil of the thirties and forties gradually disappeared; whatever stigma remained was reserved for the dependent and unrespectable poor, those who existed on the margins of society or were outcasts from society. The bulk of the poor, the 'working classes' as they were increasingly called, were seen as respectable, deserving, worthy, endowed with the puritan virtues which had served the middle classes so well, and which were shortly to earn the working classes that coveted badge of respectability, the suffrage.[41]

10   Pauper Apprentices – Bromyard

The most vulnerable paupers under the Old Poor Law were the children: orphaned children, abandoned children, and destitute children from large families. Under the Old Poor Law infants and small children were often put into the care of 'nurses' – local women who were paid 1s 6d or 2s per week from the poor rates to rear the children. Five of the six parishes in Hereford City who responded to the Poor Law Commission's request for information in 1832 stated that children were provided for in that way, or that a similar allowance was given to their parents, scaled in relation to the age of the child.[1] Bromyard answered in a similar manner and confirmed that weekly payments were made when necessary. The Overseer and the Curate for Kington stated: 'We allow them 1s 6d a head until nine years of age, when they are put out as apprentices'.[2] At Ross the Overseer, John Hardwick, stated that the children were: 'Mostly under the care of their parents, who occasionally apply to the Vestry, where their petition is received: and if it appears that they need assistance, it is ordered, which forms the major part of our casualties. At nine years old they are put out as parish apprentices.'[3] The allowances to parents were, however, often withdrawn if they refused to let their children be apprenticed at that age.

It would appear from the evidence available that in Herefordshire there existed a fairly general policy of leaving young children with their families as far as possible and of making small allowances as and when absolutely necessary, rather than taking them into the poorhouses where such existed. Although this system of subsidising families was probably the most economic and humane solution to the problem of low wages, it would not have been at all acceptable to Edwin Chadwick and other orthodox Benthamites as the New Poor Law was formulated. On the one hand, the removal of children deemed to be neglected by their parents was the cause of resentment and on the other, it was certainly pertinent to question whether children removed to a poorhouse would have been endangered by its lax atmosphere and management. In some parishes, All Saints and St Nicholas in Hereford, for example, the dangers of placing children in a poorhouse where they might have been subjected to the

wrong type of influences appeared to be recognised, and orphaned or abandoned infants were put out to nurses, even though these parishes maintained
their own poorhouses. At the tender age of 9 or 10, sometimes even as young
as 7, boys were placed with farmers or tradesmen as parish apprentices, but
it is likely that for many the training they received was insufficient to teach
them a trade which would provide them with a living for the rest of their lives.
Boys were frequently apprenticed to 'husbandry', which really meant farm
labouring, and girls were often apprenticed to 'housewifery', which probably
meant that they were merely house servants. Although proper apprenticeship
indentures were usually completed, it was unusual for an apprenticeship fee
to be paid for children apprenticed in this way, which suggests that ratepayers
were often put under pressure to take parish apprentices from time to time in
order to relieve pressure on the poor rates. In some parishes where a ratepayer
was reluctant to take a particular individual as an apprentice, he could absolve
himself by paying a £10 fine. Where indentures survive, it is clear that apprenticeship fees tended to be paid only to dressmakers, tailors, shoemakers or
milliners – trades which might really provide a youngster with an income for
life. Thus, there seemed to be a dual system of apprenticeships in operation:
one for children who were employed as gardeners, farm labourers or house
servants simply to meet the social obligations of ratepayers, and a second
for able children who were apprenticed to a tradesman who really needed an
apprentice and accepted a fee from the parish for his training.

A large number of apprenticeship indentures have survived for the townships of Norton, Winslow and Linton in the parish of Bromyard. They begin in
the year 1730, and although some are incomplete, they provide a glimpse into
the world of parish apprenticeships and also indicate that they were a means of
providing for pauper children for generations. Amongst these indentures there
are nine for boys apprenticed to husbandry who were bound to their masters
until the age of 24, with no mention of the customary release from apprenticeship on the day of marriage if that should occur before the fixed term of
years. These date from 1741 to 1775 and thereafter the usual age was 21.
The only indenture for a girl being apprenticed to the age of 24 was for Mary
Jones[4] of Norton Township, who was bound to William Inett in August 1817,
to be trained in housewifery, and once again, there was no mention of release
from the agreement on the day of marriage. The nature of parish apprenticeships probably changed over several generations, as a result of changing social
and economic circumstances. It was possible that ratepayers were finding it
increasingly costly to maintain apprentices until the age of 24 and that many
apprentices, even in situations where they had been well or at least fairly
treated, were anxious to be able to pursue adult life free from interference.
By the late 1770s, all existing indentures entered into by the Overseers of
the Bromyard townships did not extend beyond the age of 21. Although the

wording of parish indentures varied a little over time, the general format and conditions remained very much the same. Occasionally, however, when a boy was apprenticed to a recognised tradesman and apprenticeship fees were paid by his parish, he might be bound only until he was 18 years of age. In January 1798, Thomas James, aged 11, of Linton Township was apprenticed to William Jay, a shoemaker of Bromyard, until the age of 18, for which the parish paid a fee of £2 1s.[5]

An analysis of the 50 indentures with dates nearest to the introduction of the New Poor Law, 1788-1834, indicates that 36 were for boys, most of whom were apprenticed to 'husbandry', one was for tailoring, one for shoemaking and on four indentures no profession was given. Of the 14 girls, 10 were apprenticed to 'housewifery' and for the remainder no profession was given. The majority of the children, both boys and girls, were placed as apprentices between the ages of 8 and 11, and these findings appear to correlate with the responses given in the Poor Law Report of 1834. The vexed problem of supporting destitute children had existed for generations and while parish apprenticeships may have eased the pressure on the parish rates for a while, they were not a solution. Once a child was apprenticed, the parish transferred responsibility for the child to his master until the end of the apprenticeship. At the end of the apprenticeship, however, if the young adult was unemployed he once more became the responsibility of the parish, unless he had been apprenticed in another parish, in which case that parish became responsible.

In Bromyard most children were apprenticed in their own parish or one very near to it, with very few moving more than four or five miles. In such a rural area it was likely that the opportunity to do otherwise was severely limited, but there were exceptions. In July 1820, Ann Cost, aged 11, was apprenticed to William Porter of Hereford to be trained in housewifery.[6] In August 1823, two boys, probably brothers, Francis Totney, aged 11, and Henry Totney, aged 9, of the township of Norton, were apprenticed to one William Correy of Dudley in Worcestershire, but no trade was recorded.[7] Under the Old Poor Law these were parish decisions, and an insular rural community such as Bromyard may have adopted the policy of keeping parish apprentices near to home. If children were apprenticed in their own parish or one close to it, it would have been possible for a child who was being badly treated to go home or to the parish overseer or the vicar to seek help. It may be that this was the course followed by William Hinton, a boy who was released from his apprenticeship after only a few months.

William Hinton was apprenticed, aged 10, to one Elizabeth Vale on the usual terms. He was apprenticed on 10 December 1832 and released from his apprenticeship on 1 April 1833. The case was considered by two Justices of the Peace for Herefordshire who upheld the boy's complaints:

Whereas complaint has been made before us John Barnaby Esquire and Charles Scott Luxmore Dean of Saint Asaph two of his Majesty's Justices of the Peace in and for the said County by William Hinton a Parish Apprentice to Elizabeth Vale of the Parish of Avenbury in the said County of Hereford that she the said Elizabeth Vale has misused and evil treated him the said apprentice and whereas the said Elizabeth Vale has appeared before us in pursuance of our Summons for that purpose yet has not cleared herself of and from the said accusation and complaint, but on the contary [*sic*] the said William Hinton has made full proof of the truth thereof before us upon Oath. We therefore by these presents do discharge him ... of and from his apprenticeship to said Elizabeth Vale any thing in the Indentures of Apprenticeship, whereby the said William Hinton is bound to the said Elizabeth Vale to the contary notwithstanding. And we do hereby order that she ... shall upon due notice hereof forthwith deliver up to the said Apprentice his clothes and wearing apparel and also pay immediately to the Churchwardens or Overseers of the Poor of the Township of Winslow in the said County to which Parish the said Apprentice belongs, some or one of them, the Sum of Five Pounds, to be applied by them, ... under our order for the benefit of the said Apprentice as to us shall seem meet. Given under our hands and seals the first day of April One thousand eight hundred and thirty three.[8]

The Justices did not specify the manner in which William Hinton was abused, but they clearly recognised that he had been unfairly treated and had little hesitation in cancelling his indentures.

In a rural county such as Herefordshire, it was more than likely that most parish apprentices would be working on farms if they were boys and as house servants if they were girls. Their masters would have been able to maintain them relatively cheaply and control them easily from the ages of 10 to 16, but once they reached adulthood, costs and difficulties might grow once the apprentice tried to assert some independence. It may also have been the case that some apprentices did not complete their apprenticeships, absconding in their late teens to seek higher wages in towns and cities. Apprentice masters perhaps came to accept that it was easier to be rid of them at 17 and take on a new, younger and more malleable apprentice. The rudimentary nature of apprenticeship administration makes it impossible to arrive at a definite point of view; there is insufficient evidence but there are clues which throw some light on ratepayers' views.

In response to the Poor Law Commission's question on settlement laws and extending the labour market, the Assistant Overseer of Weobley, John Whiting, made the point that: 'Parish apprentices should be bound till 17 years of age instead of 21; parishioners object to having them bound till they are 21.'[9] It is impossible to know just how far this opinion obtained amongst ratepayers of other parishes, but if it was a commonly held view, it may be supposed that once apprentices reached adulthood they were likely to become too much of a financial liability, particularly in the case of girls. Parishioners' objections to having apprentices bound until the age of 21 would make more sense if the parish in question was operating a modified or disguised form of the Roundsman System; under this system individual parish ratepayers were required to take unemployed labourers for fixed periods of time and to pay them the current rate for their labour, whether they had work for them to do or not, and then, when the fixed time had expired, the labourers were moved on to the next ratepayer whose turn it was to take them. In the Poor Law Report of 1834, however, the Herefordshire parishes which responded either denied any use of the Roundsman System or left the relevant question unanswered. John Whiting of Weobley stated quite clearly that the Roundsman System was not in use in that parish, although it was quite apparent that a modified form of the system had been in use in the past. The evidence for this can be seen in an entry in the Weobley Vestry Minutes dated 25 September 1800:

> At a Vestry meeting it was agreed by the Parishioners then present to allow the present Overseer of the Poor a Rate or Assessment at the Rate of 5/6 in the pound and ... also do agree to send what children are fit to go [*sic*] apprentices into the Cotton Manufactory at Sheffield in Yorkshire and the cost of indenturing and taking them there to be paid by the persons whose turn it is to take apprentices in the parish.[10]

If, as this passage suggests, the ratepayers of Weobley had apprentices imposed upon them, it would have been understandable, as the Assistant Overseer stated, if they objected to apprentices being bound until the age of 21. Although no evidence has been found to prove that the parishioners of Bromyard thought similarly, the apprenticeship indentures of one Bromyard lad were cancelled by mutual consent when he reached the age of 17. It may be significant that he was apprenticed to a woman; that is, if he was intelligent and a strong personality, Anne Lawrence, his 'master' may have found it difficult to order his work, duties and routine. This, however, is pure conjecture, and there may have been any number of innocent or circumstantial reasons for the cancellation of his apprenticeship.

As the 19th century dawned and parishes such as Weobley prepared to send more batches of vulnerable young children to cotton factories many miles from home, the Overseers and Churchwardens of Ledbury, by comparison, continued to sustain a gentler attitude towards the treatment of children in their care. The minutes of the Overseers' meetings for the years 1803 to 1818[11] show that orphaned and abandoned infants and young children were not farmed out to nurses, but were reared at the workhouse in Church Lane and were the responsibility of the Matron. This is likely to have been the best arrangement to ensure their survival. The workhouse appears to have been generally well regulated and it was inspected on a daily basis by one of the eight members of the Board of Assistants who were elected from amongst the ratepayers to help the overseer in his duties. The visiting Assistants recorded their findings in a log book and these entries were checked and considered at each weekly meeting and the names of the visiting Assistants for the following week were recorded. Their signed comments indicate that they were quite diligent in their inspections, suggesting that the children reared in Ledbury Workhouse were probably safer and better cared for than those in many others which were less well regulated.

In his book *Workhouse Children*,[15] Frank Crompton notes that by 1780 three distinct types of parish apprenticeship had evolved: local labouring apprenticeships which provided no real training; those where precise training was given by a tradesman who received an indenture fee; and those in which batches or small groups of children were sent to distant cotton or carpet factories as cheap labour to carry out menial tasks. It is likely that all were in general use in Herefordshire, though evidence from the records of Weobley, Bromyard and Ledbury confirm that not all parishes used all three forms. The system was rife with inconsistencies and a prey to those who were able to manipulate it to their own advantage with little regard for the children. The reforms which were brought into being with the New Poor Law meant that orphaned children, abandoned children and poor children from large families would no longer be farmed out to nurses or supported by giving their parents an allowance from the poor rate. They would be looked after in the Union Workhouse. An initial moratorium was called on apprenticeships and it lasted for almost a decade. When they were reintroduced, the nature of apprenticeships had changed; far fewer boys were apprenticed to husbandry as cheap farm labour, or girls to housewifery as cheap house servants. They were either apprenticed to an individual master to learn a particular craft, or sent many miles away to be apprenticed in a cotton factory, a flax mill or a carpet weaving factory in Kidderminster, Sheffield, Manchester or Bristol. There was, however, much tighter control; Boards of Guardians insisted on more detailed information about the conditions attached to the apprenticeship before they would give their sanction. In 1842, rules for apprenticing were created by Robert Weale, Assistant Poor Law Commissioner for the West Midlands Region, and these formed the basis of the Pauper Apprentice Regulations which were laid down in 1844. The Union Medical Officer had to certify that the apprentice was fit for the work he or she was to do; the apprentice had to be able to read and write; and the terms of the apprenticeship, including wages, living conditions and a residence address, had to be laid down on the indenture. The imposition of strict apprenticeship rules probably added to the costs of Herefordshire Unions, but was beneficial to the welfare of apprentices. If apprenticed, a youngster's apprenticeship fee had to be paid; if he was not apprenticed, however, he would probably remain in the workhouse and have to be maintained well into his teens, as opposed to being maintained to nine or ten years old under the Old Poor Law. Under the Old Poor Law children were usually maintained at home or in the workhouse until 8, 9 or 10, depending on the ratepayers' decision, and then apprenticed, usually without a fee unless precise training was to be given by a craftsman. Under the New Poor Law children (deserted or orphaned) had to stay in the workhouse unless an apprenticeship with very precise conditions was agreed. Parents with children outside the workhouse could, however, seek help with apprenticeship fees. Boards of Guardians appear to have been quite diligent in making enquiries about the conditions in which children would work and live, but the fate of these children was still not assured and remained largely a matter of luck. A youngster might receive fair treatment and be taught a trade which would enable him to earn his living for the rest of his life; on the other hand, he might have good cause to run away from his master if he was abused. Much depended on the diligence of individual Boards of Guardians in checking up on masters and their treatment of their apprentices.

In October 1845 the Guardians of Dore Union considered the problem of Henry Green[16] and his master, a Mr Seal, a tailor who lived and worked in the parish of Kingstone. It appeared that the boy had repeatedly run away, wandered about the district for a while and then asked for relief. The Guardians do not appear to have thought it necessary to ask why the boy ran away, or if they did, their deliberations were not entered into the minutes, and after due consideration, it was agreed that the Constable of Abbeydore should again be directed to return Henry Green to his master. It may simply have been the case that the boy was immature or just not suited to the work, but one wonders whether he really did have cause to run away. Whatever the reason, Dore Union Guardians did not seem to be at all concerned about it, only about having to pay another fee to the constable to ensure the boy's return to his master. In January, 1837 the Kington Guardians decided that three or four children 'who are troublesome to the parish'[17] should be apprenticed. It was not made clear why they were troublesome, whether it was their behaviour, their cost to the parish or simply that they were neglected by their parents. Whatever the reason, they were split up and apprenticed out of the way. The decision of the Kington Guardians is significant in that it reveals their real attitude to pauper children: they were a nuisance, a liability and an avoidable expense. Apprenticing them out of the parish would have transferred their maintenance to their new parish. The poor rate had to be kept down at all costs.

Later that year, Edward Lewis, a cripple, son of Edward Lewis, a pauper of Old Radnor, was apprenticed to Richard Knowles, a shoemaker of Kington, and a fee of £10 was paid by the Board of Guardians.[18] In February 1852 Leominster Guardians agreed to bind Richard Purnall as apprentice to William Child, a blanketmaker of Hereford. Both parties attended the Board and Mr Child was paid half of his fee of £15.[19] A year later, almost to the day, 18 February 1853, Mr Child applied for the second payment of £7 10s, and since master and apprentice had both declared themselves satisfied, Mr Child was paid immediately.[20] A month later it was also recorded in Leominster Union minutes that one George Thomas, a merchant of Bristol, had written to the Board and stated that he could arrange a place on a merchant vessel for James Davies, a 16-year-old in Leominster Workhouse, for a premium of £5, and the Board agreed.[21] In July 1842, James Vaughan, a dyer, agreed to take Philip Harris of the parish of Burghill in Hereford Union, aged 14, for a period of seven years, with an allowance of two suits of clothes.[22]

By the late 1840s the details of apprenticeships involving one master and one child were becoming more precise, as the following examples from Ross Union make clear. At a meeting held on 26 June 1848, the Reverend T.T. Lewis requested that the Board pay the apprenticeship fees for William Price of the parish of Bridstow, aged 14, to be bound to Charles Jones, a tailor in the neighbouring parish of Hentland. He was to be bound for five years, after a premium of £15 had been paid, but Mr Jones had to agree to pay the boy 1s per week in year four of his apprenticeship and 1s 6d per week in year five.[23] The indentures were drawn up, the boy's mother, Mary Price, signed them, and the Board's seal was added at a meeting of the Board held on 21 August 1848.[24] In February 1849 a boy named James Pymble, aged 12, was apprenticed to a Ross shoemaker, Thomas Evans, and since the Board's minute suggested a tightening of apprenticeship procedures it is quoted here in full:

> Pursuant to directions received by him to that effect, Mr Dobles made his report with reference to James Pymble a poor boy of the age of 12 years 4 months whom it was proposed to bind apprentice to Thos. Evans of Ross, Shoemaker. He also produced a certificate from Charles Edmund Thomson the Medical Officer of the District as to his fitness for the proposed Trade and such Report and Certificate being satisfactory and in compliance with the Rules and Orders of the Poor Law Commissioners, Resolved that James Pymble be bound apprentice by the Guardians to the said Thos. Evans for the term of 5 years that a premium of £11 16s 4d be paid with him of which £1 16s 4d shall be in clothes and of the residue one half be paid down and the other half in twelve months and that during the last year of the Term the said Thomas Evans shall pay the said James Pymble 1/- per week. Indentures of apprenticeship were prepared accordingly and signed by the sd. Thomas Evans and James Pymble and by John Pymble the Father of the said James Pymble as a consenting party thereto and the Common Seal of the Guardians was also affixed to the said Indentures.[25]

There were far fewer apprenticeships recorded in the minutes of Guardians' meetings for girls; it might be supposed that they would be less willing to spend money on indentures for girls who were likely to marry and thus become the responsibility of their husbands. The ease with which they could usually find employment in domestic work was also likely to have been a factor. Two apprenticeships for girls have been found, however, in the Guardians' minutes for Hereford Union. In May 1846 Anna or Hannah Wood of Fownhope parish, aged 14, was apprenticed to Mrs Susan James for three years to learn dress-making and a premium of £10 was paid.[26] In April 1847 Emma Hareland was apprenticed to Thomas Fenn, a boot and shoemaker of Church Street, Hereford, but it was not clear whether she was to learn shoemaking or to be apprenticed as a house servant; perhaps the latter was the more likely.[27]

Whilst it appears that the coming of the New Poor Law brought a tightening up of the procedures of apprenticing an individual child to an individual master to learn a specific craft, the situation seems to have been far less clear when children were apprenticed to manufacturers many miles from their home parish. It is almost certainly true that individual Boards of Guardians were aware of the dangers of apprenticing batches or small groups of children to factories in distant towns and cities – indeed the details recorded in their minute books reflect their caution – but it did also provide an opportunity to reduce Union expenses. Children from Herefordshire Unions were sometimes sent to factories in Kidderminster, Bristol and Manchester, but it was not at all clear what their apprenticeship really meant and indeed whether they would actually learn a trade or merely be cheap labour to perform menial tasks. The child's position was also unclear if the man to whom he was bound left the employment of one manufacturer and took employment with another; there appears to have been confusion about who exactly was responsible for the child's general welfare.

A number of Poor Law Unions in Herefordshire and Worcestershire appear to have had some kind of understanding about the apprenticing of boys in the carpet-weaving factories of a company named McMichael and Grierson, which had factories in Worcester, Kidderminster and Bridgnorth and perhaps other towns too. In November 1839 the Hereford Board of Guardians were corresponding with the company with the aim of sending boys as apprentices to one of their factories. The initial letter received by the Guardians was businesslike, but quite genial in tone and no doubt phrased carefully to engender confidence in the proposed arrangements. It is worth quoting in full for that reason. It also expressed some concern for the safety of the boys and it was suggested that they should not be sent to Bridgnorth alone, but in the company of an adult provided by the Board of Guardians. The letter was dated 25 November 1839:

Sir. In reply to your letter of the 21st Inst. we beg to say we have 3 men who are willing to have the 3 boys you have selected as apprentices on the same conditions as the Worcester Board have apprenticed 4 boys to some of our men viz – The boys are apprenticed for 7 years. The Board gave them each a good suit of clothes, a pair of shoes and a Bible, also paid their Coach fare to Bridgnorth and gave each of the Men a Sovereign. We shall be glad if you will not require the Men to come to Hereford, as they cannot afford to lose their time and the expenses of travelling – Should your Board agree to the above terms you may send the Boys as soon as you please – It will be quite unnecessary to send the Indentures for our perusal as the Common Indenture filled up for 7 years apprenticeship is all that is required. The Worcester Board gave the Boys a months trial before they bound them. If you should not send any one with the boys please write us saying how and when you send them and we will take care they are attended to but we think it would be better to send a person with them. Any further in formation you may require we shall be happy to give.[28]

The minutes of Hereford Board of Guardians for a meeting held on 15 November 1839 make it clear that the initiative for placing the three orphan boys or three bastards with McMichael and Grierson had come from the Assistant Poor Law Commissioner for Herefordshire, Sir Edmund Walker Head.[29] He had sanctioned their apprenticeship in the carpet-weaving factory at Kidderminster, but they were ultimately sent to Bridgnorth. Sir Edmund had clearly had similar discussions with the Bromyard Board of Guardians and probably with the other Boards in Herefordshire. At a meeting of the Bromyard Guardians held on 18 November 1839 a letter from Sir. Edmund was read on the subject of placing boys as apprentices with McMichael and Grierson and the Guardians decided to ask for further details.[30] This initiative is curious in that it occurred during the period of the moratorium on apprenticeships. The fact that it happened at all probably reflected Sir Edmund's personal influence in Herefordshire; he had many relatives, personal friends, social acquaintances and political allies within the county. He also had the powerful backing of Thomas Frankland Lewis, the Chief Poor Law Commissioner at Somerset House. The company replied that it had openings for two boys, and after a number of substitutions had been made, Joseph Wood and Samuel James were nominated, and some time later a third boy, William Caust, was included. The very casual way in which the substitutions were made perhaps says much about the nature of such apprenticeships: in the case of individual pauper apprenticeships such substitutions would have been unthinkable. A long correspondence then followed between the Board of Guardians and McMichael and Grierson and, though mundane in nature, the letters serve well to illustrate how eager the Bromyard Guardians were to get the boys bound to a master and rid themselves of their maintenance.

The Board agreed to pay the substantial sum of 20s expenses to the men to whom the boys were to be bound for each journey they were required to make to Bromyard to complete the boys' indentures.[31] The company wrote to the Board, however, stating that the men could not be spared to travel to the Board and requested that they send the nominated boys on a month's trial.[32] A week later the company wrote again concerning clothes for the boys and having agreed to their suggestions, the Guardians instructed the clerk to provide a cart to convey the boys.[33] A month later, in January 1840, the company requested a further substitution and the Guardians agreed to send Samuel James in place of Phillip Fridger, though no reason was given. Having agreed, the Board of Guardians directed the clerk 'to get the boy sent'.[34] One gets the impression that Bromyard Guardians saw this type of apprenticeship as a means of absolving themselves of responsibility for the boys; as far as they were concerned, the sooner indentures were arranged and the boys were out of the way the better. This indeed may have been the case, because in March 1840 McMichael and Grierson wrote complaining that one of the boys had the 'itch' and had been sent before he was properly cured,[35] and the Board agreed to pay compensation of £3 for medical expenses and lost time.[36] The 'itch' was endemic in workhouses but was also widespread in the community at large, and the ready agreement of the Bromyard Guardians to pay for medical treatment and loss of earnings expenses is perhaps further evidence of how keen they were not to lose the opportunity to apprentice more boys in the future.

The company may have been having second thoughts about some of the boys from Bromyard because it procrastinated somewhat over the completion of their indentures; and it may have had good cause, because in March 1841 Joseph Wood was dismissed. McMichael and Grierson wrote to the Board stating 'that they had been obliged to discharge and send home the boy Joseph Wood in consequence of his having committed several thefts'.[37] On the journey back to Bromyard, the boy went missing, but later he returned to Bridgnorth and was lodged in the Borough Prison, and the company wrote to the Guardians requesting that 'he might be sent for immediately'.[38] McMichael and Grierson were obviously sick of Joseph Wood and the trouble he had caused them and did not want him back – but nor did the Guardians want him back either. Indeed, they did not want any of the boys back, and directed the clerk to call upon Mr West, the Justices' Clerk, and 'request him to have the other two boys bound apprentices without further delay'.[39] It might be presumed that had Joseph Wood already been bound, McMichael and Grierson would have been obliged to keep him and the Bromyard Board of Guardians could have washed their hands of him.

In April 1841 the indentures for the other two boys had still not been received by the clerk to Bromyard Union and, having informed the Board, he was directed to write once more to McMichael and Grierson 'and express the anxious desire of the Guardians for the business to be concluded forthwith'.[40] Shortly afterwards the Board received a letter from the company enclosing the indenture for William Caust, who had been apprenticed to Thomas Southwell of Bridgnorth but also stating that Samuel James was not bound because the man to whom he was to have been apprenticed had removed to Kidderminster. The Board wrote requesting the company to get the boy bound 'without this Board being put to any further expense'.[41] In the middle of June 1841 McMichael and Grierson wrote to Bromyard Board of Guardians concerning the binding of Samuel James as an apprentice and stated that 'they had got the boy back from Kidderminster and had put him on trial with another man and promising to have him bound a week hence if both parties like each other'.[42]

It was not at all clear that boys who were apprenticed into manufacturing areas would be taught a craft, despite having indentures of apprenticeship. As a result of extensive research into apprenticeships in the carpet-weaving mills in Kidderminster, Worcestershire, Frank Crompton has suggested that there were probably two types of apprentice: craft apprentices who received training which enabled them to become journeyman weavers, and parish apprentices who did not receive such training and were employed in unskilled work such as setting up the frames on which carpets were woven.[43] Craft apprenticeships appear to have been a closed shop in some areas, as the following quotation makes clear:

> Craft apprentices were recruited in the Kidderminster area, where there grew up a tradition that one generation arranged employment for the next, a suggestion supported by an employee of Brinton's Carpets since 1926, who was the third generation of his family employed in the carpet industry. His grandfather had first been employed in Brinton's carpet mill in the 1860s, where a system of internal recruitment had certainly operated for several generations.[44]

In April 1841[45] the Hereford Board of Guardians considered the employment terms offered by the Great Western Cotton Works in Bristol to able-bodied girls of 13 years and over, but it was not clear whether any girls were sent. Two groups of paupers from Ross Workhouse, however, were provided with new clothing and transport to Bristol – one in June 1840 and one in March 1841.

At a meeting of Ross Guardians at the beginning of June 1840 the clerk read a letter from Clarke, Mazet and Company of the Great Western Cotton Works concerning possible employment for pauper children. Commendably, the Board wanted to know more about the conditions in the factory and consideration of the company's offer was deferred for a fortnight, Mr T. Powell, one of the Guardians, undertaking to make further enquiries at Bristol in the meantime. Having visited the factory, Mr Powell reported to the Guardians and it was resolved that 'such children and young women in the workhouse as are eligible for the employment be called in and that the offer of the Company and the terms of remuneration be explained to them by the Chairman'.[46] At that time seven young women were informed of the terms of employment and were given one week to consider the proposition. This procedure suggests that they were not to be 'normal' parish apprentices, but merely employees.

The following week six of the seven young women concerned elected to take up the company's offer and it was arranged for each of them to be provided with a suit of clothes and 1s and to proceed to Bristol under the care of the Master of Ross Workhouse.[47] Only one other group of people from Ross Union Workhouse was recorded as having been supplied with new clothes and transport to the Bristol Cotton Factory. This group consisted of 12 girls and young women between 12 and 27 years of age, one woman of 60 years of age and a man of 47, his wife aged 51 and their four children, the ages of whom were not recorded.[48] Since apprenticeships were not mentioned at all in relation to any of the children in either of these groups, it might be assumed that these paupers were simply employees and it is quite likely that the same process was being enacted in other unions elsewhere.

As early as 1836, Sir Edmund Walker Head discussed with Guardians of Ledbury Union the possibility of sending pauper children to work in cotton, wool, flax and silk factories in Manchester. A letter from Mr R.M. Muggeridge, the Head of the Migration Office in Manchester, was read and the very fact that

Bromyard Workhouse around 1900 (courtesy of Bromyard & District History Society, ref: 002369)

such a post existed indicated that there was keen interest in drawing paupers and pauper children into manufacturing areas where there appeared to be an ever-increasing demand for labour. The terms and conditions of employment were duly considered; they were restricted to children over the age of 9, except in silk factories where there were no age restrictions.[49] They were not allowed to migrate until work had been found for the family, but this said nothing about orphaned or abandoned children, who were particularly vulnerable to exploitation or abuse. The subject does not appear to have been raised on any other occasion, so it might be presumed that the offer was not accepted. The Guardians were perhaps concerned about sending children so far away. Indeed, that does seem to have been the case, because in January 1838 the clerk was directed to provide a list of the boys and girls in the workhouse who required positions as servants and to see that 100 copies were printed and circulated in the town and district of Ledbury.[50]

In April 1839,[51] the education committee of the Ledbury Guardians reported that there were 31 boys and 33 girls in the workhouse, which might well suggest that the Guardians continued to sustain the policy of Ledbury's Old Poor Law administrators in not sending children to factories many miles from their own area. Considerable public disquiet about sending children so far from the Ledbury district may also have been significant. As the 1840s advanced, parish apprenticeships became fewer as the drive for education and industrial training in workhouses ensued. In relation to the New Poor Law in Norfolk, Anne Digby has suggested that the notion of industrial training for children in workhouses was considered desirable by the Poor Law authorities for moral as well as practical and financial purposes. She says:

> To counteract the debasing effect of other paupers, the poor law inspectors argued that industrial training was essential for the children. It would also serve as an alternative to apprenticeship; a good training would fit the child for independent employment and the consequent savings on apprenticeship premiums would help pay for the schooling. Under the New Poor Law apprenticeship in Norfolk was reserved for the few physically handicapped children who would not otherwise find employment. Normal children would get an industrial training, which in Kay-Shuttleworth's view would give them a training as much in the habit of industry as in the skills of industry. Industrial training was central to his perception of the relationship between education, pauperism and the social order, since through inculcating industrious habits an upright, hard-working member of the community would be created from the offspring of feckless parents. This educational philosophy proved congenial to the propertied classes in Norfolk, and hence to the ex officio members of boards of guardians, whose view of the New Poor Law was essentially that of a means to impose social discipline on the poor.[52]

In Herefordshire Unions the notion of providing industrial training for pauper children in workhouses was a vexed problem; for the most part it was not a practical consideration. In Unions which were heavily dependent on agriculture, the opportunities for children in workhouses to be trained in any specific trade were severely limited and references to industrial training in Union minute books were few and far between. In March 1839, Kington Guardians

resolved that all able-bodied women and girls should be employed in knitting or the spinning of wool and flax; able-bodied men and boys, on the other hand, were to be employed in the construction of a footpath from the turnpike to the workhouse.[53] This was no doubt an opportunity to occupy the men and boys in a useful activity and also to reduce turnpike charges. It is evident, however, that by 1841 there were attempts to provide some industrial training because in a minute relating to education in the

Two views in 2008 of Bromyard Workhouse which, like most of the other workhouse buildings in Herefordshire, has since been converted into housing

workhouse, the Guardians directed that the boys whose lessons were inter-rupted by time spent learning trades should be given extra tuition by the Schoolmistress.[54] At Ledbury, the Guardians stated in August 1841 that boys over the age of 10 should be given work appropriate to their age, when it was available.[55] At Bromyard, as early as July 1839, the boys were receiving some training, for a minute dated 8 July 1939 recorded that John Harris, a local shoe-maker, was to be paid 2s 6d for one day each week to repair paupers' shoes and to instruct the boys in the workhouse, and similarly Robert Bridgewater, a local tailor, was to be paid 3s for one day per week for mending and instruction.[56]

In September 1841 Ross Workhouse was inspected by Mr J.B. Farrall, who pointed out the need for industrial training for the boys[57] and the same point was made when Dore Union Workhouse was inspected in August 1848.[58] At Leominster, Jelinger C. Symons, Her Majesty's Inspector of Workhouse Schools, made the following points in the visitors' book in March 1854:

> Have examined the school today and find the children fairly instructed except in the common things and acts of life in which they want more practical knowledge. A systematic training in spade husbandry would do the boys more good than anything else.[59]

Boards of Guardians in rural areas were frequently dominated by farmers. They accepted the ideological need to provide pauper children with the means to support themselves, but only in so far as it did not conflict with their own vested interests. They needed a readily available pool of labour for haymaking, harvest and other seasonal work, but resented paying higher poor rates at times of the year when labourers were not needed. In managing the local labour market in this way, farmers were effectively imposing social control over paupers in their own business interests. In the minds of some Guardians there was also the lingering problem of Less Eligibility; to educate or give industrial training to the children of paupers was to be seen to give them benefits which did not accrue to the children of independent labourers outside the workhouse. Progress in lifting paupers out of long-term poverty would always be impeded whilst these conflicting interests and attitudes prevailed.

11   Settlement, Removal and Vagrancy – Weobley

The notion of possessing legal settlement in a particular parish was probably not an issue for most people unless they fell on hard times and were forced to approach the Overseer for relief. It was, however, an issue for the payers of poor rates, and parish officers did everything within their powers, and sometimes outside them, to avoid providing for paupers for whom responsibility lay elsewhere. A pauper's case would be considered but even though interim relief might be allowed, if there existed any question about his legal settlement, he might be removed from the parish, even if costly legal proceedings ensued.

In 18th and 19th century legislation and in parish vestry books throughout the land, the labouring poor were frequently referred to as being suitable or unsuitable 'objects' for relief, and in many respects this was an accurate description of their place in society. They were objects in the sense that they were there to be employed and used when the owners and occupiers of land needed them, but could be cast aside when the immediate need for their labour had passed. This harsh and patronising attitude was sustained by powers enshrined in the Act of Elizabeth 1601, which defined the parish as the administrative unit responsible for poor relief, and in the Settlement Act of 1662, which defined an individual's legal right to settlement and, thereby, to parish assistance.

> For more than two centuries a civil war was waged between the separate parishes of England and Wales. The military commanders were the owners and occupiers of land, their adjutants were the parish overseers, and the casualties in the front line were the labouring poor.[1]

The system was outmoded, unjust, ripe for exploitation and in urgent need of reform, but determined opposition from the property-owning classes successfully avoided significant change until the passing of the Union Chargeability Act of 1865, which allowed the burden of maintaining the poor to be spread more evenly. The prolonged civil war between parishes was aimed at minimising the number of poor people in a parish in order to hold down the amount of poor rates which the parish had to raise. The strategy for achieving this was the manipulation of the complex laws relating to settlement and rating. The parishes which gained most from these tactics were the small parishes, known as 'close' parishes and the parishes which lost most were known as 'open' parishes. The 'close' parishes tended to have one or only a small number of landowners who could effectively control the number of settlements in the parish. It was not uncommon for them to pull down cottages so that the labourers they employed had to live in contiguous parishes and thereby fall on the poor rates of those parishes when in need of relief. In 'open' parishes the land ownership tended to be more fragmented which meant that settlements were more difficult to control. As a result of these tactics, some 'close' parishes had a small number of landowners who were easily able to pay the poor rates required to support the parish's small number of poor; conversely, in 'open' parishes in which land was held by numerous landowners of no great wealth, the payers of poor rates were often burdened with the high cost of financing numerous poor. It was understandable, therefore, that settlement cases were often hotly contested. There were several ways in which settlement might be achieved: serving a properly indentured apprenticeship; possession of a substantial amount of property; completion of an annual hiring; holding a parish office; and, under certain circumstances, renting a tenement. Settlement claims were examined very carefully and evidence for such proceedings was recorded in the Weobley vestry book on 10 June 1807, when several cases were examined by one Robert Phillipps, probably a solicitor acting on behalf of the parish.

Robert Phillipps expressed the view that William Fowler, having purchased a property valued £30 called 'The Marsh' and having been in residence above 40 days, could consider himself settled; Edward Griffiths had gained settlement through a year's service; Thomas Colcombe, now a pauper, having been resident for three years in a tenement valued at £10 per annum, was now settled; William Tonge had gained settlement having been in the service of Mr Roger Powell for a year and from a subsequent hiring; and Benjamin White was entitled to settlement because he had been resident for several years in a tenement valued at £10 per annum and had also paid the poor rate. Herbert Williams was less fortunate, because he had been employed only temporarily, had failed to pay his land tax assessment, and could provide no evidence of holding a parish office. Robert Phillipps concluded, therefore, that having gained no settlement in Weobley for himself, 'the derivative settlement of his father in the Borough or Parish of New Radnor remains'.[2]

The most common ways of achieving legal settlement were by parentage, by birth and, in the case of women, by marriage. Even marriage, however, did not mean that parish Overseers might not challenge the validity of a woman's right to settlement, as the following case taken from the parish records for Clodock makes abundantly clear. In October 1775 the Vestry Clerk recorded that:

> We the landowners of the Township of Longtown do make the following orders. We order the overseers of the poor to take Suzannah Prichard to the Justices Meeting to swear her marriage and to summon witnesses to prove in what parish her late husband was born.[3]

Women with children, widows and single girls often appear to have faced the greatest opposition and to have suffered most in settlement cases, because if their claims succeeded they were likely to be a heavy burden on the poor rates for some years. In November 1814, Betty Nott and her five children were taken from Woolhope to Ledbury under removal orders and on arrival was granted 8s per week for one month whilst the circumstances of their removal were investigated.[4] In August 1826, widow Abigail Birch of Ledbury applied for relief but a decision was deferred until the next vestry meeting whilst the necessary enquiries were made about her husband's settlement.[5] In October 1829 Elizabeth Symonds was removed from Ledbury to Weston-under-Penyard, but having been notified of a likely appeal, the overseers of Ledbury forewarned Mr Holbrook, the parish solicitor, and instructed him to take all possible steps to defend the parish's interests.[6] The interests of the parish rate-payers were clearly of paramount importance.

The most vulnerable people in settlement disputes were young girls who had been abandoned because they were pregnant. Martha Owens was perhaps just such a young girl, and her situation led to much distress and heartache on her part and a lengthy dispute between the parishes of Weobley and Dilwyn. At a vestry meeting held at Weobley in April 1802 it was agreed by the assembled parishioners that counsel's advice should be sought in connection with the 'illegal proceedings of the overseers and other inhabitants of the Parish of Dilwyn in bringing Martha Owens, being in labour, an inhabitant of the said parish ... without a regular order of removal, whereby she was delivered of a child and became chargeable to this parish ...'.[7] On examination by Robert Phillipps, it appeared that after a family argument Martha had been forced to leave home by her stepmother. Her father had escorted her to Weobley where, after several hours of trudging around the town in an unsuccessful search for either the Overseer or the parish priest, she was taken in by one Mary Jones. Later that day Mr Baskerville, the Overseer, ordered Mary Jones to turn the girl out, but she refused because she said that Martha Owens was already in labour and would be delivered before morning. The child, of course, had legal settlement in Weobley by right of birth and as a result both mother and child became the responsibility of that parish because the child needed its mother although the settlement lay elsewhere and was in dispute by the Weobley Overseer. The treatment received by Martha Owens and many others like her was harsh but in the total absence of any poor law funding from central government, it was understandable.

The legal costs involved in fighting settlement cases could be very considerable but the long-term maintenance of a pauper family whose settlement was doubtful or had been gained fraudulently would almost certainly have been far more expensive, so once Overseers were reasonably sure that they could win a case they did not hesitate in taking matters forward. At a vestry meeting held at Weobley in June 1796, for example, the ratepayers agreed 'to empower and authorise the overseers of the poor to employ counsel to try the legality of William Thatcher's settlement at the next Quarter Sessions'.[8] In January 1816 they ordered the Overseers to remove John Newall and his wife to the township of Walton in the parish of Old Radnor, his legal place of settlement, and also instructed them to seek redress at the Quarter Sessions if the Overseers of Old Radnor challenged the removal.[9] In 1830 the ratepayers of Ledbury were burdened with the expense of removing a family named Rhodes to their legal settlement parish in Liverpool or of continuing to support them, perhaps for many years.[10] They also had to consider the cost of challenging the settlement claim of William Partridge, who was in prison. Doubts had been raised about the legality of his claim in March that year but the case was deferred until he had completed his sentence. In September 1830, however, Partridge was indicted 'for perjury committed by him in respect of his settlement'.[11] A similar case was pursued in the autumn of 1832, when the ratepayers agreed to give the wife of James Bosworth £2 as occasional relief 'to enable her to get her husband out of prison',[12] and in the following January it was ordered that enquiries be made of Mr Dunn 'as to the settlement of his tenant James Bosworth by renting a house from him in Ledbury'.[13] In February 1833 Ledbury parish officers called a special meeting of the ratepayers to consider what legal measures might be taken against the overseers of Woolhope for moving a family of paupers, namely Thomas Ford, his wife and four children 'into this parish contrary to law'.[14] By the early 1830s it was evident that settlement issues were becoming unmanageable for many parishes and the need for reform was urgent. The Settlement Act of 1662 was repealed by the Poor Law Amendment Act of 1834, but the conflict between parishes was not over, and the outcome of settlement cases continued to be an important factor in the financial status of individual parishes.

Running parallel to the issues involved in settlement cases were the equally difficult and expensive problems arising from vagrancy. In the early 1840s, the management of vagrants appears to have been a particular problem for the Master of Weobley Workhouse, and though the reasons for this remain unclear, one important factor was without doubt the rather indifferent leadership provided by the Board of Guardians. The New Poor Law was essentially urban in nature and largely inappropriate for agricultural communities, so much so that many small rural Unions like Weobley struggled with its implementation for years. Astute Guardians realised from the outset that the huge expense of building a new workhouse would lead to an increase, rather than a decrease, in parish expenditure and they therefore had little zeal to ensure that the new relief system worked effectively. Although only sparse records have survived for the first 30 years of Weobley Union the material contained in the Guardians' minute books has suggested a distinct lack of enthusiasm on their part, if not apathy. This must have been acutely embarrassing for both Sir Thomas Frankland Lewis and Sir George Cornewall Lewis – socially in Weobley because of family connections and politically in London because of their high standing at the Poor Law Commission.

The most effective Unions appear to have been those led by an efficient group of 10 or 12 energetic and wealthy Guardians who provided a firm and consistently businesslike direction over a number of years. This ought to have been possible at Weobley, but despite there being a wealth of social, financial and political connections to draw upon amongst the members of the Board, of the eight Poor Law Unions in Herefordshire it was probably the least well run and the least successful in implementing the 1834 Act. This was especially strange considering that the first Board of Guardians included several of Sir Thomas Frankland Lewis's relatives: Samuel Peploe of Garnstone Castle; the Reverend John Birch Webb, Rector of Weobley; and his own son, the Reverend Gilbert Frankland Lewis, Rector of Monnington-on-Wye. No doubt the Chief Poor Law Commissioner thought that Weobley Union would be in safe hands because at that time, before their respective marriages, his son Gilbert shared Monnington rectory with family friend Sir Edmund Walker Head, an arrangement which should have aided the flow of poor law information at all levels. It is possible, however, that these advantages engendered an indolent attitude; few were likely to question the actions of such powerful men. Attendance at Guardians' meeting was often very poor and on some occasions the Union

Weobley Workhouse in 2008

Clerk waited in vain for any of the gentlemen of the Board to arrive. This was a very poor example for Union officers; neither a deterrent to the lazy and slipshod, nor encouragement to the diligent who were struggling to manage complex situations created by difficult paupers and vagrants.

Vagrants were entitled to seek one night's lodging at any workhouse and could not be turned away, even if they had no money to pay for it. Males who were deemed to be in reasonable health were expected to break stone for one hour before breakfast and two hours afterwards before going on their way. Seasoned tramps who trod regular routes and desired no other way of life knew which workhouses made the best provision for them and also those where understaffed or lax regimes could be exploited. In small rural work-houses such as Weobley, where the number of officers was minimal, a sudden influx of vagrants could cause difficult situations in which the Master, Matron, Porter and Schoolmistress could find themselves overwhelmed and in urgent need of assistance from the parish Constables. The problem was that on some occasions the Master was confronted with 20 or 30 vagrants, many of whom claimed that they had no money but, having been given food and shelter for the night, refused to carry out their tasks in the morning. They did, however, rejoice in breaking workhouse windows in order to be arrested and sent to gaol, where the food provided was much better than that given to them at the workhouse. In the autumn of 1844 numerous incidents involving trou-blesome vagrants took place at Weobley Workhouse and after much discus-sion, the Board of Guardians instructed the Union Clerk to write to the Poor Law Commissioners to seek advice and information about the extent of their powers in finding appropriate and legal solutions to the problem.

The Guardians requested to know if they could instruct the workhouse Master just to dismiss any vagrant refusing to work, with or without his breakfast, because it would be far cheaper for the Union to forego the stone-breaking which should have been done than to meet the costs of arrest and committal. Alternatively, they wondered if they might be permitted to direct the Relieving Officers to send all vagabonds to one of the lodging houses in Weobley instead of giving them an order of admission to the workhouse. It would cost the Union 3d or 4d per head per night, but would still be cheaper than meeting legal costs and the expense of repairing broken windows in the workhouse. The Commissioners' reply arrived three weeks later at the begin-ning of December 1844, and they were unequivocal in their disapproval. They considered that the Guardians' plan would be holding out a 'direct and strong encouragement to the increase of vagrancy'[15] and that they could 'best meet the evil by a steady adherence to relief in the vagrant wards under proper regulations, and by uniformly taking offenders before the justices, when they refuse to work or destroy the property of the union'.[16] The Guardians accepted the Commissioners' advice, but the problems continued. In January 1845 the

Master reported that he had found it necessary to convey 11 vagabonds before the justices for refusing to work;[17] 10 more were committed at the beginning of February for refusing to work and breaking windows;[18] and later that month, of 25 vagrants admitted to the workhouse, 9 were taken before the justices[19] and all the men received sentences of 14 days hard labour.

There might have been a greater incentive to going to gaol than the simple fact that it provided more comfortable sleeping arrangements and better food than the workhouse, because the clerk was directed to enquire if there was any truth in a statement made to the Board 'that each vagrant committed to gaol receives from the authorities there the sum of 2/6 on being discharged ...'.[20] The Guardians no doubt thought that such a policy added insult to injury as far as they were concerned and began to devise and impose deterrent measures. They ordered that in future all vagrants admitted to the workhouse should be thoroughly searched and that any combustible or dangerous substances should be removed. Any man found to have enough money to provide food and lodging for a night should be turned out 'to shift for himself'[21] at one of the town's lodging houses; and the fireplace in the vagrant ward was to be bricked up permanently.

The buildings so delicately described as vagrant 'wards' were often little more than unheated outbuildings or barns, sometimes open to the elements on one side except for a tarpaulin. Inside there were no facilities for washing either clothes or bodies and beds were often vermin-ridden straw mattresses and blankets on a cold floor. In some workhouses there were separate wards for men and women, but in others there was a single ward for all, which almost certainly sometimes led to serious fights as well as lewd and promiscuous behaviour. As they tramped from place to place it was evident that vagrants exchanged useful information about the workhouses they had visited, guiding each other away from those where regulations were very strictly enforced to those where officers were a little more malleable and life was slightly easier. Workhouse officers were aware, for example, that they might see a marked rise in the number of vagrants seeking a night's lodging if it were known that they were awaiting the delivery of a fresh supply of stone, only to see numbers fall away again once it had arrived. Vagrant networks circulated information very efficiently, sometimes over long distances in just a few days.

In the 1840s, the 'hungry forties', there was a huge increase in the number of men walking the roads in search of employment. Many were respectable men, previously hard working and independent, but driven to a nomadic way of life as a result of trade recession, unemployment and poverty. The problem was exacerbated by the arrival of thousands of Irish people fleeing from the potato famine in the hope of a fresh start in England. The poor law administrators, both national and local, tended to treat them all as if they were seasoned tramps. The sudden appearance of 20 or 30 men, sometimes more, in the centre of Weobley, Ross, Ledbury, Bromyard or any other small market town must have been very unsettling, if not intimidating, for householders, shopkeepers, merchants, innkeepers and particularly the Master of the workhouse and the parish Constables. The cost of Weobley's vagrant problem was shared, perhaps unfairly, by otherwise unaffected Union parishes because it was charged to the Union's common fund. In 1845, however, a Bill was presented to parliament the contents of which would have had serious implications for the ratepayers in market towns because it proposed to allow paupers to claim settlement if they had lived in a parish for five years or more and also proposed to make the provision retrospective. This was perceived as manifestly unfair to ratepayers, particularly those of modest income, who might well impoverish themselves in trying to pay increased rate demands. The battle lines for disputation were drawn.

The Guardians of Ledbury Union quickly grasped the financial implications of the proposed new legislation and decided to voice their concerns in a petition to parliament, copies of which were to be forwarded to the House of Lords by Earl Somers and to the House of Commons by Thomas Mynors Baskerville Esq. They resolved 'that this Board is apprehensive that the Bill now before Parliament entitled "A Bill to consolidate and amend the laws relating to Parochial Settlement and the Removal of the Poor" will work unfavourably, both to the Rate-payers, and to the Poor'.[22] They also refuted the notion that there would be substantial savings in legal expenses as fewer settlement disputes between parishes were fought through the courts because: 'The opinion of the Magistrates in Petty Sessions always have been deemed decisive, and relief given accordingly, without the expenses of orders of removal'.[23] That statement, of course, was not strictly true but considering how complex settlement issues had become, relatively few protracted legal cases were pursued through the courts. The Kington Guardians were also very apprehensive about the proposed new measures and in January 1846 they wrote to 15 of the Poor Law Unions nearest to Kington stating that they would accept any paupers whose settlement was clearly in one of the parishes of their Union without the need for removal orders,[24] and urged other Unions to follow the same procedure in order to save time and expense for everyone.

The Boards of Guardians were right to be apprehensive. When the Bill became law as the Irremovable Poor Act of 1846 it created new problems and caused administrative chaos. It established legal settlement after five years' residence, but did not make clear whether relief for the unsettled poor was or was not retrospective:

> The Law Officers held that it was not retrospective, and the Poor Law Board felt obliged so to advise the Boards of Guardians. The result was that, up and down the country, non-resident relief began to be stopped;

and at the same time the Relieving Officers found themselves faced by many new applicants for relief in their parishes of residence.[25]

In December 1846 the clerk to Hereford Union wrote in the minute book that:

> A letter was read from the Poor Law Commissioners drawing the attention of the Guardians to the necessity of relieving non-settled paupers in the same manner as settled paupers and holding the Officers of the Union responsible for any neglect in such cases.[26]

It is not clear whether this was a general letter sent out to all Poor Law Unions or simply to those who were thought to be neglecting their responsibilities under the new legislation. Whatever the case, it suggests that there was general opposition to the notion of irremovability and that the Poor Law Commissioners were at pains to make it absolutely clear that if cases of neglect amongst the unsettled poor did occur, the Guardians would be held responsible. The Commissioners were, of course, under very close scrutiny at that time, as the reverberations of the Andover Scandal rolled on and the Commission's effectiveness was being questioned. They could not risk further accusations of neglect as a result of their lack of direction to Boards of Guardians.

In May 1846 the Ledbury Guardians had petitioned the government for a second time, this time about the difficulty of collecting poor rates on properties occupied by the poor. The Central Authority seems to have been reluctant to accept that some people would never be in a position to pay poor rates. Ledbury Guardians pointed out that they had no means of collecting rates on properties let at annual rents of £6 or less but 'which nevertheless yields the owner a larger interest of money than any other rateable property in which he can invest his capital'.[27] The petition went on to say that the poor rates were virtually a tax on the landlord and that since every other description of property was rated it was manifestly unfair that the cottages of the poor should be exempt. It was 'utterly impossible to collect the rates of cottages'[28] and in their opinion the only remedy was to make landlords liable to pay their rates. The Board ended the petition stating: 'Your petitioners pray your Honourable House will forthwith pass a law making the landlords of all cottages whose Rents are under £6 per annum liable to the payment of Poor Rates.'[29] As far as putting Poor Law finance on a firm footing was concerned, however, this was mere tinkering with a system which needed radical reform of the settlement laws, if not their total abolition, as well as changes in the rating system.

The problem rumbled on for some years, but when legislation eventually came in 1850, it simply gave powers to rate the owners of such properties rather than occupiers, which resulted in landlords passing on the rates to their tenants in the form of higher rents. The unfortunate labourer was faced, there-fore, with the problem of paying rent which in past times would have been paid for him and rates from which he had previously been exempt. Despite the need for further reform, no significant changes were attempted until 1854, 'when M.T. Baines, who had become for the second time president of the Poor Law Board, introduced a Bill proposing complete Union Chargeability, and with it the complete abolition of the power of removal of the unsettled poor, coupling with these provisions a proposal for the gradual introduction of Union rating ...'.[30] This would have greatly improved the lives of people who, having moved to find work, found themselves removed to a settlement parish where, with the passing of the years, they no longer had any family or social connections. As public feeling about the treatment of paupers began to soften in the wake of the Andover Workhouse cruelties, there also appeared to be a growing unease about the need to remove people from an area where they had lived and worked for many years as soon as they became unemployed or too old to work. In August 1853 the Guardians of Leominster Union petitioned parliament through the auspices of Lord Bateman of Shobdon Court and of George Arkwright, MP for Leominster, on just that point, stressing the injus-tice of the procedure and the hardship and distress it caused.[31]

In March 1854, Sir George Cornewall Lewis wrote to Sir Edmund Walker Head in Canada, apprising him of events in parliament, and stating that Baines had made a good speech proposing the complete abolition of the Law of Settlement and that: 'The Bill consists of a clause abolishing removals, and half-a-dozen clauses embodying a plan similar to that proposed in your article. The abolition of settlement can be carried, but there will be great resistance to union chargeability'.[32] In 1848 Sir Edmund had written an article for the radical publication *The Edinburgh Review*, in which he had advocated the adoption of the Union as the unit of finance instead of the parish. The Bill introduced by Baines had advocated Union rating and the complete abolition of removals, but it did not become law because it excluded the Irish who at that time were travelling to England in large numbers in search of work. It was esti-mated that 300,000 arrived in 1847[33] alone, and most were in desperate need of relief. The Irish MPs resented the omission of the Irish poor and lobbied the Home Secretary, Lord Palmerston, who, without any discussion with the Poor Law Board, agreed to their demands. Baines, who was President of the Poor Law Board, quite understandably took exception to Lord Palmerston's intervention and tendered his resignation and, largely as a result of the ensuing ministerial crisis, the Bill was lost and no major changes were attempted again until 1865.

The Central Authority at Somerset House frequently got what it wanted in the end but it was often the case that changes which could not be effected by direct action were accomplished by stealth. The powers granted to the Poor Law

Commission in 1834, for example, were initially just for a period of five years and, in the teeth of opposition, were renewed annually for some years after; the permanence of the Commission was thus achieved step by step until it was replaced by the Poor Law Board in 1847. The same process appears to have been employed in order to achieve permanent changes to the settlement laws, Union rating and Union Chargeability. The Irremovable Poor Act of 1846 had caused immense problems for many people of modest income because of the dramatic increase in the size of rate demands, and the injustice of the situation was relieved only when, in 1847, W.H. Bodkin, MP for Rochester, succeeded in passing a Private Member's Bill which transferred the cost of maintaining the irremovable poor from the parish of residence to the Union common fund. Bodkin's Act was presented as a temporary piece of legislation as a means of getting it through parliament, but in reality, it was renewed every year until 1865. More costs were transferred to a common fund under the terms of the Poor Law Amendment Act of 1848, and the Irremovable Poor Act of 1861 reduced the five year residence rule to three years and adopted Union rating for any costs charged to a common fund. 'The following year, unions had to appoint guardians to Union Assessment Committees, who were to work with parish overseers to prepare valuation lists of property as a basis for contributions to common fund'.[34] This brought Union rating a little closer and, step by step, moves towards change were advanced to the point where some Unions began to realise that Union rating and Union Chargeability would be beneficial to them.

In February 1863, the Guardians of Hereford Union wrote a long and detailed letter to the Poor Law Board which showed that the central authority's tactics in effecting change were producing results. They stated: 'That after an experience of many years [we] are convinced that the partial operation of the common fund is injurious to the interest of the Union and liable to great abuses,'[35] and also pointed out 'that it had been the source of endless disputes and trouble without any corresponding benefit ...'.[36] The Guardians greatly resented the powers given to district auditors to revise, retrospectively, their decisions about common fund charges and were possibly just as resentful about the amount of their own time they were having to expend in resolving such issues. They had obviously realised the situation was muddled, confused and illogical because they continued by saying that in the Union they represented 'more than one half of the Paupers are already on common fund and that such portion with Lunatics and other charges placed on common fund represent more than two thirds of the whole expenses of the Union'.[37] They ended their communication with the plea that: '[We] therefore respectfully pray your honourable Board will forward a measure in the present Session of Parliament having for its object one common fund in every Union from which every Pauper in the Union shall receive relief'.[38]

A survey of the minutes for the Unions of Kington, Ledbury, Bromyard, Leominster and Weobley for the years from 1860 to 1866 suggests, however, that there the subject had not been discussed or that the clerk had been directed not to include such discussion in the minutes. It is also possible, of course, that the Boards realised that there was little point in objecting to measures that seemed inevitable and that their silence would be seen to signify acquiescence. In May 1865 the clerk to Dore Union read a letter to the Guardians in which the Poor Law Board asked for their opinion of the Union Chargeability Bill and he was directed to write back to say 'that this Board is not in favour of the Bill'.[39] Ross Union Guardians, however, fully supported the Bill and stated:

> That your petitioners have long been of the opinion that such a Bill was much required, and that its enactment would be an act of justice to the ratepayers, and at the same time prove one of mercy to the poor. They submit that the present mode of charging the Poor rates in separate parishes is unjust and oppressive, as it throws a very large portion of the cost on those parishes where the labouring classes can obtain a house, while on the contrary, parishes occupied by the wealthy, are exempt from all but a nominal charge for that purpose. They therefore pray your honourable House to pass the said Bill.[40]

The reason for the difference in opinion on this issue is probably explained by the wording of the statement made by Ross Guardians. They had often appeared to hold less insular views than other Herefordshire Unions and, as mentioned in other chapters, the same small group of able men influenced the affairs and running of the Union for many years. The consistency of their service, and their ability as businessmen and members of the professions, perhaps gave them a broader view of practical problems than other Guardians with less poor law experience.

There was, in the end, little effective opposition to the Bill and the new Act adopted the Union as the unit for finance and for settlement and conferred on the unsettled poor the right of irremovability after just one year's residence. Sir George Cornewall Lewis had been quite right when he told Sir Edmund Walker Head that there would be enormous opposition to Union rating; it could not be otherwise when vested interests were at risk.

The victims in the conflict between parishes were, of course, the poor. They had been the victims of harsh settlement and removal laws for many generations, and had been treated as little better than livestock or merchandise. The poor called for reform of the settlement laws and for fairer treatment; the propertied classes called for a halt to spiralling poor rates. The passing of the Union Chargeability Act of 1865 did provide for a fairer system for ratepayers and it did bring greater freedom of movement for the poor, but those improvements were a long time coming – more than a generation.

Conclusion

It is important to remember that the New Poor Law was an experiment with a form of administration not hitherto attempted by a British Government: the creation of a Central Commission, in this case to oversee the management of poor relief throughout England and Wales. This fundamental change in the nature of management became a pattern for administration in other areas of social policy such as lunacy, with the appointment of the Commissioners in Lunacy. The Poor Law Amendment Act was founded on Benthamite Principles: the deterrent effect of the 'Workhouse Test', the Principle of Less Eligibility, and the Principle of National Uniformity. It failed in its objectives in part because of the inadequate nature of the legislation; it was largely an urban answer to an urban problem, but was imposed equally on rural areas, where its provisions were very quickly seen to be inappropriate. Indeed, the inappropriateness of the New Poor Law in rural counties such as Herefordshire can be illustrated by two simple examples.

As the implementation of the Act began to take place, the local Boards of Guardians were encouraged to build new and imposing workhouses which deliberately resembled prisons as part of the deterrent effect. All the Herefordshire Unions, with the exception of Leominster, built new workhouses at considerable expense to the ratepayers. This was almost certainly very irritating and illogical to the Boards of Guardians of Kington and Ledbury Unions, because in former years the ratepayers of those towns had concluded that it was cheaper to relieve the poor in their own homes than to maintain a workhouse, and had closed their workhouses in consequence. In those circumstances it would be easy to understand why opponents of the New Poor Law might take the view that the new law was more to do with the uniformity of control than the uniformity of poor relief. Another example of the inappropriateness of government policy in rural areas was its drive to introduce district schools for pauper children in the late 1840s. Her Majesty's Inspector of Workhouse Schools, Jelinger C. Symons, suggested that the Guardians of Ross, Ledbury and Newent Unions should hold a meeting to discuss the establishment of a district school, but his suggestion was rejected, indeed probably never received serious consideration. The Guardians of all three Unions would no doubt have seen instantly how impractical the establishment of such a school would have been for so large a geographical area. This again highlights the fact that urban thinking was being applied to rural situations under the assumption that a measure that proved to be practical in a metropolitan area would be equally effective in a rural one.

There can be little doubt that in rural areas many parishes incurred higher poor relief costs as a result of the New Poor Law. Not only did they have to pay for their own parish poor in the Union Workhouse and those receiving out relief; they also had to contribute to the common fund costs of running the Union to which they belonged.

The New Poor Law also failed in its objectives because of the fundamental weaknesses of the Poor Law Commission itself, weaknesses which were exposed during the enquiry into the Andover scandal of 1845. The Central Authority had failed to develop a sufficiently rigorous administrative structure and controls to prevent individual Boards of Guardians from exerting their independence by interpreting regulations in the manner which they considered best suited the needs of their Union. In this, the Poor Law Commission was in a very weak position. It was originally given a life of five years and thereafter its powers were renewed annually until its abolition and replacement by the Poor Law Board in 1847. In that situation it was arguable as to whether the Poor Law Commission could ever afford to be too autocratic, because the public fear of centralism meant that those who opposed the New Poor Law would have been swift to make political capital from any perceived abuse of power. The implementation of the New Poor Law therefore varied throughout England and Wales which in effect meant that any notion of National Uniformity was lost almost from the very beginning. The result was that there were as many variations in the relief of poverty under the New Poor Law as there had been under the Old Poor Law. This no doubt gave ammunition to those who considered the new law to be unnecessary, as well as being more expensive than the law it had sought to amend. It might be argued that the New Poor Law was invalidated by virtue of the fact that National Uniformity was very quickly seen as unattainable, and, that being so, that parish autonomy was being destroyed to no purpose. This was almost certainly the case in very rural counties such as Herefordshire, where ratepayers could see that they were losing control of parish affairs in the name of economy – an economy that was actually increasing expenditure, although it was intended to reduce the spiralling cost of poor relief. Some ratepayers could, however, seek to influence the implementation of the new Act by being elected to the Board of Guardians or, in the case of Magistrates, by sitting as ex-officio Guardians. The dominant members of the Boards of Guardians, usually the ex-officio Guardians, were in a strong position to steer Board proceedings in the manner they thought appropriate, and in Herefordshire it was certainly the case that individual Unions were steered, managed or dominated by particular families or groups of interrelated Guardians for many years.

It must have been clear to the Poor Law Commissioners from the very beginning that effecting National Uniformity would be extremely difficult, if not impossible, given the opposition to central control. That being so, one wonders whether the outward concern to control poor relief expenditure was an outward veneer to what was in fact the most efficient means of controlling the poor. The propertied classes had been severely shaken by the Swing Riots of 1830 in the counties of the south and east of England and had not forgotten the threat of revolution and bloodshed in Paris that same year. They knew that during that year England had been perhaps only a small step away from civil disorder and loss of life. The Poor Law Commission of 1832 and the resultant Poor Law Amendment Act of 1834 were enacted against a background of serious disturbance amongst some of the labouring classes and extreme anxiety amongst the propertied classes. During the first three decades of the 19th century the cost of poor relief rose relentlessly, but the relief was unevenly distributed and ranged from almost indiscriminate almsgiving to extreme parsimony. The poor called for a fairer system of poor relief; the propertied classes called for control of spiralling poor rates. The New Poor Law was introduced in an attempt to fulfil both these objectives, but in fact it failed to do justice either to the ratepayers or to the poor. It *was* successful, however, in its attempt to control the poor. By strict adherence to the laws of settlement and tight supervision of the terms on which the poor were relieved through the Boards of Guardians, church and state came neatly together to control the poor and, at the same time, impose upon them an Anglican morality. In Herefordshire Unions the clergy were powerful influences in the running of Union business as Guardians and as Magistrates, as well as in their capacity as clergymen with a duty of care to the poor. The control of poor relief was, in effect, control of the poor.

The Poor Law Commissioners certainly found it difficult to control individual Boards of Guardians on some occasions, but over a period of weeks, months or in some cases years, they usually managed to persuade Guardians to acquiesce to their wishes. At local level, however, the nature and structure of the Boards of Guardians demonstrated a clear line of control from the Chairman of the Board right down to the poor to whom relief was dispensed. In Ross Union a small group of Guardians retained effective control of the Union's affairs for a decade and more, through their marriage alliances, networks, social connections and power as Magistrates and landowners. Similarly, Dore Union was sustained, if not controlled, by the Clive family, their clerical connections and their neighbours. Leominster Union was heavily influenced for many years by the presence of Edward Evans of Eyton Hall, who supported Thomas Woolley and his wife as Master and Matron of the workhouse, with serious consequences for the poor inmates. In many cases the dominant group of ex-officio Guardians on Boards was also in a powerful position to influence the thinking and voting of the elected Guardians, some of whom were their tenant farmers. In these circumstances powerful and influential men could form an impenetrable coalition to manage Union business as they wished.

In Herefordshire, members of the clergy were heavily involved and highly influential in the implementation of the New Poor Law, from Bishop and Dean, particularly the Dean, right down to the humble parish priests who sometimes sat as elected Guardians. Clergymen were the Chairmen of several Boards of Guardians, often for long periods of time. Indeed, during the period of the Poor Law Commission, 1834-1847, all the Herefordshire Unions had five or six clerical Guardians for most of the time. Some were very high profile members of the clergy. The Dean of Hereford, Doctor John Merewether, sometimes attended the meetings of Hereford Board of Guardians and, more frequently, the meetings of Dore Union. He was Vicar of Madley in Dore Union and the Dean and Chapter of Hereford Cathedral also had large holdings of land in that area. The Reverend Charles Scott Luxmore, Dean of St Asaph, was a Guardian of Bromyard Union, a landowner, a tithe owner and an active Magistrate as well. The Venerable Archdeacon Waring was an elected Guardian for Leominster Union. These clerical gentlemen no doubt saw their participation in the administration of poor relief as being wholly compatible with their calling, but their role was far more complex than their duty of care to the poor as priests. They were often members of the most wealthy and politically powerful families in Herefordshire.

The implementation of the New Poor Law in Herefordshire was certainly unique in its close association with the most powerful figures at the Poor Law Commission in London. The first Chief Poor Law Commissioner was Thomas Frankland Lewis who lived at Harpton Court, near Kington, where he sat as an ex-officio Guardian on the Kington Board of Guardians. He was followed as Chief Commissioner by his son Sir George Cornewall Lewis. Thomas Frankland Lewis's second son, the Reverend Gilbert Frankland Lewis, Canon of Worcester, was Rector of Monnington-on-Wye in Weobley Union where his uncle, Samuel Peploe was the Chairman. The first Assistant Poor Law Commissioner for Herefordshire, Sir Edmund Walker Head, the son of a clergyman, married Anna Maria Yorke, the daughter of a clergyman, and was actually residing at Monnington-on-Wye Rectory with the Reverend Gilbert Frankland Lewis at the time of his marriage. It has been noted in previous chapters that Head and George Cornewall Lewis had been friends for many years and that they corresponded regularly until Lewis's death. It will also be remembered that Sir Edmund was appointed a full Commissioner at Somerset House in 1841 and that he and Lewis remained there until the demise of the Commission in 1847. The Lewises had powerful political friends in the Clives and remained on good terms with the family for many years. Edward Bolton Clive, MP for Hereford, was the Chairman of Dore Union and, aided by his son Colonel Clive and his son-in-law, the Venerable Archdeacon Wetherell, was the sustaining figure of that Union for many years. He was followed by his son and heir, the Reverend Archer Clive, who also served that Union for many years. All these social, political and clerical connections were no doubt valuable to those most closely involved in the running of Herefordshire Poor Law Unions, but they might prove very embarrassing and politically dangerous when serious problems arose, such as the possible potentially very damaging scandal at Leominster Workhouse.

The Boards of Guardians for all the Unions of Herefordshire appear to have had a strong social, political or marital link which led back directly to Edward Bolton Clive MP, to Sir Edmund Walker Head, or to one of the Lewises. It is impossible to quantify just how much these connections affected the implementation of the New Poor Law in Herefordshire, but it is highly unlikely that the conduct of the Boards of Guardians would not have been tempered by the presence of men with such enormous power and influence at the Poor Law Commission. It is almost certain, too, that the leading members of Boards of Guardians of Herefordshire Unions would have had fairly easy access to advice from their Assistant Commissioner, Sir Edmund Walker Head, through his many social and political connections in the county. It would have been quite easy for men such as Ross Guardian Colonel Henry Clifford of Perrystone Court near Ross, or Ledbury Guardian Earl Somers of Eastnor Castle, both relatives of Sir Edmund through his marriage to Anna Maria Yorke, to take discrete soundings about Poor Law policy over the port after dinner if they chose to do so. It would also have been quite simple for Head to impart off-the-record warnings if he felt that a Board of Guardians was straying too far from official policy. There is some evidence, however, that Sir Edmund himself gave Herefordshire Unions advice and support on the vexed problem of pauper apprenticeships while there was, in fact an official moratorium on apprenticing pauper children. The moratorium was in place for approximately the first decade of the New Poor Law, but in the 1830s Head was writing to Herefordshire Boards of Guardians suggesting the apprenticing of pauper boys to the carpet factories of McMichael and Grierson in Worcester, Kidderminster and Bridgnorth. Connections were obviously to be used.

In general terms, Herefordshire Poor Law Unions conformed to the policies and directives of the Central Authority, except in the case of pauper education. In this respect they procrastinated and used numerous ploys in order to avoid paying the salary of a suitably literate person to act as a Schoolmaster or Schoolmistress. In this, however, Herefordshire Unions were not unusual. Many Unions in different parts of the country adhered strictly to the view that to educate pauper children was to give them advantages over the children of the independent poor and therefore to infringe the Principle of Less Eligibility. They all experienced problems with dishonest Relieving Officers and negligent Medical Officers, as well as complaints against workhouse Masters for neglect of duty, drunkenness and dishonesty. All the Unions appointed a workhouse Chaplain during the 1830s, but they did not appear to play a very significant part in the running of Union affairs. Perhaps these men felt overwhelmed by the presence of high-ranking clergymen. Indeed, some of the latter clergymen were very wealthy men, and their financial interests must at times have compromised their pastoral concerns and their duty of care to the poor. Their role was an extremely complicated one; some must have experienced serious conflicts of interest which severely taxed their consciences.

Once inside the workhouse walls, paupers were subjected to rigid and monotonous routines and as a result, a workhouse morality was imposed on them by the upper classes, who assumed that they knew what was best for those below them. Those who paid the rates called the tune. The morality imposed was that of the Guardians and the workhouse Chaplain; that is, an Anglican morality. While the Victorians liked to preach the benefits and rewards of self-help in adversity, many Anglican clergymen took the view that paupers should accept their position in the social hierarchy because it was ordained by divine intervention and that to try to alter it was to oppose the will of God. In such a conflicting maelstrom even the most respectable of paupers could not hope to do the right thing. As far as the doctrine of Uniformity was concerned, once moral issues entered the judgement of Boards of Guardians, objectivity would be difficult, if not impossible, to sustain; the notion of uniformity would be lost and with it any real hope of universal fairness in the relief of poverty. Choosing between those paupers who were perceived as deserving and those who were undeserving could never be equitable.

In the meantime, the notion of parsimony was embraced by Boards of Guardians as a general policy from two standpoints: the self-interest of keeping down the rates and the convenient pursuit of the Principle of Less Eligibility.

In effect, the application of the New Poor Law depended to a very large degree on the moral stance of individual Boards of Guardians which in turn led to considerable variations in Union spending. This is quite evident in a table of Herefordshire Union expenditures prepared by Sir Edmund Walker Head in 1840. In September that year, Sir Edmund was preparing to leave Herefordshire to take up a new position as a Poor Law Commissioner at Somerset House, but clearly wished to set straight some troubling matters before he left. In order to illustrate his concern about the high level of spending of Ross Union he produced a table of comparisons between Ross and neighbouring Unions, details of which were recorded in the minutes of a meeting held on 14 September. This was a simple and perhaps crude table in which he divided the Unions' 1839 expenditure by the number of their populations in 1831 to give a per capita sum. The per capita figures were: Hereford 7s, Ledbury 6s, Weobley 6s 11d, Monmouth 5s 5d, Newent 6s 11d, Dore 8s 8d, Kington 8s 4d, with Ross at the top of the list with a per capita sum of 8s 10d. The average was 6s 10d. It is evident from these figures that some Unions were not applying the 'Workhouse Test' as firmly as others and indeed, they suggest that National Uniformity was unattainable.

The manner in which the New Poor Law was applied varied from Union to Union depending on the nature and make-up of the Board of Guardians. To take Hereford and Ross Unions as examples, the Hereford Guardians appear to have been less motivated as a group than the Ross Guardians, who were well known to each other and in many cases closely related. In addition to this, Hereford Union had experienced a great deal of anti-Poor Law criticism in the 1840s, which probably made Guardians cautious and defensive and inclined to serve as a member of the Board for only a year or two. Ross Guardians, however, appeared not to excite any real criticism of their running of the Union and were therefore confident and prepared to serve as Guardians year after year, in some cases for 10 or 20 years without a break. Ross Guardians were comfortable, perhaps too comfortable, in their position; Hereford Guardians, on the other hand, were never quite comfortable and thus applied the law firmly, if not cruelly. The Union in the county town was, however, always likely to attract more criticism than a Union in a small market town and in those circumstances, strict adherence to the letter of the law, even if it appeared hard and uncaring, was the best policy.

By the late 1840s the public's attitude to the poor was softening, particularly in the wake of the Andover Scandal. The policy of the Central Authority had begun to soften too, in that it seemed to be accepted that some groups of paupers were not culpable in their own destitution and could never really be held to account for it. The old, the sick, and orphaned and abandoned children could not be blamed for their circumstances and deserved to be treated more gently than other classes of pauper. Thus, the 'Workhouse Test', the Principle of National Uniformity and the Principle of Less Eligibility which Edwin Chadwick and other orthodox Utilitarians had imposed on the relief of poverty were found to be unsustainable. On the surface the New Poor Law had failed in its objective of uniformity and fairness in the provision of poor relief throughout England and Wales. As a means of bringing the poor under a national system of control, however, it was very effective. Social control was perhaps the real reason for the Poor Law Amendment Act of 1834 all the time.

Bibliography

Primary Sources

The Poor Law Reports on Herefordshire, 1834, Irish University Press Reprints of British Parliamentary Papers of the Nineteenth Century; Poor Law, Vol. 3, Dublin 1972.

The Irish University Press Reprint of the Census Report of 1851 (Population Vol. 8.).

Acts of Parliament

The Poor Law Amendment Act 1834 (4 and 5 Will. IV. c.76).

The Irremovable Poor Act of 1846 (9 and 10 Vic. c.66).

Bodkin's Act of 1847 (10 and 11 Vic. c.110).

The Poor Law Amendment Act of 1848 (11 and 12 Vic. c.110).

The Irremovable Poor Act of 1861 (24 and 25 Vic. c.55).

The Parochial Assessment Act of 1862 (25 and 26 Vic. c.105).

The Union Chargeability Act of 1865 (28 and 29 Vic. c.79).

Papers held at Herefordshire Record Office, Harold Street, Hereford

Minutes in Herefordshire Record Office - Ref. K42.

Ross Union Minutes.

Kington Union Minutes.

Dore Union Minutes.

Hereford Union Minutes.

Ledbury Union Minutes.

Bromyard Union Minutes.

Leominster Union Minutes.

Weobley Union Minutes.

Other Papers held at Herefordshire Record Office

The Wallwyn Papers HRO Ref. RC/C/778.

The Kerne Bridge Co. Papers, HRO Ref. D48/52.

Hereford Union Register of Births, HRO Ref. BJ6.

British and Foreign School Papers, HRO Ref. AP72/11.

Ross Parish Registers.

Kington Parish Registers.

List of Magistrates 1842/1843, HRO Ref. G42/39 (ii) Box 59.

Madley Vestry Minutes, HRO Ref. BK52/50, September, 1836.

Leominster Vestry Minutes, HRO Ref. AK3/72.

Clodock Vestry Book, HRO Ref. G71/4.

Ledbury Union Workhouse, Building Schedule. HRO Ref. W31/1.

Shobdon Burial Register.

Ledbury Overseers' Minutes, HRO Ref. BO 92/56 - BO92/74.

Ledbury Overseers' Disbursements, 1822-1830. HRO Ref. AG1/39-49.

Ledbury Overseers' Poor Rate Assessment and Collection, 1824-1835. HRO Ref. AG1/2/38.

Ledbury Overseers' Coal Account, 1832. HRO Ref. AG1/50.
Ledbury Overseers Clothing Account, 1832. HRO Ref. AG1/51.
Bromyard Indentures. HRO Ref. E38/47/1-50, E38/28/1-28, E38/71/26.
Weobley Vestry Minutes 1793-1820, HRO Ref. N3/3.
Leominster Union Workhouse Visitors' Book, 31.3.1854.
The Southall Papers, HRO Ref. BG99.

Papers held at the Public Record Office at Kew in respect of Leominster Union
The Poor Law Commissioners' Letter Books. PRO Ref. MH/12/4385, 4386, 4387.

Papers in Private Collection
Nathaniel Morgan, private journals.

Contemporary Newspapers
The Hereford Times, 1830s and 1840s.
Hereford Journal, 1830s.
The Hereford Independent, 1825.

Secondary Sources
Books
Anstruther, I., *The Scandal of the Andover Workhouse*, Alan Sutton, Gloucester, 1973.
Armstrong, A., *Stability and Change in an English Country Town*, CUP, 1974.
Bannister, A.T., *Diocese of Hereford Institutions*, Wilson and Phillips, Hereford, 1923.
Baxter, G.W., *The Book of Bastiles*, John Stephens, Hereford, 1841.
Blacklock, F.G., *The Suppressed Benedictine Minster and other Ancient and Modern Institutions of the Borough of Leominster*, The Mortimer Press, (undated).
Brundage, A., *England's 'Prussian Minister'*, The Pennsylvania State University, 1988.
Burke's Peerage 1888, Harrison and Sons.
Chadwick, O., *The Victorian Church - Part 1*, (Third Edition), Black, 1949.
Checkland, S.G. and E.O.A. (eds.), *The Poor Law Report of 1834*, Penguin, 1974.
Clive, M., (ed.), *Caroline Clive, (Diaries and Letters)*, Bodley Head, 1949.
Cole, M., *Beatrice Webb's Diaries 1924-1932*, Longman, Green and Co., 1956.
Cragoe, M., *An Anglican Aristocracy*, Clarendon, 1996.
Crompton, F., *Workhouse Children*, Sutton Publishing, Stroud, Gloucestershire, 1997.
Crowther, M.A., *The Workhouse System 1834-1929*, Methuen, 1981.
Digby, A., *Pauper Palaces*, RKP, 1978.
Donajdrodski, A.J. (ed.), *Social Control in Nineteenth Century Britain*, Croom Helm, 1977.
Driver, F., *Power and Pauperism*, CUP, 1993.
Edsall, N.C., *The anti-Poor Law Movement 1834-1844*, Manchester UP, 1971.
Fenn, R.W.B. and Sinclair J.B., *The Bishops of Hereford and their Palace*, The Friends of Hereford Cathedral, Hereford, 1990.
Finer, S.E., *The Life and Times of Sir Edwin Chadwick*, Barnes and Noble Inc., New York, 1952.
Fraser, D., *Power and Authority in the Victorian City*, Blackwell, Oxford, 1979.
Goffman, E., *Asylums*, Penguin, 1991.

Goss, E., *Father and Son*, Penguin in Association with Heinemann, 1983.

Gray, H.J., *English Field Systems*, Harvard University Press, 1959.

Himmelfarb, G., *The Idea of Poverty*, Faber and Faber, 1984.

Hobsbawm, E.J. and Rude, G., *Captain Swing*, Lawrence and Wishart, 1972.

Inglis, K.S., *Churches and the Working Classes in Victorian England*, RKP, 1963.

Jones, E.J., *The Contentious Tithe*, RKP, 1976.

Marshall, W., *The Review and Abstract of the County Reports of the Board of Agriculture., Vol.2 - Western Department*, (Reprint of Report of 1818) Augustus M. Kelley, New York, 1968.

Molloy, P., *And They Blessed Rebecca*, J.L. Lewis and Sons Ltd., Gomer Press, Llandysul, 1983.

Morgan, C.A.V., *Nathaniel Morgan 1775-1854 of Ross-on-Wye, Herefordshire*, Ross-on-Wye and District Civic Trust, 1995.

Percival, J., *The Great Famine: Ireland's Potato Famine 1845-1851*, BCA in Association with BBC Books, (undated).

Pigot and Co., *National Commercial Directory, 1835*, Facsimile Edition, Michael Winton, Norwich, 1996.

Robinson, Rev. C.J., *A History of the Mansions and Manors of Herefordshire*, Scolar, Yorkshire, 1872.

Rowdon, H.H., *The Origins of the Brethren*, Pickering and Inglis Ltd., 1967.

Rule, J., *The Labouring Classes in Early Industrial England 1750-1850*, Longman, 1986.

Selleck, R.J.W., *James Kay-Shuttleworth, Journey of an Outsider*, Woburn Press, Ilford, Essex, 1994.

Smith, F.B., *The People's Health, 1830-1910*, Weidenfeld and Nicholson, 1979.

Webb, S. and B., *English Poor Law History*, Part 2, Vol. 1, Cass, 1929.

Webb, S. and B., *English Poor Law Policy*, Vol. 10, Cass, 1963.

Williams, D., *The Rebecca Riots*, University of Wales Press, Cardiff, 1986.

Woodward, Sir Llewellyn, *The Age of Reform 1815-1870*, OUP, 1962.

The Dictionary of National Biography, Smith, Elder and Company, 1909.

The Letters of Sir George Cornewall Lewis Bart. to Various Friends, Longman, Green and Company, 1870.

The Transactions of the Woolhope Naturalists' Field Club, Vol. XLVI, Part 3. 1990.

Journal Articles

Apfel, W. and Dunkley, P., 'English Rural Society and the New Poor Law: Bedfordshire 1834-1847', *Social History*, Vol. 10, No. 1, January, 1985.

Banks, S., 'Nineteenth-century Scandal or Twentieth-century Model? A New look at 'open' and 'closed' parishes'', *Economic History Review*, Second Series, XLI, I, 1988.

Davies, A.E. 'The New Poor Law in Rural Areas, 1834-1850', *The Ceredigion Antiquarian Society*, Vol. 8, 1978.

Holderness, B.A., 'Open' and 'Closed' Parishes in England in the Eighteenth and Nineteenth Centuries', *Agricultural History Review*, February, 1972.

Williams, G., 'The Administration of the New Poor Law in the Union of Thorne, 1834-1852', *Journals On-Line*, Vol.17 No. Winter, 1997.

Unpublished Theses, Dissertations and Studies

Briffet, J. 'The Operation of the Poor Law Union 1890-1914.' (1977)

Burrows, H., 'Religious Provision and Practice in some Mainly Rural Poor Law Districts of the Lower Marches 1836-1871', unpublished Ph.D. Thesis, C.N.A.A. (Wolverhampton Polytechnic), 1991.

McKay, K.P., 'Education under the Poor Law in Gloucestershire', unpublished M.Ed. Thesis, Bristol University, 1983.

Moscrop, W.M., 'The Deserving and the Undeserving Poor and Policy Decisions Concerning Them', unpublished M.Sc. Thesis, University of Salford, 1967.

Thompson, K.M., 'The Leicester Poor Law Union 1836-1871', unpublished Ph.D. Thesis, University of Leicester, 1988.

References

Chapter 1 Parish Relief and Parish Autonomy

1. Digby, A., *Pauper Palaces*, p.105.
2. Woodward, Sir Llewellyn, *Age of Reform*, p.77.
3. Ibid p.78.
4. Ibid.
5. The Poor Law Report of 1834, Appendix B1 and Appendix B2.
6. Hobsbawm, E.J. and Rude, G., *Captain Swing*, p.231.
7. Ibid p.118.
8. Ibid p.158.
9. Ibid p.112.

Chapter 2 Union Relief and Union Control

1. Driver, F., *Power and Pauperism*, p.61.
2. Ibid p.59.
3. Chadwick, O., *The Victorian Church - Part 1*, p.96.
4. Crompton, F., *Workhouse Children*, p.112.
5. Apfel, W. and Dunkley, P, 'English Rural Policy and the New Poor Law, Bedfordshire 1834- 1847', *Social History*, p.52.
6. Williams, G., 'The Administration of the New Poor Law in the Union of Thorne 1834-1852', *Journals On-Line*.
7. Digby, A., *Pauper Palace*s, p.177.
8. Ibid.
9. Crowther, M.A., *The Workhouse System 1834-1929*, p.31.
10. Baxter, G.W., *The Book of Bastiles*, p.5.
11. Ibid
12. Ibid p.113.
13. Ross Union Minutes, 21 Nov. 1853 – 29 Sept., 1856, p.152.
14. Webb, S. and B., *English Poor Law Policy*, Vol. 10, p.108.
15. Ibid p.109.
16. Crompton, F., *Workhouse Children*, p.232.
17. *The Letters of Sir George Cornewall Lewis Bart. to Various Friends*, p.183.

Chapter 3 Old Poor Law – Ledbury

1. The Poor Law Report of 1834, Irish University Reprints of British Parliamentary Papers of the Nineteenth Century; Poor Law, Vol. 3, Dublin 1972. Appendix B1, Part 4.
2. Ledbury Overseers' Accounts, HRO Ref. BO92/70, 9 July 1803.
3. Ibid, 29 September 1803.
4. Ibid, 24 June 1804.
5. Ibid, 22 October 1804.
6. Ibid, 10 April 1805.
7. Ibid, 20 August 1803.
8. Ibid, 5 July 1803.
9. Ibid, 6 July 1803.
10. Ibid, 17 August 1803.
11. Ibid, 27 July 1803.
12. Ibid, 6 July 1804.
13. Ibid.
14. Ibid, 2 May 1803.
15. Ibid, 20 July 1803.
16. Ibid, 27 July 1803.
17. Ibid, 26 November 1803.
18. Ibid, 30 November 1803.
19. Ibid.
20. Ledbury Overseers' Minutes 1802-1822, HRO Ref. BO92/59, 3 July 1816.
21. Ibid, 1 November 1821.
22. Ledbury Overseers' Accounts, HRO Ref. BO92/70 9 March 1804.
23. Ledbury Apprentice Register 1805-1825, HRO Ref. BO92/62.
24. Ledbury Overseers' Accounts, HRO Ref. BO92/70. 29 June 1816.
25. Ledbury Overseers' Minutes, HRO Ref. BO92/59. 3 December 1817.

26. Ibid, 11 December 1817.
27. Ibid, 19 February 1818.
28. Ledbury Register of Putative Fathers, HRO Ref. BO92/70.
29. Ledbury Overseers' Minutes, HRO Ref. BO92/59, 6 December 1818.
30. Ibid, 4 April 1819.
31. Ibid, 10 June 1819.
32. Ibid, 24 June 1819.
33. Ibid, 2 March 1820.
34. Ibid, 2 August 1821.
35. Ledbury Overseers' Accounts 1821-1831, HRO Ref. BO92/65.
36. Ledbury Overseers' Accounts, HRO Ref. BO92/70. 2 December 1816.
37. Ibid, 12 March 1817.
38. Ibid, 7 April 1817.
39. Ibid.
40. Ledbury Overseers' Minutes, HRO Ref. BO92/59. 11 December 1817.
41. Ibid, 14 February 1815.
42. Ibid, 25 March 1815.
43. Ibid, 24 January 1816.
44. Ibid.
45. Ibid.
46. Ledbury Overseers' Accounts, HRO Ref. BO92/70, 29 October 1817.
47. Ledbury Overseers' Minutes, HRO Ref. BO92/59. 5 November 1817.
48. Ibid, 18 December 1817.
49. Ibid, 11 March 1818.
50. Ibid.
51. Ibid, 3 May 1818.
52. Ibid.
53. Ibid, 2 May 1816.
54. Ibid.
55. Ibid.
56. Ibid.
57. Ledbury Overseers' Accounts, HRO Ref. BO92/70, 29 June 1816.
58. Ledbury Overseers' Minutes, HRO Ref. BO92/59, 4 September 1816.
59. Ibid, 11 December 1817.
60. Ledbury Overseers' Accounts, HRO Ref. BO92/70. 30 September 1816.
61. Ibid, 23 April 1817.
62. Ibid, 26 June 1817.
63. Ibid.
64. Ibid, 2 August 1817.
65. Ibid, 10 September 1817.
66. Ledbury Overseers' Minutes, HRO Ref. BO92/59., 3 September 1817.
67. Ledbury Overseers' Accounts, HRO Ref. BO92/70, 10 September 1817.
68. Ibid, 17 September 1817.
69. Ibid.
70. Ledbury Overseers' Minutes, HRO Ref. BO92/59, 5 November 1817.
71. Ibid, 26 March 1818.
72. Ibid.
73. Ibid.
74. Ibid, 9 September 1818.
75. Ledbury Overseers' Accounts, HRO Ref. BO92/70, 23 April 1818.
76. Ibid.
77. Ledbury Overseers' Minutes, HRO Ref. BO92/59, 3 May 1818.
78. Ibid, 26 March 1818.
79. Ibid, 1 November 1818.
80. Ibid.
81. Ibid, 24 June 1819.
82. Ibid, 24 June 1818.
83. Ibid, 13 January 1820.
84. Ibid, 8 October 1820.
85. Ibid, 1 November 1821.
86. Ibid, 29 March 1821.
87. Ibid, 31 August 1821.
88. Ledbury Overseers' Minutes, HRO Ref. BO92/60, 3 October 1822.
89. Ibid.
90. Ibid, 19 February 1835.
91. Ibid, 6 January 1831.
92. Ibid, 3 February 1831.
93. Ibid, 19 February 1835.
94. Ledbury Overseers' Minutes, HRO Ref. BO92/61, 22 November 1831.
95. Ledbury Overseers' Minutes, HRO Ref. BO92/60, 25 March 1832.
96. Ibid, 26 July 1832.
97. Ibid, 7 July 1836.

**Chapter 4 The New Poor Law
– Ledbury**

1. Ledbury Union Minutes, 3 June 1836, p.2.
2. Ibid.
3. Ibid, 3 June 1836, p.7 and 28 June 1836, p.20.
4. Ibid, 5 July 1836, p.25.
5. Ibid, 19 July 1836, p.34.
6. Ibid, 26 July 1836, p.42.
7. HRO Ref. W31/1.
8. Ledbury Union Minutes, 9 August 1836, p.55.
9. Ibid, 4 October 1836, p.87.
10. Ibid, 19 July 1836, p.37.
11. Ibid, 17 June 1836, p.14.
12. Ibid, 16 August 1836, p.65.
13. Ibid, 4 October 1836, p.89.
14. Ibid, 24 January 1837, p.164.
15. Ibid, 14 February 1837, p.179.
16. Ibid, 13 September 1836, p.76.
17. Ibid, 27 December 1836, p.146.
18. Ibid, 18 April 1837, p.219.
19. Ibid, 2 May 1837, p.239.
20. Ibid, 17 January 1837, p.157.
21. Ibid, 28 November 1836, p.106.
22. Ibid, 24 January 1837, p.163.
23. Ibid, 2 August 1836, p.50.
24. Ibid, 2 May 1837, p.239.
25. Ibid, 16 May 1837, p.252.
26. Ibid, 2 May 1837. p.237.
27. Ibid, 30 May 1837, p.265.
28. Ibid, 20 June 1837, p.290.
29. Ibid, 18 July 1837, p.324.
30. Ibid, 19 September 1837, p.367.
31. Ledbury Overseers' Accounts, HRO Ref. BO92/60 8 December 1838.
32. Ibid, 20 December 1838.
33. Ibid.
34. Ibid, HRO Ref. BO92/57, 25 April 1839.
35. Ledbury Union Minutes, 7 November 1837, p.415.
36. Ibid, 21 November 1842, p.152.
37. Ibid, 21 November 1842, p.153.
38. Ibid.
39. Ibid, 21 November 1842, p.155.
40. Ibid, 17 October 1837, p.391.
41. Ibid, 9 January 1838, p.9.
42. Ibid, 21 November 1842, p.154.
43. Ibid, 26 June 1838, p.71.
44. Ibid, 23 April 1839, p.9.
45. Ibid.
46. Ibid, 30 May 1843, p.22.
47. Ibid, 13 August 1844, p.147.
48. Ibid, 10 November 1846, p.3.
49. Ibid, 3 November 1846, p.210.
50. Ibid.
51. Ibid, 30 January 1844, p.94.
52. Ibid, 15 December 1846, p.15.
53. Ibid, 2 February 1847, p.30.
54. Ibid, 9 February 1847, p.33.
55. Ibid, 2 February 1847, p.30.
56. Ibid, 23 February 1847, p.37.
57. Ibid, 9 March 1847, p.50.
58. Ibid, 27 April 1847, p.56.
59. Ibid, 11 May 1847, p.60.
60. Ibid, 17 October 1848, p.22.
61. Ibid, 30 January 1849, p.59.
62. Ibid, 10 April 1849, p.71.
63. Ibid, 30 October 1849, p.152.
64. Ibid, 15 December 1846, p.15.
65. Ibid, 25 July 1848, p.206.
66. Ibid.
67. Ibid, 28 November 1848, p.39.
68. Ibid, 22 May 1849, p.106 and 19 June 1849, p.109.
69. Ibid, 6 November 1849, p.154.
70. Ibid, 30 October 1849, p.152.
71. Ibid.
72. Ibid.
73. Ibid, 30 October 1849, p.153.
74. Ibid, 30 October 1849, p.152.
75. Ibid, 11 December 1849, p.164.
76. Ibid, 30 October 1849, p.153.
77. Ibid, 9 February 1847, p.33.
78. Ibid, 23 February 1847, p.37.
79. Ibid, 29 May 1849, p.101.
80. Ibid, 30 April 1850, p.11 and 25 March 1850, p.200.
81. Ibid, 15 January 1850, p.178.
82. Ibid.

83. Ibid, 5 May 1850, p.193.
84. Ibid.
85. Ibid, 18 June 1850, p.25.
86. Ibid, 9 September 1851, p.151.
87. Ibid, 16 September 1851, p.154.
88. Ibid, 28 September 1852, p.42.
89. Ibid, 12 May 1856, p.179.
90. Ibid, 19 August 1856, p.205.
91. Ibid, 26 August 1856, p.208.
92. Ibid, 7 October 1856, p.13.
93. Ibid.
94. Ibid, 14 October 1856, p.16.
95. Ibid, 17 April 1849, p.87.

**Chapter 5 Confidence and
    Independence – Ross**

1. Brundage, A., *England's 'Prussian
   Minister'*, p.40.
2. Finer, S.E., *The Life and Times of Sir
   Edwin Chadwick*, p.108.
3. Brundage, A., *England's 'Prussian
   Minister'*, p.40.
4. Ross Union Minutes, 25 April 1836,
   p.1.
5. Robinson, Rev. C.J., *A History
   of the Mansions and Manors of
   Herefordshire*, p.118.
6. Ibid p.119.
7. Weobley Union Minutes, 11 April
   1836, p.1.
8. Dore Union Minutes, 11 April 1837,
   p.2.
9. Ibid
10. Ibid
11. Robinson, Rev. C.J., *A History
    of the Mansions and Manors of
    Herefordshire*, p.313.
12. *Burke's Peerage 1888*, p.669.
13. Ibid.
14. Baxter, G.W., *The Book of Bastiles*,
    p.559.
15. Ross Union Minutes, 25 April 1836
    p.1.
16. Crowther, M.A., *The Workhouse
    System 1834-1929*, p.36.
17. Robinson, Rev. C.J., *A History
    of the Mansions and Manors of
    Herefordshire*, p.281.
18. Ibid.
19. The Kerne Bridge Company Papers,
    HRO ref. D48/52
20. *Burke's Peerage 1888*, p.669.
21. Ibid.
22. Ross Parish Register, 8 May 1841.
23. Nathaniel Morgan's Private Journal,
    3 August 1824.
24. Morgan, C.A.V., *Nathaniel
    Morgan 1775-1854 of Ross-on-Wye,
    Herefordshire*, p.12.
25. Ibid p.19.
26. Ibid p.4.
27. Ibid.
28. Nathaniel Morgan's Private Journal,
    17 December 1825.
29. Ross Union Minutes, 25 April 1836.
    p.1.
30. Ibid p.2.
31. Ibid p.12.
32. Ibid p.16.
33. The British and Foreign School
    Papers, HRO Ref. AP72/1.
34. Ross Union Minutes, 9 June 1836.
    p.29.
35. Ibid, 23 March 1840. p.287.
36. Ibid, 30 March 1840, p.292.
37. Ibid.
38. Ross Parish Register, August 1838.
39. Crowther, M.A., *The Workhouse
    System 1834-1929*, p.118.
40. Ross Union Minutes, 17 April 1848,
    p.204.
41. Ibid, 3 September 1838. p.37.
42. Ibid.
43. Ibid.
44. Ibid, 10 March 1845, p.66.
45. Ibid, 25 April 1836, p.6.
46. Ibid, 13 April 1837, p.176.
47. Ibid, 8 November 1841, p.70.
48. Ibid, 20 December 1841, p.83.
49. Ibid, 14 August 1843, p.312.

50. Ibid, 1 April 1844, p.356.
51. Ibid 30 September 1846, p.316.
52. Ibid, 19 April 1847, p.67.
53. Ibid, 14 June 1847, p.82.
54. Ibid, 18 October 1847, p.126.
55. Ibid, 25 April 1836, p.3.
56. Ibid, p.4.
57. Ibid, 16 January 1838, p.367.
58. Ibid, June 1838, p.441.
59. Ibid, 9 July 1838, p.13.
60. Ibid, 22 October 1838, p.71.
61. Ibid, 8 November 1838, p.78.
62. Webb, S. and B., *English Poor Law History*, Part 2, Vol. 1, p.249.
63. Ross Union Minutes, 3 September 1846, p.306.
64. Ibid, 17 September 1846, p.321.
65. Ibid, 15 October 1846, p.338.
66. Ibid, 3 April 1848, p.199.
67. Ibid, 17 April 1848, p.203.
68. Ibid, November 1853, p.4.
69. Ibid, 12 March 1855, p.152.

Chapter 6 Poor Law and Anti-Poor Law – Hereford

1. Chadwick, O., *The Victorian Church - Part 1*, p.53.
2. Fenn, R.W.D. and Sinclair J.B., *The Bishops of Hereford and their Palace*, p.30.
3. *Dictionary of National Biography*, p.275.
4. Chadwick, O., *The Victorian Church - Part 1*, p.226.
5. *The Letters of Sir George Cornewall Lewis Bart. to Various Friends*, p.223.
6. Ibid.
7. Chadwick, O., *The Victorian Church - Part 1*, p.53.
8. Dore Union Minutes, 11 August 1837, p.57.
9. Digby, A., *Pauper Palaces*, p.211.
10. Ibid.
11. Nathaniel Morgan's Private Journal, 18 December 1832.
12. *The Transactions of the Woolhope Naturalists' Field Club*, Vol. XLVI, 1990, Part 3, p.503.
13. Ibid.
14. Hereford Union Minutes, 29 November 1837, p.336.
15. Ibid.
16. *The Hereford Times*, 24 February 1841.
17. *The Transactions of the Woolhope Naturalists' Field Club*, Vol. XLVI, 1990, Part 3, p.503.
18. Ibid, p.504.
19. Ibid, p.507.
20. Digby, A., *Pauper Palaces*, p.25.
21. Baxter, G.W., *The Book of Bastiles*, p.107.
22. Ibid, p.109.
23. Hereford Union Minutes, 6 March 1841, p.161.
24. Ibid, 13 June 1836, p.29.
25. Ibid, 14 July 1836, p.50.
26. Ibid, 23 July 1836, p.57.
27. Ibid, 29 October 1836, p.102.
28. Ibid, 26 November 1836, p.118.
29. Ibid, 19 November 1836, p.112.
30. Ibid, 9 November 1836, p.110.
31. Ibid, 14 October 1836, p.248.
32. Hereford Union Workhouse Register of Births, HRO Ref. BJ6.
33. Hereford Union Minutes, 31 July 1839, p.256.
34. Ibid, 15 November 1839, p.308.
35. Ibid, p.328.
36. Ibid.
37. Ibid, 6 June 1838, p.35.
38. Ibid, 13 June 1838, p.48.
39. Ibid, 5 September 1838, p.82.
40. Ibid, 10 October 1838, p.98.
41. Ibid, 21 November 1838, p.119.
42. Ibid, 23 January 1839, p.161
43. Ibid, 1 May 1839, p.213.
44. Ibid, 8 May 1839, p.216.
45. Ibid, 22 May 1839, p.225.
46. Ibid, 31 July 1839, p.256.
47. Ibid, 7 August 1839. p.259.

48. Ibid, 14 August 1839, p.261.
49. Ibid, 18 September 1839, p.276.
50. Ibid, 28 August 1839, p.266.
51. Ibid.
52. Ibid, 4 September 1839, p.269.
53. Ibid, 25 September 1839, p.280.
54. Ibid, 9 October 1839, pp.298-9.
55. Ibid, 22 January 1840, p.347.
56. Ibid, 15 January 1840, p.345.
57. Ibid, 11 March 1840, p.372.
58. Ibid, 1 July 1840, p.39.
59. Ibid, 5 November 1842, p.51.
60. Ibid, 18 March 1840, p.377.
61. Ibid, 30 December 1843, p.288.
62. Ibid, 4 July 1838, p.50.
63. Ibid.
64. Crompton, F., *Workhouse Children*, p.138.
65. Crowther, M.A., *The Workhouse System 1834-1929*, p.195.

Chapter 7 Welsh Border Unions – Kington

1. Pigot and Co., *National Commercial Directory, 1835*, p.11.
2. Ibid.
3. Ibid.
4. Ibid.
5. Kington Union Minutes, 26 August 1836, p.1.
6. Ibid.
7. Pigot and Co., *National Commercial Directory, 1835*, p.12.
8. Davies, A.E., 'The New Poor Law in a Rural Area, 1834-1850', *The Ceredigion Antiquarian Society*, p.249.
9. Ibid.
10. *The Letters of Sir George Cornewall Lewis Bart. to Various Friends*, p.79.
11. Ibid.
12. Ibid.
13. Ibid.
14. Williams, D., *The Rebecca Riots*, p.145.
15. Ibid.
16. The Poor Law Report, 1834. Appendix B2, Part 2.
17. Kington Union Minutes, 30 August 1836, p.105.
18. Ibid, 21 December 1836, p.73.
19. Ibid, 29 March 1837, p.159.
20. Ibid, 18 January 1837, p.105.
21. Ibid, 31 August 1839, p.308.
22. Ibid.
23. Ibid, 12 October 1839, p.325.
24. Ibid, 27 July 1838, p.104.
25. Ibid, 18 January 1837, p.107.
26. Ibid.
27. Ibid, 1 February 1837, p.119.
28. Ibid, 29 November 1837, p.325.
29. Ibid, 25 march 1838, p.231.
30. Ibid, January 1838, p.372.
31. Ibid, p.375.
32. Digby, A., *Pauper Palaces*, p.153.
33. Crompton, F., *Workhouse Children*, p.43.
34. Williams, D., *The Rebecca Riots*, p.143.
35. Ibid.
36. Kington Union Minutes, 8 October 1836, p.27.
37. Ibid, 11 July 1840, p.103.
38. The Poor Law Report 1834, Appendix B2, Part 2.
39. Kington Parish Marriage Register, HRO Ref. AF16/19 and 20.
40. Crowther, M.A., *The Workhouse System 1834-1929*, p.15.
41. The Census Report of 1851, The Irish University Press Reprint of the Census Report of 1851, Population Vol. 8. p. XLIV.
42. Bannister, A.T., *Diocese of Hereford Institutions*, p.153.
43. Kington Union Minutes, 1836.
44. Ibid, 1837.
45. 1843 List of Magistrates, HRO Ref. G42/39 (ii) Box 59.
46. Kington Union Minutes, 10 February 1838 and 15 February 1838, pp.391-3.

47. Ibid, 22 September 1838, p.135.
48. Ibid, 30 September 1846, p.135.
49. Donajdrodski, A.J., (ed.) *Social Control in Nineteenth Century Britain*, p.109.
50. Ibid, p.108.
51. Ibid, p.114.
52. Ibid, p.109.

Chapter 8 Welsh Border Unions – Dore

1. Dore Union Minutes, 11 April 1837, p.2.
2. Robinson, Rev. C.J., *A History of the Mansions and Manors of Herefordshire*, p.313.
3. Ibid.
4. List of Magistrates for 1843, HRO Ref. G42/39 (ii) Box 59.
5. Dore Union Minutes, 11 April 1837, p.1.
6. Robinson, Rev. C.J., *A History of the Mansions and Manors of Herefordshire*, p.313.
7. Clive, M., (ed.), *Caroline Clive, (Diaries and Letters)*, p.27.
8. Ibid.
9. Ibid, p.36.
10. Dore Union Minutes, 11 April 1837, p.11.
11. Ibid, p.3.
12. Ibid, 1 May 1837, p.23.
13. Ibid, 16 June 1837, p.31.
14. Ibid, 2 June 1837, p.29.
15. Ibid, 15 September 1837, p.76.
16. Ibid, 17 November 1837, p.119.
17. Ibid, 18 April 1837, p.14.
18. Ibid, 1 May 1837, p.23.
19. Ibid, 13 October 1837, p.98.
20. Ibid, 11 April 1837, p.11 and 18 April 1837, p.14.
21. Ibid, 21 July 1837, p.48.
22. Ibid, 4 August 1837, p.52.
23. Ibid, 28 September 1838, p.319.
24. Ibid, 25 August 1837, p.66.
25. Ibid, 30 March 1838, p.235.
26. Ibid, 31 August 1838, p.305.
27. Ibid, 7 December 1838, p.354.
28. Ibid, 23 April 1841, p.254.
29. HRO Ref. BK52/50 September 1836.
30. Dore Union Minutes, 11 April 1837, p.12.
31. Nathaniel Morgan's Private Journal, 27 March 1849.
32. Dore Union Minutes, 22 October 1841, p.305.
33. Ibid, 9 September 1842, p.4.
34. Ibid, 18 May 1843, p.85.
35. Ibid, 3 December 1847, p.207.
36. Ibid, 20 April 1849, p.336.
37. Ibid, 7 July 1837, p.41.
38. Ibid, 27 October 1837, p.102.
39. Ibid, 18 November 1842, p.21.
40. Ibid.
41. Kington Union Minutes, 14 April 1838, p.25.
42. Ibid, 28 April 1838, p.43.
43. Ibid, 26 May 1838, p.61.
44. Ibid, 13 June 1838, p.95.
45. Ibid, 11 September 1841, p.252.
46. Digby, A., *Pauper Palaces*, p.187.
47. Ibid, p.183.
48. Kington Union Minutes, 18 December 1841, p.287.
49. Ibid, 6 November 1841, p.276.
50. Ibid, 30 April 1842, p.338.
51. Ibid, 14 May 1842, p.342.
52. Ibid, 11 June 1842, p.352.
53. Ibid, 26 June 1842, p.352.
54. Ibid, 9 July 1842, p.362.
55. Ibid, 21 December 1844, p.261.
56. Ibid, 15 December 1845, p.284.
57. Ibid, 7 June 1845, p.343.
58. Ibid, 6 December 1845, p.6.
59. Digby, A., *Pauper Palaces*, p.187.
61. Ibid, 19 August 1846, p.116.
62. Ibid, 8 July 1846, p.103.
63. Digby, A., *Pauper Palaces*, p.183.
64. Dore Union Minutes, 21 February 1840, p.130.
65. Ibid, 13 January 1843, p.43.

66. Ibid, 10 February 1843, p.53.
67. Ibid, 24 February 1843, p.59.
68. Ibid, 28 January 1847, p.60.
69. Ibid, 12 March 1847, p.76.
70. Ibid, 9 April 1847, p.87.
71. Ibid, 23 April 1847, p.93.
72. Ibid, 31 November 1847, p.215.
73. Ibid, 7 August 1848, p.245.
74. Ibid, 26 January 1849, p.313.
75. Ibid, 9 March 1849, p.325.
76. Ibid, 7 May 1841, p.258.
77. Kington Union Minutes, 2 March 1839, p.218.
78. Ibid, 7 April 1840, p.43.
79. Ibid, 26 May 1847, p.235.
80. Williams, D., *The Rebecca Riots*, p.137.
81. Ibid, p.138.
82. Brundage, A., *England's 'Prussian Minister'*, p.32.
83. Ibid, p.33.
84. Ibid, p.52.
85. Ibid, p.14.

Chapter 9 Workhouse Scandals – Andover and Leominster

1. Leominster Vestry Minutes 1796-1843, HRO Ref. AK3/72.
2. Ibid.
3. Ibid.
4. Ibid.
5. Poor Law Commission Letter Book, PRO Kew, Ref. MH12/4387.
6. Blacklock, F.G., *The Suppressed Benedictine Minster and other Ancient and Modern Institutions of the Borough of Leominster*, p.187.
7. Leominster Union Visitors' Book 1854-1855, 4 May 1855.
8. Poor Law Commission Letter Book, PRO Kew, MH12/4386.
9. Ibid.
10. Ibid.
11. Ibid.
12. Ibid.
13. Ibid.
14. Ibid.
15. Ibid.
16. Ibid.
17. Poor Law Commission Letter Book, Ref. MH12/4387.
18. Ibid.
19. Ibid, Ref. MH12/4386.
20. *The Letters of Sir George Cornewall Lewis Bart. to Various Friends*, p.150.
21. Finer, S.E., *The Life and Times of Sir Edwin Chadwick*, p.109.
22. Ibid, p.116.
23. Brundage, A., *England's 'Prussian Minister'*, p.113.
24. Finer, S.E., *The Life and Times of Sir Edwin Chadwick*, p.193.
25. Ibid, p.184.
26. Anstruther, I., *The Scandal of the Andover Workhouse*, p.19.
27. Himmelfarb, G., *The Idea of Poverty*, p.167.
28. Anstruther, I., *The Scandal of the Andover Workhouse*, p.144.
29. Shobdon Parish Burial Register, HRO Ref. AJ94/4.
30. Poor Law Commission Letter Book, Kew, Ref. MH12/4387.
31. Ibid.
32. Ibid.
33. Ibid.
34. Ibid.
35. Ibid, Ref. MH12/4385
36. Ibid, Ref. MH12/4386.
37. Leominster Union Minutes, 17 June 1853, p.172.
38. Ibid, 17 June 1853 p.176.
39. Ibid, 13 July 1853, p.186.
40. The Southall Papers, letter dated August 1838, HRO Ref. BG99/4/111.
41. Himmelfarb, G., *The Idea of Poverty*, p.529.

Chapter 10 Pauper Apprentices – Bromyard

1. The Poor Law Report 1834, Irish University Press Reprints of British Parliamentary Papers of the Nineteenth Century; Poor Law, Vol. 3. Dublin 1972. Appendix B2, Part 2.
2. Ibid, Kington.
3. Ibid, Ross-on-Wye.
4. Bromyard Pauper Apprentice Indentures, HRO Ref. E38/47/1-50.
5. Ibid, HRO Ref.E38/28/1-26.
6. Ibid, HRO Ref. E38/47/1-50.
7. Ibid, HRO Ref. E38/28/1-26.
8. Ibid, HRO Ref. E38/71/26.
9. The Poor Law Report 1834, Weobley. Appendix B1 Part 5.
10. Weobley Vestry Minutes 1793-1820, HRO Ref. N3/3.
11. Ledbury Overseers' Minutes 1803-1818, HRO Ref. BO92/70.
12. Ibid, 2 May 1803.
13. Ibid, 20 July 1803.
14. Ledbury Pauper Apprentice Register 1805-1825, HRO Ref. BO92/62.
15. Crompton, F., *Workhouse Children*, p.18.
16. Dore Union Minutes, October 1845, p.323.
17. Kington Union Minutes, January 1837, p.107.
18. Ibid, 1837 p.321.
19. Leominster Union Minutes 1852, p.4.
20. Ibid 1853, p.124.
21. Ibid, p.139.
22. Hereford Union Minutes 1842, p.2.
23. Ross Union Minutes June 1848, p.264.
24. Ibid, p.297.
25. Ibid, 1848 p.382.
26. Hereford Union Minutes 1846, p.491.
27. Ibid, 1847, p.193.
28. Ibid, 27 November 1839, p.316.
29. Ibid, 15 November 1839, p.307.
30. Bromyard Union Minutes, 18 November 1839, p.255.
31. Ibid, 25 November 1839, p.258.
32. Ibid, 2 December 1839, p.261.
33. Ibid, 9 December 1839, p.265.
34. Ibid, 3 February 1840, p.300.
35. Ibid, 30 March 1840, p.334.
36. Ibid, 13 April 1840, p.340.
37. Ibid, 8 May 1841, p.86.
38. Ibid, 15 March 1841, p.89.
39. Ibid, 8 March 1841, p.86.
40. Ibid, 5 April 1841, p.101.
41. Ibid, 12 April 1841, p.105.
42. Ibid, 14 June 1841, p.132.
43. Crompton, F., *Workhouse Children*, p.20.
44. Ibid, p.21.
45. Hereford Union Minutes, 3 February 1841, p.148.
46. Ross Union Minutes, 15 June 1840, p.333.
47. Ibid, 29 June 1840, p.345.
48. Ibid, 15 March 1841, p.427.
49. Ledbury Union Minutes, 29 November 1836, p.119.
50. Ibid, 16 January 1838, p.11.
51. Ibid, 23 April 1839, p.9.
52. Digby, A., *Pauper Palaces*, p.190.
53. Kington Union Minutes, 30 March 1839, p.229.
54. Ibid, 18 December 1841, p.287.
55. Ledbury Union Minutes, 25 August 1840, p.148.
56. Bromyard Union Minutes, 8 July 1839, p.183.
57. Ross Union Minutes, 18 September 1841, p.310.
58. Dore Union Minutes, 7 August 1848, p.245.
59. Leominster Union Workhouse Visitors' Book, 31 March 1854.

Chapter 11 Settlement, Removal & Vagrancy – Weobley

1. Digby, A., *Pauper Palaces*, p.83.
2. Weobley Vestry Book, HRO Ref. N3/3, 10 January 1807.
3. Clodock Vestry Book, HRO G71/4, 15 October 1775.
4. Ledbury Overseers' Accounts, HRO Ref. BO92/59, 3 November 1814.
5. Ibid, HRO Ref. BO92/60, 3 August 1826.
6. Ibid, 1 October 1829.
7. Weobley Vestry Book, HRO Ref. N3/3, 16 April 1802.
8. Ibid, 26 June 1796.
9. Ibid, 14 January 1816.
10. Ledbury Overseers' Accounts, HRO Ref. BO92/60, 15 July 1830.
11. Ibid, 18 March 1830 and 2 September 1830.
12. Ibid, 11 October 1832.
13. Ibid, 3 January 1833.
14. Ibid ,2 February 1833.
15. Weobley Union Minutes, 2 December 1844, p.425.
16. Ibid.
17. Ibid, 13 January 1845, p.442.
18. Ibid, 10 February 1845, p.460.
19. Ibid, 24 February 1845, p.466.
20. Ibid.
21. Ibid, p.468.
22. Ledbury Union Minutes, 22 April 1845, p.34.
23. Ibid.
24. Kington Union Minutes, 17 January 1846, p.22.
25. Webb, S. and B., *English Poor Law History*, Part 2, Vol. 1, p.423.
26. Hereford Union Minutes, 12 December 1846, p.99.
27. Ledbury Union Minutes, 5 May 1846, p.149.
28. Ibid.
29. Ibid.
30. Webb, S. and B., *English Poor Law History*, Part 2, Vol. 1, p.429.
31. Leominster Union Minutes, 1 August 1853, p.149.
32. *The Letters of Sir George Cornewall Lewis Bart. to Various Friends*, p.278.
33. Percival, J., *The Great Famine: Ireland's Potato Famine 1845-1851*, p.120.
34. Digby, A., *Pauper Palaces*, p.96.
35. Hereford Union Minutes, 28 February 1863, p.81.
36. Ibid.
37. Ibid.
38. Ibid.
39. Dore Union Minutes, 29 May 1865, p.338.
40. Ross Union Minutes, 18 May 1865, p.411.

Index

Churchwardens 9, 25
Clarendon, Earl of 148
Clifford, Emily 72
Clifford, Fanny Elizabeth Mary 72
Clifford, Henry Morgan 72, 83, 189
Clifford, William 120
Clive family of Whitfield Court 68, 89, 187
Clive, Rev Archer 18, 68, 89, 119-120, 189
Clive, Col. Edward 68, 89, 189
Clive, Edward Bolton, MP 68, 89, 94, 119, 121, 188-189
Clive, George 68, 72, 107, 120, 121-122
Clive, Harriet (wife of Edward Bolton) 119
Clive, Harriet (daughter of Edward Bolton) 120
Clodock 122, 175
Cockburn, Sir William 106
Cocks, Anna Maria 69
Cocks, Charles 69
Cocks, William Cary 71
Coke, Rev George 106
Colcombe, Thomas 174
Collins, James 53, 55
Collins, John Stratford 72, 73, 80, 126
Coniam, Elizabeth Matilda 131
Cooke, Charles 47, 50, 51
Cornewall, Sir George 68
Correy, William 159
Cost, Ann 159
Cotterell, George 28
Cotterell, Hannah 29
Cowdell, Thomas 110
Credenhill 5, 11
Crickmay, Mr
Crompton, Frank 18, 23, 104, 114, 162
Cross, Susan 133
Crowther, M.A. 116

Davies, James 99
Davies, James (Leominster) 164
Davies, James (Muir Court) 106
Davies, John (Gladestry) 111
Davies, John (Staunton) 97
Davies, Joseph 81-82
Davies, Mary (Hereford) 102
Davies, Mary (Kington) 143
Davies, T.W. 143
Davies, Thomas 81
Davies, Thomas William 50
Day, William 108
Digby, Anne 2, 19, 90, 93, 113, 132, 170
Dilwyn 175
Dix, Mary 28, 29
Dobles, Mr 164
Dodson, Rev Christopher 138, 139, 155

Dore Union x, 18, 89, 119-136, 187
    Board of Guardians 121, 123, 125-127, 163, 184, 188
        harsh decisions 124
    education 133-134, 172
    illegitimate children 123
    Medical Officers 122
    New Poor Law
        difficulty of understanding 123
        lack of enthusiasm for 121
    Overseers 124-125
    Relieving Officers 122-123, 134
Dowell, Rev 60
Dowle, Thomas 73
Dowle, William and Victoria 61, 63
Duncombe, T.S., MP 94
Dunn, Mr 176
Dyer, William and Sarah 51

Eardisland 5
Eastnor Castle 69
Eaton, Daniel and Harriet 63, 65
Edinburgh Review, the 182
education 20-22, 55-57, 83-86, 130-135
Egerton, Sarah 42
Eley, William 61
Elkerton, Henry and Eliza 60
Elton, Richard 60
enclosure 11-12
Evans, Rev Charles Edward 154
Evans, Edward 143, 144, 145, 155, 187
Evans, James 102
Evans, Capt. Kingsmill 71, 72
Evans, Mary 111

farmers 2, 8, 9-10, 28, 30, 69, 107, 132-133, 135, 172
Farr, John 122, 134
Farrall, J.B. 172
Farrell, Mary Matilda 131
fathers, putative 32-33, 42, 53, 97, 114-115
Fenn, Thomas 165
Finer, S.E. 147
Fluck, Henry Thomas 152
Ford, Thomas 176
Fowler, William 174
Fownhope 8
Foy 72
Freeman, John 7
Fridger, Phillip 167
friendly societies 93
Fuller, Diana 99

Index

Industrial Revolution, the 3-4
irremovability 180-184
Irremovable Poor Act (1846) 180, 183

James, George 100
James, Henry 122
James, Rev Maurice 106
James, Rebecca 81
James, Samuel 166, 168
James, Susan 165
James, Thomas (Hereford) 102
James, Thomas (Linton) 159
Jauncey, John 43
Johnson, Benjamin 28
Jones family, The Cleeve 72
Jones, Rev Albert 103
Jones, Charles 164
Jones, Christopher 47, 51
Jones, Edith 72
Jones, Eleanor 114-115
Jones, Mary (Huntington) 111
Jones, Mary (Llangarron) 80
Jones, Mary (Norton) 158
Jones, Mary (Weobley) 175
Jones, Rev Matthew Henry 70, 73

Kay-Shuttleworth, James 170
Kentchurch 122
Kidderminster 32, 162, 165, 168
Kington 105
    under Old Poor Law 108-109
    under New Poor Law 109-114
Kington Parish Church 115
Kington Union x, 5, 7, 68, 105-118, 130-133
    Board of Guardians 106-107, 112-113,
        163-164, 188
    education 130-133, 171-172
    illegitimate children 113-116
    influence of Thomas Frankland Lewis 105
    settlement laws 180
    workhouse, new 109-110
Knowles, Richard 163
Kyrle family, Walford/Much Marcle 72

Labour Rate, the 1
labourers, living conditions 11, 13
Lane, Mr 122
Lanwarne, Nicholas 19-20, 97, 114, 125, 129
Law, William and Sarah 60
Lawrence, Elizabeth 101
Ledbury, under Old Poor Law 25-46, 161-162
    poor relief at home 27, 30, 48, 55
    settlement claims 176
Ledbury Union ix, 5, 18, 22, 25-66, 68

apprenticeships 31-32, 43
Board of Assistants 27, 30, 35-36, 40, 41,
    43
Board of Guardians 45, 47, 53, 58-62,
    64-66
Chaplain 56, 57, 59-60, 61-63
children 45, 54-63, 169-170, 172
difficulty of retaining staff 56-63
education 55-57
finances 34-36, 41-43, 51-55, 66
Master 34, 49, 51, 53, 63, 65
Matron 37, 40-41, 49, 53
Medical Officers 50, 51
New Poor Law in 47-66
pauper numbers, increase 54
paupers, bad behaviour 62
pin factory 28
Overseers and Churchwardens 31, 33-36,
    43, 48, 50, 55
poor rates, collection of 181
records falsified 63-65
Relieving Officers 50, 51, 57
reorganisation 43
settlement laws and 180
staff conduct 61-63
Union Clerk 63-65
Visiting Committee 53, 57, 61
workhouse, old 26-30, 33-34, 38-42, 48
workhouse, new 47-49
Leominster, under Old Poor Law 139-140
Leominster Union x, 7, 68, 137-156, 164, 187-
    188
    abuses at 137-156, 189
    Board of Guardians 137, 142-145, 164,
        182, 188
    Chaplain, failure to appoint 153-155
    children 172
    Master 137
    Medical Officer 152
    Union Clerk 143
    Visiting Committee 152, 154
    workhouse 57, 139-145, 152-153
Less Eligibility, Principle of ix, 15, 19, 20,
    22-23, 55, 85, 172, 185, 189-191
Lewis, Edward (Dore) 132
Lewis, Edward (Old Radnor) 163
Lewis, Rev Gilbert Frankland 68, 177, 188
Lewis, Sir Thomas Frankland 67, 68, 74, 105,
    106, 121, 135, 147, 166, 177, 188
Lewis, Sir George Cornewall 20, 24, 68, 88,
    107-108, 146, 147, 150, 177, 182, 188
Lewis, Rev T.T. 164
Lincoln Hill House 72
Lister, Lady Teresa 148